2-79

To: Rev. ⟨...⟩
from: Mr. & Mrs. Mike Kern

May this book enrich your study of God's word.

UNDERSTANDING GOD

by

Patricia Beall Gruits

WHITAKER HOUSE
Pittsburgh and Colfax Streets
Springdale, PA 15144

Dedicated to
My Father and Mother

HARRY AND MYRTLE BEALL

To whom I owe so much.

Wisdom is the principal thing;
therefore get wisdom: and with all
thy getting get understanding.

PROVERBS 4:7

PREFACE TO THE SECOND EDITION

God is pouring out His Spirit upon hungry people everywhere, in all denominations, from all walks of life, of all ages. Along with the excitement of discovering a fresh relationship with God comes a new hunger for truth, and a desire to experience the doctrines as they are related in the Scriptures.

"UNDERSTANDING GOD" is a textbook on Christian doctrine designed to satisfy hunger for knowledge of God by teaching how to experience the doctrines and sacraments which were once only tradition. All basic topics are covered in this book, presented with fresh appeal and simplicity because God has restored life to these truths through the revelation of the Holy Spirit.

This book uses the oldest and most rewarding technique of religious instruction . . . a systematic question and answer method. The catechism has proved its value in the field of Christian education because it teaches by provocative questions and by concise, clear and definite answers. It presents Biblical truth in logical organization and progressive steps. It lays out the work of both pupil and teacher within the specific limits of definite assignments. It emphasizes the permanent character of truth and most important of all, it gives the student a firm and intelligent grasp on the Christian faith.

The benefits of the catechism are many. It develops spiritual understanding, stimulates growth in grace, fortifies against temptation, creates hunger for further searching the scriptures, encourages personal witnessing and strengthens for Christian life and service.

The demand for the publishing of this second edition has come from those who have observed the benefits of the first edition in their own lives and in the lives of others. Many groups throughout the country are realizing the need for a textbook such as this as a guide into personal experience of the foundational doctrines of Christ.

As the students learn about the Christian experiences which are ours in Jesus Christ, the teacher should pray with them until they come into the experience of that particular truth. This has been the secret of the success of the first edition.

Upon the completion of the entire course only those students who have had genuine experiences of justification, water baptism, and the baptism of the Holy Spirit, should be confirmed. This is done by presenting the confirmants to the congregation by the laying on of the hands of the local ministers, thus establishing them in the faith as it is in Christ Jesus.

The method of teaching found in "UNDERSTANDING GOD" has been tested for many years at the Bethesda Missionary Temple in Detroit, and in many other churches throughout the country. We believe this catechism will help students, parents, and teachers to understand the Bible better, to love God more and to serve Christ more confidently. Teachers and students alike are urged to seek the aid of the Holy Spirit in studying these pages, that the use of the catechism will lead many to salvation and to steadfastness in the Christian life.

"And Judas and Silas . . . exhorted the brethren with many words, and confirmed them." Acts 15:32

PATRICIA BEALL GRUITS

Detroit, Michigan
1972

TABLE OF CONTENTS

THE CHRISTIAN GUIDEBOOK

Chapter 1

THE BIBLE

1. WHAT IS THE BIBLE?

The Bible is a book written under the divine inspiration of God and accepted by Christians as the Word of God.

All scripture is given by inspiration of God. II Tim. 3:16.

2. WHO WROTE THE BIBLE?

Holy men of God wrote the Bible. The prophets and priests wrote the books of the Old Testament. Evangelists and apostles wrote the books of the New Testament.

. . . Holy men of God spake as they were moved by the Holy Ghost. II Pet. 1:21.

3. WHY IS THE BIBLE THE WORD OF GOD EVEN THOUGH IT WAS WRITTEN BY MEN?

The Bible is the Word of God because it was written by the inspiration of God.

All Scripture is given by inspiration of God . . .
II Tim. 3:16.

4. WHAT DOES "BY INSPIRATION OF GOD" MEAN?

The Holy Ghost guided the minds of the holy men so the thoughts and words which they expressed and wrote were directed and dictated by God.

. . . Holy men of God spake as they were moved by the Holy Ghost. II Pet. 1:21.

We speak, not in the words which man's wisdom teacheth, but which the Holy Ghost teacheth. I Cor. 2:13.

5. WHY DID GOD GIVE US THE BIBLE?

God gave us the Bible to reveal Christ to us.

And that from a child thou hast known the holy scriptures, which are able to make thee wise unto salvation through faith which is in Christ Jesus. II Tim. 3:15.

6. HOW DOES THE BIBLE REVEAL CHRIST TO US?

Throughout the Old Testament God uses the prophets to foretell the coming of Jesus Christ as the Messiah. In the New Testament through the Holy Spirit, we recognize that Christ is the fulfillment of these prophecies.

Search the scriptures; for in them ye think ye have eternal life: and they are they which testify of me. John 5:39.

Then said I, Lo, I come: in the volume of the book it is written of me. Ps. 40:7.

7. WHAT USE SHOULD WE MAKE OF THE BIBLE?

Since the renewing of the mind is received through revelation of Christ, we should use the Bible as a guide to salvation and holy living that we might believe, understand, know, love and follow Christ.

Thy word is a lamp unto my feet and a light unto my path. Ps. 119: 105.

8. WHAT ARE THE TWO GREAT TEACHINGS OF THE BIBLE?

Law and Gospel are the two great teachings of the Bible.

For the law was given by Moses, but grace and truth came by Jesus Christ. John 1:17.

9. WHAT WAS THE LAW?

The Law was the judgments, ordinances, and the Ten Commandments given by God to Moses to instruct the people of Israel, to motivate them to obey God, and to make them conscious of sin. Its Purpose was to teach man how God expects him to live and to show man that he cannot obey God through his own efforts alone, without Christ and without the indwelling of the Holy Spirit.

And knowest his will, and approvest the things that are more excellent, being instructed out of the law. Rom. 2:18.

The law of the Lord is perfect, converting the soul: the testimony of the Lord is sure, making wise the simple. The statutes of the Lord are right, rejoicing the heart: the commandment of the Lord is pure, enlightening the eyes. Ps. 19:7,8.

. . . for by the law is the knowledge of sin. Rom. 3:20.

Wherefore the law was our schoolmaster to bring us unto Christ, that we might be justified by faith. Gal. 3:24.

0. WHAT IS THE GOSPEL?

The Gospel is the good news of our salvation.

To wit, that God was in Christ, reconciling the world unto himself, not imputing their trespasses unto them; and hath committed unto us the word of reconciliation. II Cor. 5:19.

In this was manifested the love of God toward us, because that God sent his only begotten Son into the world that we might live through him. I John 4:9.

STUDY QUESTIONS—Chapter 1

1. What is the Bible?
2. Who wrote the Bible?
3. Why is the Bible the Word of God even though it was written by men?
4. What does "by inspiration of God" mean?
5. For what purpose did God give us the Bible?
6. What use should we make of the Bible?
7. What are the two great teachings of the Bible?
8. What is the Law? What is the Gospel?
9. Memorize Ps. 119:105, II Tim. 3:16, John 1:17.

Chapter 2

USING THE BIBLE

11. **HOW OFTEN SHOULD WE READ THE BIBLE?**

We should read the Bible prayerfully every day. Along with strengthening our faith, daily reading of the Scriptures will give us help, strength, guidance, comfort, hope and love.

> *So then faith cometh by hearing, and hearing by the word of God. Rom. 10:17.*

> *And that from a child thou hast known the holy scriptures, which are able to make thee wise unto salvation through faith which is in Christ Jesus. All scripture is given by inspiration of God, and is profitable for doctrine, for reproof, for correction, for instruction in righteousness: That the man of God may be perfect, thoroughly furnished unto all good works. II Tim. 3:15–17.*

12. **WHAT HAPPENS WHEN WE READ THE BIBLE?**

God prepares our hearts that we might receive a revelation of Christ who changes our carnal minds into spiritual minds.

> *And beginning at Moses and all the prophets, he expounded unto them in all the scriptures the things concerning himself . . . And their eyes were opened, and they knew him . . . And they said one to another, Did not our heart burn within us, while he talked with us by the way, and while he opened to us the scriptures? Luke 24:27, 31, 32.*

13. **WHY MUST OUR MINDS BE CHANGED?**

From early childhood, we have been taught (conditioned) to respond to certain situations in certain ways. Our ways of response have not always been pleasing to God. We even tend to respond to the things of God as we have been taught to respond. This limits God. We cannot serve God effectually if we do not think like He does. Our thoughts must be in agreement with His thoughts if we are to become spiritual.

> *For my thoughts are not your thoughts, neither are your ways my ways, saith the Lord. For as the heavens are higher than the earth, so are my ways higher than your ways, and my thoughts than your thoughts. For as the rain cometh down, and the snow from heaven, and returneth not thither, but watereth the earth, and maketh it bring forth and bud, that it may give seed to the sower, and bread to the eater: So shall my word that goeth forth out of my mouth: it shall not return unto me void, but it shall accomplish that which I please, and it shall prosper in the thing whereto I sent it. Isa. 55:8–11.*

> *This people honoreth me with their lips, but their heart is far from me. Howbeit in vain do they worship me, teaching for doctrines the commandments of men. For laying aside the commandment of God, ye hold the tradition of men, as the washing of pots and cups: and many other such like things ye do. And he said unto them, Full well ye reject the commandment of God, that ye may keep your own tradition. Mark 7:6b–9.*

14. WHAT IS REVELATION?

Revelation is a divine understanding or knowledge given to us by God concerning Himself or what He is doing.

> *That the God of our Lord Jesus Christ, the Father of glory, may give unto you the spirit of wisdom and revelation in the knowledge of him. Eph. 1:17.*

> *How that by revelation he made known unto me the mystery. . . . Eph. 3:3.*

15. WHY MUST WE BECOME SPIRITUALLY MINDED?

Unless we become spiritually minded, we cannot have life and peace.

> *For to be carnally minded is death: but to be spiritually*

minded is life and peace. Because the carnal mind is enmity against God: for it is not subject to the law of God, neither indeed can be. So then they that are in the flesh cannot please God. Rom. 8:6–8.

16.   HOW DO WE BECOME SPIRITUALLY MINDED?

By reading the Bible under the direction and guidance of the Holy Spirit.

It is the spirit that quickeneth; the flesh profiteth nothing: the words that I speak unto you, they are spirit, and they are life. John 6:63.

17.   HOW DO WE RECEIVE THE DIRECTION AND GUIDANCE OF THE HOLY SPIRIT?

First of all, the Holy Spirit gives us a desire or longing for knowledge. Then we pray and ask the Holy Spirit to reveal to us, through the Scriptures, what God is doing or what God wants us to know.

I have yet many things to say unto you, but ye cannot bear them now. Howbeit when he, the Spirit of truth, is come, he will guide you into all truth: for he shall not speak of himself; but whatsoever he shall hear, that shall he speak: and he will shew you things to come. John 16:12,13.

18.   WHY SHOULD WE MEMORIZE THE NAMES OF THE BOOKS OF THE BIBLE?

Knowing the names of the books in their proper order will enable us to find Scripture verses quickly and easily. By studying them in groups, we can learn them much faster.

THE OLD TESTAMENT (39 Books)

Historical Books (17)

Genesis	Joshua	I and II Chronicles
Exodus	Judges	Ezra
Leviticus	Ruth	Nehemiah
Numbers	I and II Samuel	Esther
Deuteronomy	I and II Kings	

Poetical Books (5)

Job	Ecclesiastes
Psalms	Song of Solomon
Proverbs	

Prophetic Books (17)—*The Major Prophets*

Isaiah	Ezekiel
Jeremiah	Daniel
Lamentations (also Poetical)	

The Minor Prophets

Hosea	Jonah	Zephaniah
Joel	Micah	Haggai
Amos	Nahum	Zechariah
Obadiah	Habakkuk	Malachi

THE NEW TESTAMENT (27 Books)

Historical Books (5)

Matthew	John
Mark	The Acts
Luke	

Doctrinal Books (The 21 Epistles)

A. The Epistles of St. Paul (13)

Romans	Colossians
I and II Corinthians	I and II Thessalonians
Galatians	I and II Timothy
Ephesians	Titus
Philippians	Philemon

B. The Epistle to the Hebrews

C. The Seven General Epistles

James	I, II, III John
I and II Peter	Jude

Prophetic Book
Book of Revelation—St. John

Note: The word "Bible" is derived from the Greek word "Biblia" which means "books", so we know that it is not just one book but a combination of books. It was written by forty-four authors over a period of many centuries and is composed of sixty-six books.

STUDY QUESTIONS—Chapter 2

1. How often should we read the Bible?
2. What should be our main objective in reading the Bible?
3. Why must our minds be changed?
4. How do we become spiritually minded?
5. How does the Holy Spirit direct and guide us?
6. How many books are in the Bible? How many are in the Old Testament? How many are in the New Testament?
7. Into what three classes is the Old Testament divided?
8. Write and be able to recite the books of the Old Testament.
9. Write and be able to recite the books of the New Testament.
10. How many writers wrote the Bible?

IN THE BEGINNING

Chapter 3

THE PRE-EXISTENCE OF GOD

19. WHAT IS MEANT BY THE PRE-EXISTENCE OF GOD?

God existed before time began.

> *Lord, thou hast been our dwelling place in all generations. Before the mountains were brought forth, or ever thou hadst formed the earth and the world, even from everlasting to everlasting, thou art God. Ps. 90:1,2.*

20. WHAT HAS GOD REVEALED ABOUT HIMSELF IN THE BIBLE?

He revealed to us that He is one God, He is Spirit, Life, Light and Love.

> *Hear, O Israel: the Lord our God is one Lord. Deut. 6:4.*

> *God is a Spirit: and they that worship him must worship in spirit and truth. John 4:24.*

> *This is the true God, and eternal life. I John 5:20.*

> *God is light, and in him is no darkness at all. I John 1:5.*

> *God is love. I John 4:8.*

21. WHAT IS GOD?

> *God is spirit. John 4:24 RSV.*

22.   WHAT IS A SPIRIT?

A spirit is a being that has intelligence and free will but has no body and therefore, cannot be destroyed.

A spirit hath not flesh and bones. Luke 24:39.

Now unto the King eternal, immortal, invisible, the only wise God, be honour and glory for ever and ever. Amen. I Tim. 1:17.

23.   WHAT ARE SOME OF THE CHARACTERISTICS OF GOD?

He is:

A. Eternal.

Lord, thou hast been our dwelling place in all generations. Before the mountains were brought forth or ever thou hadst formed the earth and the world, even from everlasting to everlasting, thou art God. Ps. 90:1,2.

B. Unchangeable.

For I am the Lord, I change not. Mal. 3:6.

C. Omnipotent (Almighty, All-powerful).

I am the almighty God. Gen. 17:1.

God hath spoken once; twice have I heard this; that power belongeth unto God. . . . Ps. 62:11.

. . . With God all things are possible. Matt. 19:26.

D. Omniscient (All-knowing).

O Lord, thou hast searched me and known me. Thou knowest my downsittings and mine uprisings, thou understandest my thought afar off. Thou compassest my path and my lying down and art acquainted with all my ways. For there is not a word in my tongue, but, O Lord, thou knowest it altogether. Ps. 139:1–4.

E. Omnipresent (He is everywhere).

Can any hide himself in secret places that I shall not see him? saith the Lord. Do not I fill heaven and earth? saith the Lord. Jer. 23:24.

F. Holy (Sinless)

. . . I the Lord your God am holy. Lev. 19:2.

G. Just (Fair and impartial).

. . . A God of truth and without iniquity, just and right is he. Deut. 32:4.

H. Faithful (Keeping His promises).

. . . He abideth faithful: He cannot deny himself. II Tim. 2:13.

I. Benevolent (Good, kind).

The Lord is good to all: and his tender mercies are over all his works. Ps. 145:9.

J. Merciful (Full of pity).

The Lord, the Lord God, merciful and gracious, longsuffering, abundant in goodness and truth, keeping mercy for thousands, forgiving iniquity and transgression and sin. Exod. 34:6,7a.

K. Gracious (Showing undeserved kindness, forgiving).

. . . God is love. I John 4:8.

24. **HOW BIG IS GOD?**

No one knows. God is bigger than the entire universe.

Who hath measured the waters in the hollow of his hands, and meted out heaven with the span, and comprehended the dust of the earth in a measure, and weighed the mountains in scales, and the hills in a balance? Behold, the nations are as a drop of a bucket, and are counted as the small dust of the balance: behold, he taketh up the isles as a very little thing. It is he that sitteth upon the circle of the earth, and the inhabitants thereof are as grasshoppers; that stretcheth out the heavens as a curtain, and spreadeth them out as a tent to dwell in. Isa. 40:12,15,22.

25. **WHERE IS GOD?**

God is everywhere. We cannot hide nor escape Him for His eyes are in every place; however, His home and throne are in heaven.

The eyes of the Lord are in every place, beholding the evil and the good. Prov. 15:3.

For the eyes of the Lord run to and fro throughout the whole earth, to shew himself strong in the behalf of them whose heart is perfect toward him. . . . II Chron. 16:9a.

Whither shall I go from thy spirit? or whither shall I flee from thy presence? If I ascend up into heaven, thou art there: if I make my bed in hell, behold, thou art there. Ps. 139:7,8.

. . . Heaven is my throne, and the earth is my footstool. Isa. 66:1.

STUDY QUESTIONS—Chapter 3

1. What is meant by the pre-existence of God?
2. What five things has God revealed about Himself in the Bible?
3. What is God?
4. Describe God in eleven ways.
5. How big is God?
6. Where is God?
7. Write and memorize Matt. 19:26, Prov. 15:3, John 4:24.

Chapter 4

THE MYSTERY OF THE TRIUNE GOD

26. WHAT IS MEANT BY THE MYSTERY OF THE TRIUNE GOD?

It means that in God there are three divine and distinct identities —the Father, Son and Holy Spirit.

> *And Jesus, when he was baptized, went up straightway out of the water: and lo, the heavens were opened unto him, and he saw the Spirit of God descending like a dove, and lighting upon him; And lo a voice from heaven, saying, This is my beloved Son, in whom I am well pleased. Matt. 3:16,17.*

27. HOW ARE THE THREE IDENTITIES DISTINCT FROM ONE ANOTHER?

To the Father is credited the work of creation; to the Son, the work of redemption; to the Holy Spirit, the work of sanctification.

> *In the beginning God created the heaven and the earth. Gen. 1:1.*

> *But when the fulness of the time was come, God sent forth his Son, made of a woman, made under the law, To redeem them that were under the law, that we might receive the adoption of sons. Gal. 4:4,5.*

> *Elect according to the foreknowledge of God the Father, through sanctification of the Spirit, unto obedience and sprinkling of the blood of Jesus Christ: Grace unto you, and peace, be multiplied. I Peter 1;2.*

28. HOW CAN THREE DISTINCT IDENTITIES BE ONE?

Because they are all of the same substance. God has revealed Himself to us through Jesus Christ and the Holy Spirit.

That they may be ONE, as WE are. John 17:11b.

In the beginning was the Word, and the Word was with God and the Word was God. John 1:1.

Hear, O Israel: The Lord our God is one Lord. Deut. 6:4.

29. WHEN WE REACH HEAVEN, WILL WE SEE THREE PERSONS OR ONE?

We will see ONE God. God has three identities but He is only one God. A man can be a father, a son, and a husband but he is still only one person.

30. HAS ANY MAN EVER SEEN GOD?

No man has ever seen God because God is a Spirit but He has revealed Himself to man in various forms.

No man hath seen God at any time: the only begotten Son, which is in the bosom of the Father, he hath declared him. John 1:18.

31. IN WHAT FORMS HAS GOD REVEALED HIMSELF TO MAN?

God has revealed Himself as:

A. The Rock.

Behold, I will stand before thee there upon the rock in Horeb; and thou shalt smite the rock, and there shall come water out of it, that the people may drink. Exod. 17:6.

And did all drink the same spiritual drink; for they drank of that spiritual Rock that followed them; and that Rock was Christ. I Cor. 10:4.

B. The Pillar of Fire.

C. A Cloud.

And the Lord went before them by day in a pillar of a cloud, to lead them the way; and by night in a pillar of fire, to give them light; to go by day and night: He took not away the pillar of the cloud by day, nor the pillar of fire by night, from before the people. Exod. 13:21,22.

D. The Angel of the Lord.

And the angel of the Lord found her by a fountain of water in the wilderness, by the fountain in the way to Shur. And he said, Hagar, Sarai's maid, whence camest thou? and whither wilt thou go? And she said, I flee from the face of my mistress Sarai. And the angel of the Lord said unto her, Return to thy mistress, and submit thyself under her hands. And the angel of the Lord said unto her, I will multiply thy seed exceedingly, that it shall not be numbered for multitude. And the angel of the Lord said unto her, Behold, thou art with child, and shall bear a son, and shalt call his name Ishmael; because the Lord hath heard thy afflictions. Gen. 16:7–11.

And the angel of the Lord appeared unto him in a flame of fire out of the midst of a bush: and he looked, and, behold, the bush burned with fire, and the bush was not consumed. And Moses said, I will now turn aside, and see this great sight, why the bush is not burnt. And when the Lord saw that he turned aside to see, God called unto him out of the midst of the bush, and said, Moses, Moses. And he said, Here am I. Exod. 3:2–4.

And an angel of the Lord came up from Gilgal to Bochim, and said, I made you to go up out of Egypt, and have brought you unto the land which I sware unto your fathers; and I said, I will never break my covenant with you. Judges 2:1.

E. In the Flesh as Jesus Christ.

And without controversy great is the mystery of godliness: God was manifest in the flesh, justified in the Spirit, seen of angels, preached unto the Gentiles, believed on in the world, received up into Glory. I Tim. 3:16.

F. The Holy Spirit.

. . . As God hath said, I will dwell in them, and walk in them; and I will be their God, and they shall be my people. II Cor. 6:16b.

STUDY QUESTIONS—Chapter 4

1. What is meant by the Mystery of the Triune God?
2. What is the work of the Father?
3. What is the work of the Son?
4. What is the work of the Holy Spirit?
5. How can three distinct identities be one?
6. In what forms has God revealed Himself to man?
7. Write Matt. 3:16,17; Deut. 6:4; I Tim. 3:16.

Chapter 5

THE ANGELS

32. WHAT ARE ANGELS?

Angels are spirit beings who were created by God. Their power and intelligence is greater than that of natural man.

> *But one in a certain place testified, saying, What is man, that thou art mindful of him? or the son of man, that thou visitest him? Thou madest him a little lower than the angels; thou crownedst him with glory and honour, and didst set him over the works of thy hands. Heb. 2:6,7.*

33. WHY DID GOD CREATE THE ANGELS?

God created the angels to worship and to serve Him.

> *Bless the Lord, ye his angels, that excel in strength, that do his commandments, hearkening unto the voice of his word. Bless ye the Lord, all ye his hosts; ye ministers of his, that do his pleasure. Ps. 103:20,21.*

> *Thou, even thou, art Lord alone; thou hast made heaven, the heaven of heavens, with all their host, the earth, and all things that are therein, the seas, and all that is therein, and thou preservest them all; and the host of heaven worshippeth thee. Neh. 9:6.*

> *And he said, Hear thou therefore the word of the Lord: I saw the Lord sitting on his throne, and all the host of heaven standing by him on his right hand and on his left. I Kings 22:19.*

34. ARE ALL ANGELS EQUAL IN POWER AND STRENGTH?

No. They are divided into orders according to their power and strength.

1. Seraphs—They minister at God's throne. They have six wings.

   In the year that king Uzziah died I saw also the Lord sitting upon a throne, high and lifted up, and his train filled the temple. Above it stood the seraphims: each one had six wings; with twain he covered his face, and with twain he covered his feet, and with twain he did fly. And one cried unto another, and said, Holy, holy, holy, is the Lord of hosts: the whole earth is full of his glory. Isa. 6:1-3.

2. Cherubs—They guard and cover the throne of God. They have two wings.

   And the cherubims shall stretch forth their wings on high, covering the mercy seat with their wings, and their faces shall look one to another; toward the mercy seat shall the faces of the cherubims be. Exod. 25:20.

   So he drove out the man; and he placed at the east of the garden of Eden Cherubims, and a flaming sword which turned every way, to keep the way of the tree of life. Gen. 3:24.

   Thou art the anointed cherub (Lucifer) that covereth; and I have set thee so; thou wast upon the holy mountain of God; thou hast walked up and down in the midst of the stones of fire. Ezek. 28:14.

3. Archangels—The princes of the angels.

   For the Lord himself shall descend from heaven with a shout, with the voice of the archangel, and with the trump of God: and the dead in Christ shall rise first. I Thess. 4:16.

   Yet Michael the archangel, when contending with the devil he disputed about the body of Moses, durst not bring against him a railing accusation, but said, The Lord rebuke thee. Jude 9.

4. Angels—The agents of God sent forth to do his bidding. These superior beings are very numerous and possess different ranks of dignity and power.

   Bless the Lord, ye His angels, that excel in strength, that do his commandments, hearkening unto the voice of his word. Bless ye the Lord, all ye his hosts; ye ministers of his, that do his pleasure. Ps. 103:20,21.

... thousand thousands ministered unto him, and ten thousand times ten thousand stood before him. ... Dan. 7:10.

Then said he unto me, Fear not, Daniel: for from the first day that thou didst set thine heart to understand, and to chasten thyself before thy God, thy words were heard, and I am come for thy words. But the prince of the kingdom of Persia withstood me one and twenty days: but, lo, Michael, one of the chief princes, came to help me; and I remained there with the kings of Persia. Dan. 10:12,13.

Note: There are also Thrones, Dominations or Dominions, Virtues, Powers, Principalities or Princedoms.

35. **DO ANGELS HAVE POWER TO MAKE THEMSELVES VISIBLE TO MAN?**

Yes. There are numerous instances in the Bible where angels have appeared to man.

BIBLE NARRATIVES: An angel wrestled with Jacob, Gen. 32:24. An angel set Peter free, Acts 12:5–11; An angel saved Daniel from the lion, Dan. 6; The angel Gabriel announced to Mary that she would become the mother of Jesus, Luke 1:26–33; An angel appeared to the shepherds, Luke 2:8–14; An angel appeared to the women at Christ's tomb, Luke 24:1–10; Angels carried Lazarus into Abraham's bosom, Luke 16:22.

36. **DID GOD CREATE THE ANGELS MALE OR FEMALE?**

God created the angels as males. They are called the "sons of God".

Now there was a day when the sons of God came to present themselves before the Lord, and Satan came also among them. Job 1:6.

Yea, whiles I was speaking in prayer, even the man Gabriel, whom I had seen in the vision at the beginning, being caused to fly swiftly, touched me about the time of the evening oblation. Dan. 9:21.

When the morning stars sang together, and all the sons of God shouted for joy? Job 38:7.

37. DO THE ANGELS HAVE THE FREEDOM TO OBEY OR DISOBEY GOD?

Yes. Just as God gave Adam and Eve the will to choose to obey or disobey Him, so He also gave the angels the same freedom.

> *For thou (Lucifer) hast said in thine heart, I will ascend into heaven, I will exalt my throne above the stars of God: I will sit also upon the mount of the congregation, in the sides of the north: I will ascend above the heights of the clouds; I will be like the most High. Isa. 14:13,14.*

38. DO ANGELS MINISTER TO MAN TODAY?

Yes. Angels minister in time of need to the heirs of salvation.

> *Are they not all ministering spirits, sent forth to minister for them who shall be heirs of salvation? Heb. 1:14.*

> *Be not forgetful to entertain strangers; for thereby some have entertained angels unawares. Heb. 13:2.*

39. WHAT ELSE DOES THE BIBLE TELL US ABOUT THE ANGELS?

A. They behold the face of God the Father in heaven.

> *Take heed that ye despise not one of these little ones; for I say unto you, That in heaven their angels do always behold the face of my Father which is in heaven. Matt. 18:10.*

B. They are great in number and power.

> *Suddenly there was with the angel a multitude of the heavenly host . . . Luke 2:13a.*

> *. . . Thousand thousands ministered unto him, and ten thousand times ten thousand stood before him. Dan. 7:10.*

> *Thinkest thou that I cannot now pray to my Father, and he shall presently give me more than twelve legions of angels? Matt. 26:53.*

> *The chariots of God are twenty thousand, even thousands of angels. . . . Ps. 68:17a.*

BIBLE NARRATIVES: One angel slew 185,000 of Sennacherib's army, II Kings 19:35; Elisha and his servant were protected by the heavenly hosts, II Kings 6:15–17.

C. They rejoice over penitent sinners.

Likewise, I say unto you, there is joy in the presence of the angels of God over one sinner that repenteth. Luke 15:10.

D. They watch over Christ's little ones (children) and serve the Christians.

Take heed that ye despise not one of these little ones; for I say unto you, That in heaven their angels do always behold the face of my Father which is in heaven. Matt. 18:10.

The angel of the Lord encampeth round about them that fear him, and delivereth them. Ps. 34:7.

STUDY QUESTIONS—Chapter 5

1. What are angels?
2. Why were angels created?
3. Do angels have the power to make themselves visible?
4. In what form do they appear to man?

Chapter 6

THE CREATION

40. WHEN DID GOD CREATE THE HEAVENS AND THE EARTH?

In the beginning. According to Radio Metric Dating, the earth is 4.7 billion years old.

In the beginning God created the heaven and the earth. Gen. 1:1.

41. HOW DID GOD CREATE THE HEAVENS AND THE EARTH?

He created them by ordering them to come into existence.

Let them praise the name of the Lord; for he commanded, and they were created. Ps. 148:5.

For by him were all things created, that are in heaven, and that are in earth, visible and invisible, whether they be thrones, or dominions, or principalities, or powers: all things were created by him, and for him: And he is before all things, and by him all things consist. Col. 1:16,17.

42. HOW BIG IS THE UNIVERSE THAT GOD CREATED?

No one knows except God. Scientists tell us that the nearest star, Alpha Centauri, is 25 trillion, 206 billion, 797 million 800 thousand miles from the earth. It takes four years and four months for its light, which is traveling at the speed of 186 thousand miles a second, to reach the earth. According to Albert Einstein, man can never reach the speed of light because if he did, he would cease to exist. Traveling at the speed of light, a round trip to Alpha Centauri would take nine years.

STUDY QUESTIONS—Chapter 6

1. When was the earth created?
2. How was the earth created?
3. How far is the nearest star?

Chapter 7

THE FALL OF LUCIFER AND HIS ANGELS

43. WHO WAS LUCIFER?

He was the anointed cherub who led the angels in their worship and adoration of God.

> *You were the anointed cherub that covers with overshadowing (wings), and I set you so. You were upon the holy mountain of God; you walked up and down in the midst of the stones of fire (like the paved work of gleaming sapphire stone upon which the God of Israel walked on Mount Sinai). Ezek. 28:14 Amp.*

44. WHAT WAS LUCIFER LIKE?

He was a most beautiful creature, perfect in beauty and in wisdom.

> *Thou sealest up the sum, full of wisdom, and perfect in beauty. Thou hast been in Eden the garden of God; every precious stone was thy covering, the sardius, topaz, and the diamond, the beryl, the onyx, and the jasper, the sapphire, the emerald, and the carbuncle, and gold: the workmanship of thy tabrets and of thy pipes was prepared in thee in the day that thou was created. Ezek. 28:12–13.*

> *Thou was perfect in thy ways from the day that thou wast created. Ezek. 28:15.*

45. WAS LUCIFER FAITHFUL TO GOD?

No. He coveted the worship and adoration that belonged to God and attempted to take God's place by overthrowing the throne of God.

*For thou hast said in thine heart, I will ascend into heaven,
I will exalt my throne above the stars of God: I will sit also
upon the mount of the congregation in the sides of the
north; I will ascend above the heights of the clouds; I will
be like the most High. Isa. 14:13–14.*

46. WHAT HAPPENED TO LUCIFER?

He was cast out of heaven because he took glory to himself that
belonged to God.

*And he (Jesus) said unto them, I beheld Satan as lightning
fall from heaven. Luke 10:18. (A warning against pride).*

*How art thou fallen from heaven, O Lucifer, son of the
morning! how art thou cut down to the ground, which didst
weaken the nations! Isa. 14:12.*

*I am the Lord: that is my name: and my glory will I not
give to another, neither my praise to graven images.
Isa. 42:8.*

47. WHO FELL FROM HEAVEN WITH LUCIFER?

Many thousands of angels who sinned with Lucifer. They became
demons.

*And the great dragon was cast out, that old serpent, called
the Devil and Satan, which deceiveth the whole world: he
was cast out into the earth, and his angels were cast out
with him. Rev. 12:9.*

48. WHAT HAPPENED TO THE WORLD WHEN LUCIFER WAS CAST OUT OF HEAVEN?

When Lucifer and his followers were thrown from heaven, the
world was turned upside down, underwent a terrible upheaval
and was made without form and void.

*And the earth was without form, and void; and darkness
was upon the face of the deep. And the Spirit of God moved
upon the face of the waters. Gen. 1:2.*

*Behold, the Lord maketh the earth empty, and maketh it
waste, and turneth it upside down, and scattereth abroad
the inhabitants thereof. Isa. 24:1.*

> *I beheld the earth, and lo, it was without form, and void; and the heavens, and they had no light. I beheld the mountains, and lo, they trembled, and all the hills moved lightly. I beheld, and lo, there was no man, and all the birds of the heavens were fled. I beheld, and lo, the fruitful place was a wilderness, and all the cities thereof were broken down at the presence of the Lord, and by his fierce anger. For thus hath the Lord said, The whole land shall be desolate; yet will I not make a full end. Jer. 4:23–27.*

Note: The time element between the first and second verses of Genesis is sometimes referred to by theologians as the "Gap Theory".

49. WHERE IS LUCIFER NOW?

Lucifer and his demons inhabit the earth and its atmosphere.

> *And the Lord said unto Satan, Whence comest thou? Then Satan answered the Lord, and said, From going to and fro in the earth and from walking up and down in it. Job 1:7.*

> *Be sober, be vigilant; because your adversary the devil, as a roaring lion, walketh about, seeking whom he may devour. I Pet. 5:8–9.*

> *The whole world lieth in wickedness. I John 5:19b.*

50. DO DEMONS HAVE POWER TO SHOW THEMSELVES?

Yes. Although they are disembodied spirits, they are able to make their power felt either by possessing the body of a man or animal or by means of an apparition.

> *Put on the whole armour of God, that ye may be able to stand against the wiles of the devil. For we wrestle not against flesh and blood, but against principalities, against powers, against the rulers of the darkness of this world, against spiritual wickedness in high places. Eph. 6:11–12.*

STUDY QUESTIONS—Chapter 7

1. Who was Lucifer?
2. What happened to Lucifer?
3. What are demons?
4. Where is Lucifer now?
5. Do demons have power to make themselves visible?
6. Write and memorize Eph. 6:11–12.

THE RE-CREATION

Chapter 8

THE RE-CREATION

51. WHEN DID GOD RESTORE THE EARTH?

About 4,000 B.C. (About 6,000 years ago.)

52. DID GOD RE-CREATE LIGHT AND DARKNESS, THE SUN, MOON AND STARS, LAND AND SEA?

No. These things were created in the beginning. God called them back into operation in the re-creation. He commanded the water to be gathered together in one place and dry land once again appeared. The Scriptures say that water covered the face of the deep after the earth had undergone a convulsive change as a result of divine judgment.

> *And God SAID, Let there by light and there WAS light. Gen. 1:3.*

> *And God SAID, Let there be a firmament in the midst of the waters and let it divide the waters from the waters. Gen. 1:6.*

> *And God SAID, Let the waters under the heaven be gathered together unto one place and let the dry land APPEAR and it WAS SO. Gen. 1:9.*

53. HOW DID GOD CREATE THE BEASTS OF THE FIELD AND THE FOWL OF THE AIR?

Every beast and fowl was formed out of the dust of the ground.

> *And out of the ground the Lord God formed every beast of the field, and every fowl of the air. Gen. 2:19.*

54. HOW DID THEY GET THEIR NAMES?

Adam named every living creature God made, including his wife Eve.

> *And Adam gave names to all cattle, and to the fowl of the air, and to every beast of the field. . . . Gen. 2:20a.*

> *And Adam called his wife's name Eve. . . . Gen. 3:20a.*

55. HOW LONG DID IT TAKE GOD TO RESTORE THE EARTH?

It took God six days to restore the earth.

> *And God saw every thing that he had made, and behold, it was very good. And the evening and the morning were the sixth day. Thus the heavens and the earth were finished, and all the host of them. And on the seventh day God ended his work which he had made; and he rested on the seventh day from all his work which he had made. Gen. 1:31; 2:1,2.*

56. WHAT IS THE THEORY OF EVOLUTION?

It is a theory, not a proven fact. It states that:

A. All matter, energy and life appeared and developed by nature (by itself) with out any divine intervention at any given point.

B. All life began by chance through an impersonal combination of matter and energy plus time.

C. All plants and animals began as very simple forms of life and developed into higher forms. Evidence of some early forms are preserved in rocks. (fossils).

D. All species came into being through a series of changes (mutations) which occurred by chance in earlier forms.

E. Man, like all other creatures, developed from simple forms of life through many stages of change.

57. DOES THE THEORY OF EVOLUTION DISAGREE WITH THE BIBLE ACCOUNT OF CREATION AND MAN?

Yes! The Bible is truth inspired by God. It states that:

A. In the beginning a personal God created all matter and energy (things visible and invisible).

In the beginning God created the heavens and the earth. Gen. 1:1.

For by him were all things created, that are in heaven, and that are in earth, visible and invisible, whether they be thrones, or dominions, or principalities, or powers: all things were created by him, and for him: Col. 1:16.

B. God created and organized matter and energy from which he specifically created plant and animal life.

And God created great whales, and every living creature that moveth, which the waters brought forth abundantly, AFTER THEIR KIND, and every winged fowl AFTER HIS KIND; and God saw that it was good. Gen. 1:21.

C. God created the higher forms of animals.

And God said, let the earth bring forth the living creatures after his kind, cattle, and creeping things, and beast of the earth after his kind, and it was so. And God made the beast of the earth AFTER HIS KIND, and cattle AFTER THEIR KIND, and everything that creepeth upon the earth AFTER HIS KIND, and God saw that it was good. Gen. 1:24,25.

D. God personally made the differences between animals.

And God made the beast of the earth after his kind. Gen. 1:25a.

E. God personally imposed Himself upon nature to create man in His own image and likeness and to impart personality.

So God created man in his own image, in the image of God created he him; male and female created he them. Gen. 1:27.

And the Lord God formed man of the dust of the ground, and breathed into his nostrils the breath of life; and man became a living soul. Gen. 2:7.

STUDY QUESTIONS—Chapter 8

1. How long ago did God re-create the earth?
2. Did God re-create the light and darkness, the sun, moon and th stars, land and sea?
3. How did God create the beasts of the field and the fowl of the air
4. Who named the animals?
5. What did God create in each of the six days?
6. Write and memorize Gen. 2:19 and Gen. 2:20.

Chapter 9

MAN

58. WHAT IS MAN?

Man is a creature composed of body, soul and spirit. He is made in the image and likeness of God.

> *And the Lord God formed man of the dust of the ground and breathed into his nostrils the breath of life; and man became a living soul. Gen. 2:7.*

> *And God said, Let us make man in our image, after our likeness: and let them have dominion over the fish of the sea and over the fowl of the air and over the cattle and over all the earth and over every creeping thing that creepeth upon the earth. So God created man in his own image, in the image of God created he him; male and female created he them. Gen. 1:26,27.*

59. WHAT IS MEANT BY THE IMAGE AND LIKENESS OF GOD?

A. When God created man in His own image, He endowed man with certain characteristics of personality similar to His own. Man was made perfectly holy and blessed and was given understanding and free will.

> *So God created man in his own image, in the image of God created he him; male and female created he them. And God blessed them, and God said unto them, Be fruitful, and multiply, and replenish the earth, and subdue it: . . . . Gen. 1:27,28a.*

> *And they heard the voice of the Lord God walking in the garden in the cool of the day: and Adam and his wife hid*

*themselves from the presence of the Lord God amongst the
trees of the garden. And the Lord God called unto Adam,
and said unto him, Where art thou? And he said, I heard
thy voice in the garden, and I was afraid, because I was
naked; and I hid myself. Gen. 3:8–10.*

B. The likeness of man to God is chiefly in the spirit. It is throug
the spirit that man has an awareness of God.

*But there is a spirit in man; and the inspiration of the Al-
mighty giveth him understanding. Job 32:8.*

60. DOES MAN STILL BEAR THE IMAGE OF GOD?

No. Man lost the image of God through the fall of Adam an
Eve. In believers, a beginning of its renewal is made. Only
heaven, however, will this image be fully restored.

*(Adam) begat a son in his own likeness, after his own
image. Gen. 5:3.*

*But we all, with open face beholding as in a glass the glory
of the Lord, are changed into the same image from glory to
glory, even as by the Spirit of the Lord. II Cor. 3:18.*

*. . . the dead shall be raised incorruptible, and we shall
be changed. I Cor. 15:52.*

*I will behold thy face in righteousness; I shall be satisfied,
when I awake, with thy likeness. Ps. 17:15.*

61. IS MAN A SPIRIT BEING?

Man is more of a spirit being than he is a physical being. There i
a spirit in man, inbreathed by God, which gives man a far greate
capacity for eternal things and for the spiritual realm than fo
temporal things and the material realm.

*And God said, Let us make man in our image after our own
likeness. Gen. 1:26.*

*And I pray God your whole spirit, and soul, and body be
preserved blameless unto the coming of our Lord Jesus
Christ. I Thess. 5:23.*

*God has set the world (eternity) in their hearts . . .
Eccles. 3:11.*

... Man does not live by bread alone, but by every word that proceedeth out of the mouth of God. Matt. 4:4.

2. WHAT IS THE DIFFERENCE BETWEEN BODY, SOUL, AND SPIRIT?

The body, through the five senses, makes us world-conscious—it is fed by natural food. The soul, which is the personality of man, makes us self-conscious (ego)—it is fed by love. The spirit makes us God conscious and thus, enables us to communicate with God —it is fed by God's word.

For the word of God is quick, and powerful and sharper than any twoedged sword, piercing even to the dividing asunder of soul and spirit, and of the joints and marrow, and is a discerner of the thoughts and intents of the heart. Heb. 4:12.

3. HOW WAS WOMAN CREATED?

Woman was created by God out of a rib which the Lord removed from Adam's side.

And the Lord God caused a deep sleep to fall upon Adam, and he slept; and he took one of his ribs, and closed the flesh instead thereof; And the rib, which the Lord God had taken from man, made he a woman, and brought her unto the man. Gen. 2:21–22.

4. WHY WAS WOMAN CREATED?

God created woman because He saw that it was not good for man to be alone. She was also created to mother the people of the earth.

... But for Adam there was not found an help meet for him. Gen. 2:20.

And the Lord God said, It is not good that the man should be alone; I will make him an help meet for him. Gen. 2:18.

And Adam said, This is now bone of my bones, and flesh of my flesh: she shall be called Woman, because she was taken out of Man. Therefore shall a man leave his father and his mother, and shall cleave unto his wife and they shall be one flesh. Gen. 2:23–24.

> *And Adam called his wife's name Eve; because she was the mother of all living. Gen. 3:20.*

STUDY QUESTIONS—Chapter 9

1. What is man?
2. What is meant by the image and likeness of God?
3. Does man still bear the image of God?
4. Is man a spirit being?
5. What is the difference between body, soul and spirit?
6. How was woman created?
7. Why was woman created?
8. Write Gen. 3:20; Gen. 2:7; Gen. 1:26.

THE DISPENSATIONS

Chapter 10

THE DISPENSATIONS

65. WHAT IS A DISPENSATION?

A Dispensation is a plan or method that God used during a particular period of time to reveal His mind and will to man.

> *For if I do this thing willingly, I have a reward: but if against my will, a dispensation of the gospel is committed unto me. I Cor. 9:17.*

66. HOW MANY DEFINED DISPENSATIONS WERE THERE?

There were six defined dispensations.

67. WHAT ARE THEY?

The six defined dispensations are:
1. Innocence.
2. Conscience.
3. Human Government.
4. Promise.
5. Law.
6. Grace.

68. WHY DID GOD FIND IT NECESSARY TO TEST MAN?

God tested man in six distinct ways to show man that he could not be obedient to God without undergoing an inward change.

69. WHY IS IT IMPORTANT FOR US TO STUDY THE DISPENSATIONS?

By studying the dispensations, we are able to systematically study the various periods of the Bible and to know the people with whom God dealt.

STUDY QUESTIONS—Chapter 10

1. What is a dispensation?
2. Is "dispensation" a Biblical word?
3. How many defined dispensations are there?
4. Why did God find it necessary to test man?
5. Why is it important for us to study the dispensations?
6. List the six defined dispensations.

Chapter 11

THE DISPENSATION OF INNOCENCE

70. **WHAT WAS THE DISPENSATION OF INNOCENCE?**

The Dispensation of Innocence was an age of sinlessness when Adam and Eve had fellowship with God. They enjoyed the fullness of natural and spiritual life and possessed superior intelligence and knowledge.

> *So God created man in his own image, in the image of God created he him; male and female created he them.*
> *Gen. 1:27.*

> *And out of the ground the Lord God formed every beast of the field, and every fowl of the air; and brought them unto Adam to see what he would call them: and whatsoever Adam called every living creature, that was the name thereof. And Adam gave names to all cattle, and to the fowl of the air, and to every beast of the field; but for Adam there was not found an help meet for him. Gen. 2:19,20.*

71. **HOW DID GOD TEST ADAM AND EVE?**

God tested Adam and Eve by placing two trees (The Tree of Life and The Tree of the Knowledge of Good and Evil) in the garden of Eden to give them the opportunity and freedom to obey or disobey His command.

> *And out of the ground made the Lord God to grow every tree that is pleasant to the sight, and good for food; the tree of life also in the midst of the garden, and the tree of the knowledge of good and evil. Gen. 2:9.*

72. WHAT DID GOD COMMAND THEM TO DO?

God commanded them not to eat of the tree of the Knowledge of Good and Evil.

> *And the Lord God commanded the man, saying, of every tree of the garden thou mayest freely eat: But of the tree of the knowledge of good and evil, thou shalt not eat of it: for in the day that thou eatest thereof thou shalt surely die. Gen. 2:16,17.*

73. WHAT WAS THE TREE OF LIFE?

The Tree of Life was a tree whose fruit held the power of everlasting life. It was a manifestation (unveiling or revealing) of Christ, the source of life, wisdom and knowledge.

> *In him (Christ) was life; and the life was the light of men. John 1:4.*

> *In whom (Christ) are hid all the treasures of wisdom and knowledge. Col. 2:3.*

> *I am the living bread which came down from heaven: if any man eat of this bread, he shall live for ever: and the bread that I will give is my flesh, which I will give for the life of the world. John 6:51.*

74. WHAT WAS THE TREE OF KNOWLEDGE OF GOOD AND EVIL?

The Tree of Knowledge of Good and Evil was a test for man. Man was tested as to whether he would rely on God for his knowledge or turn to a forbidden tree and gain independence from God.

> *And the serpent said unto the woman, Ye shall not surely die: For God doth know that in the days ye eat thereof, then your eyes shall be opened, and ye shall be as gods, knowing good and evil. Gen. 3:4,5.*

75. WHY DID GOD COMMAND ADAM AND EVE NOT TO EAT OF THIS TREE?

There had to be one restriction upon man. He had to have the opportunity to choose between God and Satan. Man must exercise his free will . . . he must choose.

> *But of the tree of the knowledge of good and evil, thou shalt not eat of it: for in the day that thou eatest thereof thou shalt surely die. Gen. 2:17.*

> *There is a way which seemeth right unto a man, but the end thereof are the ways of death. Prov. 14:12.*

> *O Lord, I know that the way of man is not in himself: it is not in man that walketh to direct his steps. Jer. 10:23.*

> *Man's goings are of the Lord; how can a man then understand his own way? Prov. 20:24.*

76. WHY DID SATAN TEMPT ADAM AND EVE?

Satan tempted them to disobey God because he was jealous of the power and dominion God had given to Adam over the earth.

> *And God said, Let us make man in our image, after our likeness: and let them have dominion over the fish of the sea, and over the fowl of the air, and over the cattle, and over all the earth, and over every creeping thing that creepeth upon the earth. So God created man in his own image, in the image of God created he him; male and female created he them. And God blessed them, and God said unto them, Be fruitful, and multiply, and replenish the earth, and subdue it: and have dominion over the fish of the sea, and over the fowl of the air, and over every living thing that moveth upon the earth. Gen. 1:26–28.*

77. WHY DID GOD TEST ADAM AND EVE?

God tested Adam and Eve to see if they would obey Him.

78. WHY IS OBEDIENCE TO GOD SO IMPORTANT?

God gives the knowledge of His kingdom power to those who obey Him. He gave this power to the second Adam, Jesus Christ, after His obedience unto death was complete.

> *And we are his witnesses of these things; and so is also the Holy Ghost, whom God hath given to them that obey him. Acts 5:32.*

> *(Jesus Christ) declared to be the Son of God with power, according to the spirit of holiness, by the resurrection from the dead. Rom. 1:4.*

But (Christ) made himself of no reputation, and took upon him the form of a servant, and was made in the likeness of men: And being found in fashion as a man, he humbled himself, and became obedient unto death, even the death of the cross. Wherefore God also hath highly exalted him, and given him a name which is above every name: That at the name of Jesus every knee should bow, of things in heaven, and things in earth, and things under the earth; And that every tongue should confess that Jesus Christ is Lord, to the glory of God the Father. Phil. 2:7–11.

79.   WHY DID ADAM AND EVE CHOOSE TO DISOBEY GOD?

They chose to disobey God because Satan led them to believe that the knowledge they would receive would make them self-sufficient, and therefore, independent of God.

And when the woman saw that the tree was good for food, and that it was pleasant to the eyes, and a tree to be desired to make one wise, she took of the fruit thereof, and did eat, and gave also unto her husband with her; and he did eat. Gen. 3:6.

80.   WHAT HAPPENED TO ADAM AND EVE WHEN THEY YIELDED TO TEMPTATION?

The lust for knowledge and power that was conceived in Adam and Eve when they heard God's commandment . . . "Thou shalt not" . . . became sin when they yielded to temptation.

And they were both naked, the man and his wife, and were not ashamed. Gen. 2:25.

And the eyes of them both were opened, and they knew that they were naked; and they sewed fig leaves together, and made themselves aprons. Gen. 3:7.

. . . Nay, I had not known sin, but by the law: for I had not known lust, except the law had said, Thou shalt not covet. But sin, taking occasion by the commandment, wrought in me all manner of concupiscence. (All kinds of forbidden desires—lust, covetousness.) For without the law sin was dead. Rom. 7:7,8.

81. WHAT KNOWLEDGE DID ADAM AND EVE RECEIVE?

They received an experimental knowledge of evil that manifested itself in feelings of guilt and shame.

> *And he said, I heard thy voice in the garden, and I was afraid, because I was naked; and I hid myself. Gen. 3:10.*

> *And the Lord God said, Behold, the man is become as one of us, to know good and evil . . . Gen. 3:22a.*

> *For we wrestle not against flesh and blood, but against principalities, against powers, against the rulers of the darkness of this world, against spiritual wickedness in high places. Eph. 6:12.*

82. WHY DID GOD SEVER THE RELATIONSHIP BETWEEN HIMSELF AND MAN?

God, who is light, cannot fellowship with darkness.

> *. . . what fellowship hath righteousness with unrighteousness? and what communion hath light with darkness? And what concord hath Christ with Belial? (Satan) . . . II Cor. 6:14b–15a.*

83. WHY WERE ADAM AND EVE PUT OUT OF THE GARDEN OF EDEN?

God in His mercy drove Adam and Eve out of the garden of Eden so that they could not partake of the Tree of Life. Had they eaten of its fruit, they would have been doomed to live forever in their sinful state.

> *And the Lord God said, Behold, the man is become as one of us, to know good and evil: and now, lest he put forth his hand, and take also of the tree of life, and eat, and live forever: Therefore, the Lord God sent him forth from the garden of Eden, to till the ground from whence he was taken. Gen. 3:22–23.*

84. WHAT WAS THE PUNISHMENT FOR THE SIN OF ADAM AND EVE?

A. The serpent, as a tool of Satan, was cursed above all creatures. For all his days, he will crawl upon his belly and eat the dust of the earth.

B. The woman, who before the fall was equal to man, would now be ruled by the man and childbirth would bring sorrow and pain.

C. The man was doomed to earn his bread by the sweat of his brow and his body would return to the dust from which it was created.

D. The earth was cursed by God and would now produce vegetation that would make it difficult for man to make a living ... thorns, thistles, weeds and briars.

> *And the Lord God said unto the serpent, Because thou has done this, thou art cursed above all cattle, and above every beast of the field; upon thy belly shalt thou go, and dust shalt thou eat all the days of thy life: And I will put enmity between thee and the woman, and between thy seed and her seed; it shall bruise thy head, and thou shalt bruise his heel. Unto the woman he said, I will greatly multiply thy sorrow and thy conception; in sorrow thou shalt bring forth children; and thy desire shall be to thy husband, and he shall rule over thee. And unto Adam he said, Because thou hast hearkened unto the voice of thy wife, and hast eaten of the tree, of which I commanded thee, saying, Thou shalt not eat of it: cursed is the ground for thy sake; in sorrow shalt thou eat of it all the days of thy life; Thorns also and thistles shall it bring forth to thee; and thou shalt eat the herb of the field; In the sweat of thy face shalt thou eat bread, till thou return unto the ground; for out of it was thou taken: for dust thou art, and unto dust shalt thou return. Gen. 3:14–19.*

85. DID GOD COMPLETELY ABANDON MAN AFTER THE FALL OF ADAM AND EVE?

No. God did not abandon man even though man had sinned.

> *And I will put enmity between thee and the woman, and between thy seed and her seed; it shall bruise thy head, and thou shalt bruise his heel. Gen. 3:15.*

> *For God so loved the world, that he gave his only begotten Son, that whosoever believeth in him should not perish, but have everlasting life. John 3:16.*

86. WHAT HOPE DID GOD OFFER TO MAN?

He promised man that He would send a Redeemer into the world who would free him from sin and darkness and who would reopen the way to the Tree of Life.

> *To him that overcometh will I give to eat of the tree of life, which is in the midst of the paradise of God. Rev. 2:7.*

> *For God, who commanded the light to shine out of darkness, hath shined in our hearts, to give the light of the knowledge of the glory of God in the face of Jesus Christ. II Cor. 4:6.*

> *To open their eyes, and to turn them from darkness to light, and from the power of Satan unto God, that they may receive forgiveness of sins, and inheritance among them which are sanctified by faith that is in me. Acts 26:18.*

STUDY QUESTIONS—Chapter 11

1. What was the Dispensation of Innocence?
2. How did God test Adam and Eve?
3. What was the Tree of Life?
4. What was the Tree of the Knowledge of Good and Evil?
5. Why did God command Adam and Eve not to eat of the Tree of the Knowledge of Good and Evil?
6. Why did Adam and Eve choose to disobey God?
7. Why did God sever His relationship with Adam and Eve after they sinned?
8. Why did God put Adam and Eve out of the Garden of Eden?
9. What was the punishment God gave to all who were involved in the sin of Adam and Eve?
10. Did God completely abandon man after the fall of Adam and Eve?
11. Write Gen. 2:16,17; Gen. 3:6; Gen. 3:15.

Chapter 12

THE DISPENSATION OF CONSCIENCE

87. WHAT WAS THE DISPENSATION OF CONSCIENCE?

The Dispensation of Conscience was an age during which God tested man by allowing man the freedom of either obeying or disobeying the dictates of his own conscience.

88. WHAT IS CONSCIENCE?

Conscience is an inner knowledge of good and evil given to man by God.

89. WHY DID GOD GIVE MAN FREEDOM OF CONSCIENCE?

God gave man freedom of conscience to decide and choose between good and evil according to the knowledge he possessed. Freedom of choice made man a person.

90. WHAT HAD SEPARATED MAN FROM GOD?

The sin of Adam.

> *Wherefore, as by one man sin entered into the world, and death by sin; and so death passed upon all men, for that all have sinned. Rom. 5:12.*

91. TO WHAT EXTENT DID MAN EXPLORE THE KNOWLEDGE OF EVIL?

Man explored the realm of spiritual wickedness to such an extent that the angels (sons of God) came down from heaven and married sinful women. The result of their wickedness produced a race of giants upon the earth.

And it came to pass, when men began to multiply on the face of the earth, and daughters were born unto them, that the sons of God saw the daughters of men that they were fair; and they took them wives of all which they chose. There were giants in the earth in those days; and also after that, when the sons of God came in unto the daughters of men, and they bare children to them, the same became mighty men which were of old, men of renown. Gen. 6:1,2,4.

92. WHAT HAPPENED TO THE GIANTS WHO WERE THE OFFSPRING OF ANGELS AND MORTALS?

The giants born during the Dispensation of Conscience were destroyed in the flood. The giants born after the flood fought against the people of God until they were killed.

There were giants in the earth in those days; and also after that, when the sons of God came in unto the daughters of men, and they bare children to them, the same became mighty men which were of old, men of renown. Gen. 6:4.

But the men that went up with him (Caleb) said, We be not able to go up against the people; for they are stronger than we. And they brought up an evil report of the land which they had searched unto the children of Israel, saying, The land, through which we have gone to search it, is a land that eateth up the inhabitants thereof; and all the people that we saw in it are men of a great stature. And there we saw the giants, the sons of Anak, which come of the giants: and we were in our own sight as grasshoppers, and so we were in their sight. Num. 13:31–33.

BIBLE NARRATIVE: David and Goliath—I Sam. 17. David did not fight Goliath with natural strength. He understood he was not mere flesh and blood but had a spiritual strength that could only be felled by the Spirit of the Lord. David slew Goliath with a stone that he shot at Goliath in the name of the Lord.

93. WHAT HAPPENED TO THE ANGELS THAT SINNED?

The angels that sinned are chained in the center of the earth awaiting judgment.

. . . God spared not the angels that sinned, but cast them

down to hell, and delivered them unto chains of darkness, to be reserved unto judgment. II Peter 2:4.

And the angels which kept not their first estate, but left their own habitation, he hath reserved in everlasting chains under darkness unto the judgment of the great day. EVEN as Sodom and Gomorrha, and the cities about them IN LIKE MANNER, giving themselves over to fornication, and going after strange flesh, are set forth for an example suffering the vengeance of eternal fire. Jude 6,7.

94. WERE ALL MEN CORRUPTED BY THESE ANGELS?

No, Noah and his family kept themselves undefiled and found grace in the eyes of the Lord.

But Noah found grace in the eyes of the Lord. Gen. 6:8.

95. WHO WAS NOAH?

Noah was a righteous man who served God in his generation. He was the great-grandson of Enoch, a man whom God translated to heaven without experiencing death, and the grandson of Methuselah, who lived to be the oldest man on earth (969 years).

96. HOW DID THE DISPENSATION OF CONSCIENCE END?

God destroyed all flesh that was corrupt by sending a flood of water upon the earth.

The earth also was corrupt before God, and the earth was filled with violence. And God looked upon the earth and, behold, it was corrupt; for all flesh had corrupted his way upon the earth. And God said to Noah, The end of all flesh is come before me; for the earth is filled with violence through them; . . . And, behold I, even I, do bring a flood of waters upon the earth, to destroy all flesh, wherein is the breath of life, from under heaven; and every thing that is in the earth shall die. Gen. 6:11–13,17.

97. WILL GOD EVER DESTROY THE EARTH AGAIN BY A FLOOD?

No, God made a covenant with man that He would never again destroy the earth with a flood. He put a rainbow in the sky as a reminder of the promise He made to man.

I do set my bow in the cloud and it shall be for a token of a covenant between me and the earth. And it shall come to pass, when I bring a cloud over the earth, that the bow shall be seen in the cloud: and I will remember my covenant, which is between me and you and every living creature of all flesh; and the waters shall no more become a flood to destroy all flesh. Gen. 9:13–15.

BIBLE NARRATIVE: The story of Noah and the Ark. Gen. 6,7,8,9.

STUDY QUESTIONS—Chapter 12

1. What was the Dispensation of Conscience?
2. What is conscience?
3. Why did God give man freedom of choice?
4. What separated man from God?
5. Where did the giants come from?
6. Were all men corrupted during this dispensation?
7. How did the Dispensation of Conscience end?
8. What guarantee do we have that God will never again destroy the earth with a flood?
9. What were most men doing during the age of Noah?
10. Who was Methuselah?

Chapter 13

THE DISPENSATION OF HUMAN GOVERNMENT

98. WHAT WAS THE DISPENSATION OF HUMAN GOVERNMENT?

The Dispensation of Human Government was an age during which God gave man the authority to govern himself and others.

99. WHY DID GOD INSTITUTE HUMAN GOVERNMENT?

By giving man certain laws to abide by, God gave man the opportunity to do good and avoid evil. Through obedience to the laws of human government, man would now be taught by law to do that which was good.

100. WHAT COMMANDS DID GOD GIVE TO MAN DURING THIS DISPENSATION?

God commanded man to:

A. Govern himself and gave man the power to judge and execute criminals for certain crimes.

Whoso sheddeth man's blood, by man shall his blood be shed; for in the image of God made he man. Gen. 9:6.

B. Replenish the earth.

And God blessed Noah and his sons, and said unto them, Be fruitful and multiply, and replenish the earth. Gen. 9:1.

And you, be fruitful and multiply; bring forth abundantly in the earth, and multiply therein. Gen. 9:7.

C. Not eat the blood of animals.

> *But flesh with the life thereof, which is the blood thereof, shall ye not eat. Gen. 9:4.*

Note: Man could now eat the flesh of animals—Gen. 9:3.

101. ACCORDING TO GENESIS 9:6, DOES GOD COMMAND CAPITAL PUNISHMENT?

Yes, God instituted capital punishment to protect society from dangerous criminals.

102. DID MAN OBEY THE COMMANDS OF GOD?

No. In spite of the laws of God and the laws of human government, man chose to do evil rather than good.

103. INTO WHOSE HANDS DID GOD GIVE THE RIGHT OF GOVERNMENT?

Of the three sons of Noah, Shem was to have the right of government, Japheth was to cooperate with him, and Ham was to be their servant.

> *And he said, Cursed be Canaan; a servant of servants shall he be unto his brethren. And he said, Blessed be the Lord God of Shem; and Canaan shall be his servant. God shall enlarge Japheth, and he shall dwell in the tents of Shem; and Canaan shall be his servant. Gen. 9:25–27.*

104. HOW DID MAN DEFY GOD DURING THIS AGE?

Man defied God when Nimrod, a descendant of Ham, usurped the place of government and became the world's first dictator. With slave labor he built a city and a tower called "Babel" that was to be used for the worshipping of angels, exploring spiritual wickedness and as an escape from possible destruction by another flood.

> *And they said, Go to, let us build us a city and a tower, whose top may reach unto heaven; and let us make us a name, lest we be scattered upon the face of the whole earth. Gen. 11:4.*

105. HOW DID THE DISPENSATION OF HUMAN GOVERNMENT END?

Up until this time, all men spoke one language. When God saw man's determination to stay in one place and seek spiritual wickedness, He took men's tongues and caused them to speak many different languages. The confusion that resulted forced man to scatter himself over the earth as God had originally intended.

> *And the Lord came down to see the city and the tower, which the children of men builded. And the Lord said, Behold, the people is one; and they have all one language; and this they begin to do: and now nothing will be restrained from them, which they have imagined to do. Go to, let us go down, and there confound their language that they may not understand one another's speech. So the Lord scattered them abroad from thence upon the face of all the earth: and they left off to build the city. Therefore is the name of it called Babel; because the Lord did there confound the language of all the earth: and from thence did the Lord scatter them abroad upon the face of all the earth. Gen. 11:5-9.*

106. WHY DID GOD TEST MAN'S OBEDIENCE TO THE LAW OF HUMAN GOVERNMENT?

As in previous dispensations, God wanted to show man that he could not govern himself in a way that would be pleasing to God or beneficial to himself without first undergoing a change of heart.

STUDY QUESTIONS—Chapter 13

1. What was the Dispensation of Human Government?
2. Why did God set up human government?
3. Does God command capital punishment?
4. Did man obey the laws of human government?
5. What positions did God give to each of Noah's three sons?
6. How did Nimrod defy God?
7. Why did God intervene to cause men to speak different languages?
8. Why was the building of the tower of Babel sinful?
9. What does man need to be able to obey God and govern himself?

Chapter 14

THE DISPENSATION OF PROMISE

107. WHAT WAS THE DISPENSATION OF PROMISE?

The Dispensation of Promise was an age during which God made certain promises and covenants to Abraham and his seed.

108. WHAT WAS THE PURPOSE OF THIS DISPENSATION?

God called Abraham to be the father of a nation that would be separated unto Himself and which would be the righteous line through which He would send the deliverer—Jesus Christ.

109. WHAT BLESSINGS DID GOD PROMISE TO ABRAHAM?

God promised:

1. To make of Abraham a great nation.
2. To make Abraham the father of numerous descendants.
3. To grant personal blessing to Abraham.
4. To grant personal honor to Abraham by making his name great.
5. To make Abraham a channel of blessing.
6. To bless those who honored Abraham and to curse those who did not.
7. To bless all the families of the earth through Abraham's seed, Jesus Christ.

> *Now the Lord said unto Abram, Get thee out of thy country, and from thy kindred, and from thy father's house, unto a land that I will shew thee: And I will make of thee a great nation, and I will bless thee, and make thy name great: and thou shalt be a blessing: and I will bless them that bless thee, and curse him that curseth thee: and in thee shall all families of the earth be blessed. Gen. 12:1–3.*

110.   **WHAT WERE THE PROMISES GOD MADE TO ABRA-
HAM?**

God promised Abraham and his barren wife, Sarah, a son. To
the Israelites, God promised deliverance from Egyptian slavery.

> *He hath remembered his covenant for ever, the word
> which he commanded to a thousand generations. Which
> covenant he made with Abraham, and his oath unto Isaac;
> And confirmed the same unto Jacob for a law, and to Is-
> rael for an everlasting covenant: Saying, Unto thee will I
> give the land of Canaan, the lot of your inheritance.
> Ps. 105:8–11. (Ref. Gen. 15:13,14).*

111.   **HOW DID GOD FULFILL HIS PROMISES?**

God fulfilled His promises through a series of events which included the birth of a son (Isaac) to Abraham when he was 99
years old and his wife, Sarah, was 89. Isaac's grandson, Joseph,
was sold into slavery by his brothers, but later became one of the
rulers of Egypt, the country in which he was enslaved. After Joseph's death, the Egyptians enslaved the Israelites. Then, God
raised up a deliverer, Moses, who led them out of Egypt into the
Promised Land.

> *He (Abraham) staggered not at the promise of God
> through unbelief, but was strong in faith, giving glory to
> God; And being fully persuaded that, what he had prom-
> ised, he was able to perform. And therefore it was imputed
> to him for righteousness. Now it was not written for his
> sake alone, that it was imputed to him, but for us also, to
> whom it shall be imputed, if we believe on him that raised
> up Jesus, our Lord from the dead; Who was delivered for
> our offenses, and was raised again for our justification.
> Rom. 4:20–25.*

Read Rom. 10:6–10.

BIBLE NARRATIVES: Isaac, Gen. 26:17–35; Jacob, Gen.
31,32; Joseph, Gen. 37–41; Moses, Exod. 2–7.

112.   **DID ABRAHAM KNOW HOW LONG ISRAEL WOULD BE
IN SLAVERY?**

Yes. During a deep sleep that fell upon Abraham, God told
him the Israelites would be slaves to the Egyptians for 400

years and then Israel would emerge as a strong and wealthy nation.

> *And when the sun was going down, a deep sleep fell upon Abram: and, lo, an horror of great darkness fell upon him. And he said unto Abram, Know of a surety that thy seed shall be a stranger in a land that is not their's, and shall serve them; and they shall afflict them four hundred years; And also that nation, whom they shall serve, will I judge: and afterward shall they come out with great substance. Gen. 15:12–14.*

113. HOW LONG DID THE DISPENSATION OF PROMISE LAST?

It lasted 430 years—from Abraham to Moses.

114. WHY DID IT END?

Although the Dispensation of Promise was an era of fulfillment, and Abraham's descendants saw many promises of God fulfilled, few of the descendants of Abraham had the righteousness of faith given to them. As a whole, they were unconcerned about their sinful lives. The Dispensation of Law was introduced to make the Israelites aware of sins and to prompt them to seek an inward change which would cause them to become a "peculiar treasure" and a "kingdom of priests".

> *And this I say, that the covenant, that was confirmed before of God in Christ, the law, which was four hundred and thirty years after, cannot disannul, that it should make the promise of none effect. Wherefore then serveth the law? It was added because of transgressions, till the seed should come to whom the promise was made; and it was ordained by angels in the hand of a mediator. Gal. 3:17,19.*

> *Now therefore, if ye will obey my voice indeed, and keep my covenant, then ye shall be a peculiar treasure unto me above all people; for all the earth is mine. And ye shall be unto me a kingdom of priests, and an holy nation. . . . Exod. 19:5,6a.*

STUDY QUESTIONS—Chapter 14

1. What was the Dispensation of Promise?
2. For what purpose did God call Abraham?
3. List the blessings God promised to Abraham.
4. Who was Isaac?
5. Did Abraham know the future of his descendants?
6. How long did the Dispensation of Promise last?
7. Why did the Dispensation of Promise end?
8. Why was the Dispensation of Law introduced?
9. Write Gen. 12:1–3.

Chapter 15

THE DISPENSATION OF LAW

115. **WHAT WAS THE DISPENSATION OF LAW?**

The Dispensation of Law was a period of 1520 years when God tested man's obedience to the Law of Moses.

116. **WHAT WAS THE LAW OF MOSES?**

The Law of Moses consisted of the ordinances, judgments and commandments given to the people of Israel by God through Moses for the purpose of instructing them in the moral, ceremonial and political laws by which they were to live until the coming of the Messiah.

> *And keep the charge of the Lord thy God, to walk in his ways, to keep his statutes, and his commandments, and his judgments, and his testimonies, as it is written in the law of Moses, that thou mayest prosper in all that thou doest, and whithersoever thou turnest thyself. I Kings 2:3.*

> *And this is the law which Moses set before the children of Israel: These are the testimonies, and the statutes, and the judgments, which Moses spake unto the children of Israel, after they came forth out of Egypt. Deut. 4:44,45.*

> *The law and the prophets were until John: since that time the kingdom of God is preached, and every man presseth into it. Luke 16:16.*

117. **WHAT IS THE MORAL LAW?**

The moral law consists of the Ten Commandments which tell us our duty toward God and man. It was the only law that was written into men's hearts.

Jesus said unto him, Thou shalt love the Lord thy God with all thy heart, and with all thy soul, and with all thy mind. This is the first and great commandment. And the second is like unto it, Thou shalt love thy neighbor as thyself. On these two commandments hang all the law and the prophets. Matt. 22:37–40.

For when the Gentiles, which have not the law, do by nature the things contained in the law, these, having not the law, are a law unto themselves; Which show the work of the law written in their hearts, their conscience also bearing witness, and their thoughts the meanwhile accusing or else excusing one another. Rom. 2:14–15.

118.   WHAT ARE THE TEN COMMANDMENTS?

The Ten Commandments are the basic moral laws of the Old Testament.

Note: The Lord gave the commandments but did not specify which is the first, second, third, etc. Not all churches use the same order in numbering them.

119.   HOW DID GOD GIVE THE COMMANDMENTS TO MANKIND?

In the beginning, they were written in men's hearts. Later, God wrote them upon two tables of stone and made them known through Moses.

For when the Gentiles, which have not the law, do by nature the things contained in the law, these, having not the law, are a law unto themselves; Which show the work of the law written in their hearts, their conscience also bearing witness, and their thoughts the meanwhile accusing or else excusing one another. Rom. 2:14–15.

120.   WHAT WAS THE CEREMONIAL LAW?

The ceremonial law regulated the religious practices of the Israelites in the Old Testament.

121.   WHAT WAS THE POLITICAL LAW?

It was the state law of the Israelites.

22. WHAT TWO COMMANDMENTS CONTAIN THE WHOLE LAW OF GOD?

The first is, Thou shalt love the Lord, thy God, with all thy heart, and with all thy soul, and with all thy mind. Matt. 22:37.

The second is, Thou shalt love thy neighbor as thyself. Matt. 22:39.

23. WHAT IS THE SUMMARY OF ALL THE COMMANDMENTS?

Love is the summary of all the commandments. Our love must first go to God, and then to all mankind.

> *If you love me, keep my commandments. John 14:15.*

> *. . . Love is the fulfilling of the law. Rom. 13:10.*

124. WHAT WAS THE PURPOSE OF THE LAW?

The Law was given to Israel for three reasons:

1. It was to be a schoolmaster to lead the Israelites to Christ.

   > *Wherefore the law was our schoolmaster to bring us unto Christ, that we might be justified by faith. Gal. 3:24.*

2. It was to be a factor in separating them from other nations.

   > *. . . Come out from among them, and be ye separate, saith the Lord, and touch not the unclean thing; and I will receive you. II Cor. 6:17.*

3. It was to make them a peculiar treasure unto the Lord.

   > *If ye will obey my voice indeed, and keep my covenant, then ye shall be a peculiar treasure unto me above all people. Exod. 19:5.*

125. HOW DID GOD USE THE PROPHETS DURING THIS DISPENSATION?

In addition to the Law of Moses, God spoke to the Israelites through the prophets. Failure to obey the "Word of the Lord" carried the same punishment as disobedience to the Law of Moses.

> *Yet the Lord testified against Israel, and against Judah, by all the prophets, and by all the seers, saying, Turn ye from your evil ways, and keep my commandments and my statutes, according to all the law which I commanded your fathers, and which I sent to you by my servants the prophets. II Kings 17:13.*

> *Therefore all things whatsoever ye would that men should do to you, do ye even so to them: for this is the law and the prophets. Matt. 7:12.*

126. DID ISRAEL KEEP THE LAW OF MOSES AND THE PROPHETS?

The history of Israel is one long record of disobedience.

> *And they rejected his statutes, and his covenant that he made with their fathers, and testimonies which he testified against them; and they followed vanity, and became vain, and went after the heathen that were round about them, concerning whom the Lord had charged them, that they should not do like them. And they left all the commandments of the Lord their God, and made them molten images, even two calves, and made a grove, and worshipped all the host of heaven, and served Baal. And they caused their sons and their daughters to pass through the fire, and used divination and enchantments, and sold themselves to do evil in the sight of the Lord, to provoke him to anger. II Kings 17:15–17.*

> *And the Lord rejected all the seed of Israel, and afflicted them, and delivered them into the hand of spoilers, until he had cast them out of his sight. II Kings 17:20.*

127. HOW DID THE DISPENSATION END?

After Christ had fulfilled the Law and paid the penalty for all sin on the cross of Calvary, the Dispensation of Law came to a close.

> *For what the law could not do, in that it was weak through the flesh, God sending his own Son in the likeness of sinful flesh, and for sin, condemned sin in the flesh: That the righteousness of the law might be fulfilled in us, who walk not after the flesh, but after the Spirit. Rom. 8:3–4.*

STUDY QUESTIONS—Chapter 15

1. What did God test during the Dispensation of Law?
2. How long did the Dispensation of Law last?
3. What was the Law of Moses?
4. What is the moral law and how is it different from all other laws?
5. What are the Ten Commandments?
6. What is the summary of all the Commandments?
7. For what purpose was the law given to Israel?
8. How did God use the prophets during this dispensation?
9. In one word describe Israel's history.
10. How did the Dispensation of Law end?
11. Write Matt. 22:37–39; Rom. 13:10: Rom. 8:3,4.

THE TEN COMMANDMENTS

Chapter 16

THE TEN COMMANDMENTS

28. WHY IS IT IMPORTANT FOR US TO STUDY THE TEN COMMANDMENTS?

It is important for us to study the Ten Commandments to know what sin is.

> *. . . sin is the transgression of the law. I John 3:4.*

> *. . . I had not known sin, but by the law: for I had not known lust, except the law had said, Thou shalt not covet. Rom. 7:7b.*

> *. . . for without the law sin was dead. Rom. 7:8b.*

> *. . . but sin, that it might appear sin, working death in me by that which is good; that sin by the commandment might become exceeding sinful. Rom. 7:13b.*

29. WHY MUST WE KNOW THE COMMANDMENTS?

Christ said, "If you love me, you will keep my commandments". Before we can be obedient to the commandments, we must know what they are. When we know what they are, we show our love for the Lord by keeping them.

30. WHAT DOES GOD SAY CONCERNING THE COMMANDMENTS?

He says:

> *. . . I, the Lord, thy God, am a jealous God, visiting the in-*

iquity of the fathers upon the children unto the third and fourth generation of them that hate me, and showing mercy unto thousands of them that love me and keep my commandments. Exod. 20:5,6.

131. WHAT DOES THIS MEAN?

It means that God will punish all who break His command ments, but to all who keep them, He promises grace and blessing.

132. HOW DOES GOD PUNISH THOSE WHO FAIL TO KEEP HIS COMMANDMENTS?

Those who fail to be obedient to God's commandments are subject to His wrath and displeasure, physical death and eternal damnation if they do not turn from their wicked ways.

> *. . . Cursed is everyone that continueth not in all things which are written in the book of the law to do them. Gal. 3:10.*

> *For the wages of sin is death . . . Rom. 6:23.*

133. WHAT DOES GOD MEAN WHEN HE PROMISES GRACE AND BLESSING TO THOSE WHO KEEP HIS COMMANDMENTS?

By promising grace and blessing, God graciously rewards those who are faithful in keeping His commandments.

> *. . . Godliness is profitable unto all things, having promise of the life that now is and of that which is to come. I Tim. 4:8.*

> *I am not worthy of the least of all the mercies and of all the truth which thou hast shewed thy servant. Gen. 32:10.*

134. WHAT DOES GOD MEAN WHEN HE PROMISES MERCY "UNTO THOUSANDS" THAT LOVE HIM AND KEEP HIS COMMANDMENTS?

By promising mercy "unto thousands," the descendants of His loving and obedient children are blessed by God for many generations.

Note: God blessed the Israelites for the sake of obedient Abraham. He also blessed the kings of Judah for the sake of David.

5.   WHY DOES GOD MAKE THESE PROMISES TO US?

God makes these promises to encourage us to love Him, to trust in Him, and to willingly be obedient to His commandments.

> *For this is the love of God, that we keep his commandments. . . . I John 5:3.*

> *Blessed is the man that walketh not in the counsel of the ungodly, nor standeth in the way of sinners, nor sitteth in the seat of the scornful. But his delight is in the law of the Lord; and in his law doth he meditate day and night . . . whatsoever he doeth shall prosper. Ps. 1:1–3.*

> *And it shall come to pass, if thou shalt hearken diligently unto the voice of the Lord thy God, to observe and to do all his commandments, which I command thee this day, that the Lord thy God will set thee on high above all nations of the earth. And all these blessings shall come on thee, and overtake thee, if thou shalt hearken unto the voice of the Lord thy God. Deut. 28:1,2.*

136.   IS ANY MAN CAPABLE OF KEEPING THE COMMANDMENTS PERFECTLY?

A. Natural man is not capable of keeping the commandments perfectly.

> *They are all gone aside, they are all together become filthy; there is none that doeth good, no, not one. Ps. 14:3.*

> *There is not a just man upon earth, that doeth good, and sinneth not. Eccl. 7:20.*

> *But we are all as an unclean thing, and all our righteousnesses are as filthy rags. Isa. 64:6.*

B. Christians can keep the commandments if they walk in the Spirit.

> *For what the law could not do, in that it was weak through the flesh, God sending his own Son in the likeness of sinful flesh, and for sin, condemned sin in the flesh: That the*

righteousness of the law might be fulfilled in us, who walk not after the flesh, but after the Spirit. Rom. 8:3,4.

137. CAN ANYONE BE SAVED BY THE LAW (THE COMMANDMENTS)?

No!

... No man is justified by the law in the sight of God. ... Gal. 3:11.

138. WHAT IS THE PURPOSE OF THE LAW?

The Law has a threefold purpose:

1. It acts as a curb by checking, to some extent, the outbursts of sin in the world.

    ... The law is not made for a righteous man, but for the lawless and disobedient, for the ungodly and for sinners, for unholy and profane, for murderers of fathers and murderers of mothers, for manslayers. I Tim. 1:9.

    For when the Gentiles, which have not the law, do by nature the things contained in the law, these, having not the law, are a law unto themselves; which show the work of the law, written in their hearts, their own conscience also bearing witness, and their thoughts the meanwhile accursing or else excusing one another. Rom. 2:14,15.

2. It acts as a mirror by showing to us our sins.

    ... By the law is the knowledge of sin. Rom. 3:20.

    ... And I had not known sin but by the law; for I had not known lust, except the law said, Thou shalt not covet. Rom. 7:7.

3. It acts as a rule by teaching Christians which works are pleasing to God.

    Wherewithal shall a young man cleanse his ways? By taking heed thereto according to thy word. Ps. 119:9.

    Thy word is a lamp unto my feet and a light unto my path. Ps. 119:105.

STUDY QUESTIONS—Chapter 16

1. Why is it important for us to study the Ten Commandments?
2. Why must we know the commandments?
3. How does God punish those who fail to keep His commandments?
4. How does God bless those who keep His commandments?
5. Is man capable of keeping the commandments?
6. Can we be saved by keeping the commandments?
7. What is the purpose of the Law?
8. Write Num. 14:18; Rom. 6:23; Eccl. 7:20.

Chapter 17

THE FIRST COMMANDMENT

139. WHAT IS THE FIRST COMMANDMENT?

Thou shalt have no other gods before me. Exod. 20:3.

140. WHAT ARE WE COMMANDED BY THE FIRST COMMANDMENT?

We are commanded to offer to God alone the supreme worship that is due Him.

. . . Thou shalt worship the Lord, thy God, and him only shalt thou serve. Matt. 4:10.

I am the Lord: that is my name: and my glory will I not give to another, neither my praise to graven images. Isa. 42:8.

141. WHAT IS FORBIDDEN BY THE FIRST COMMANDMENT?

A. We are forbidden to set up any creature or object as the chief object of our worship, the chief source of our happiness, or the chief teacher of truth. This is making a god out of something created.

But our God is in the heavens; he hath done whatsoever he hath pleased. Their idols are silver and gold, the work of men's hands. Ps. 115:3,4.

BIBLE NARRATIVES: Israel worshipped the golden calf, Exod. 32; The people worshipped Baal, I Kings 18:18–29; The Philistines made Dagon their god, Judges 16:23,24.

B. We are forbidden to believe in a god who is not the Triune God.

> *... All men should honor the Son, even as they honor the Father. He that honoreth not the Son honoreth not the Father, who hath sent him. John 5:23.*

C. We are forbidden to fear, love or trust in any person or thing more than we do God. It is a sin to attribute to a creature or thing a power that belongs to God alone, such as using charms or spells, believing in fortune-tellers, or going to spiritualists.

> *And fear not them which kill the body, but which are not able to kill the soul: but rather fear him which is able to destroy both soul and body in hell. Matt. 10:28.*

> *He that loveth father or mother more than me is not worthy of me: and he that loveth son or daughter more than me is not worthy of me. Matt. 10:37.*

> *Trust in the Lord with all thine heart, and lean not unto thine own understanding. Prov. 3:5.*

> *... whose God is their belly and whose glory is in their shame, who mind earthly things. Phil. 3:19.*

BIBLE NARRATIVES: The rich man thought more of costly clothes and good food than of God, Luke 16:19; The young rich man loved his possessions more than he loved Christ, Matt. 19:22.

142. WHEN DO WE LOVE GOD ABOVE ALL THINGS?

When we gladly devote our lives to His service, firmly believe what God has revealed and profess these beliefs openly whenever necessary.

> *... thou shalt love the Lord, thy God, with all thy heart, and with all thy soul, and with all thy mind. Matt. 22:37.*

143. WHEN DO WE TRUST IN GOD ABOVE ALL THINGS?

When we completely commit our lives into His keeping, rely upon Him for help in every need, and believe in God's faithfulness to keep His promises.

> *It is better to trust in the Lord than to put confidence in man. Ps. 118:8.*

> *Trust in the Lord with all thine heart . . . Prov. 3:5.*

BIBLE NARRATIVE: David trusted in the Lord when he fought against Goliath, I Sam. 17:37,46,47.

STUDY QUESTIONS—Chapter 17

1. What is the first commandment?
2. How are we to obey the first commandment?
3. What is forbidden by the first commandment?
4. When do we love God above all things?
5. When do we trust in God above all things?
6. Write Ps. 115:3,4; Prov. 3:5; Ps. 118:8.

Chapter 18

THE SECOND COMMANDMENT

144. **WHAT IS THE SECOND COMMANDMENT?**

Thou shalt not make unto thee any graven image. Exod. 20:4.

145. **WHAT DOES THE SECOND COMMANDMENT FORBID?**

It forbids us to make any likeness of any thing that is in heaven above, or in the earth beneath or in the water under the earth. We are forbidden to bow down to idols or to serve them.

146. **WHY DOES GOD FORBID IDOLATRY?**

Because He is a jealous God and will not share His glory or praise with anyone or anything.

> . . . for I thy God am a jealous God. Exod. 20:5.

> I am the Lord, that is my name: and my glory will I not give to another, neither my praise to graven images. Isa. 42:8.

147. **HOW DOES GOD LOOK UPON IDOLATRY?**

As degrading, the practice of fools and an abomination in His sight.

> Forasmuch then as we are the offspring of God, we ought not to think that the Godhead is like gold, or silver, or stone, graven by art and man's device. Acts 17:29.

> Professing themselves to be wise, they became fools; and changed the glory of the incorruptible God into an image made like to corruptible man, and to birds, and fourfooted beasts and creeping things. Rom. 1:22,23.

148.   WHAT IS AN ABOMINATION?

An abomination is an idolatrous sin that incites the wrath of God upon man.

> *When thou art come into the land which the Lord thy God giveth thee, thou shalt not learn to do after the abominations of those nations. There shall not be found among you any one that maketh his son or his daughter to pass through the fire, or that useth divination, or an observer of times, or an enchanter, or a witch, or a charmer, For all that do these things are an abomination unto the Lord: and because of these abominations the Lord thy God doth drive them out from before thee. Deut. 18:9–12.*

> *The graven images of their gods shall ye burn with fire; thou shalt not desire the silver or gold that is on them, nor take it unto thee, lest thou be snared therein: for it is an abomination to the Lord thy God. Deut. 7:25.*

149.   HOW CAN WE PLEASE GOD AND SECURE HIS BLESSINGS?

By serving the only TRUE God and Him only.

> *And shewing mercy unto thousands of them that love me, and keep my commandments. Exod. 20:6.*

STUDY QUESTIONS—Chapter 18

1. What is the second commandment?
2. What does the second commandment forbid?
3. What is idolatry?
4. What is an abomination?
5. How can we please God and secure His blessings?
6. Write Isa. 42:8; Acts 17:29.

Chapter 19

THE THIRD COMMANDMENT

150. **WHAT IS THE THIRD COMMANDMENT?**

Thou shalt not take the name of the Lord thy God in vain. Exod. 20:7.

151. **WHAT IS MEANT BY TAKING GOD'S NAME IN VAIN?**

The name of God or Jesus Christ is used to attribute an act or statement to God that is not of God. It is also sinful to use a Divine Name thoughtlessly in uncertain or unimportant matters or to express surprise or anger.

For the Lord will not hold him guiltless that taketh his name in vain. Exod. 20:7.

152. **WHAT ARE WE COMMANDED BY THE THIRD COMMANDMENT?**

We are commanded to always speak with reverence of God and to be truthful when taking oaths or vows.

153. **WHAT DOES THE THIRD COMMANDMENT FORBID?**

It forbids us to speak irreverently of God, to take the name of God as a witness without necessity, to take an oath to something that is false or to break a lawful oath. It also forbids blasphemy, cursing, using witchcraft, lying or deceiving by God's name.

... Ye have heard that it hath been said of them of old time, Thou shalt not forswear thyself, but shalt perform unto the Lord thine oaths: But I say unto you, Swear not at all; neither by heaven, for it is God's throne: nor by the earth; for it is his footstool: neither by Jerusalem; for it is

the city of the great King. Neither shalt thou swear by thy head, because thou canst not make one hair white or black. But let your communication be Yea, yea; Nay, nay: for whatsoever is more than these cometh of evil.
Matt. 5:33–37.

154.   WHAT IS AN OATH?

It is calling on God to witness what we say as truth.

I call God for a record upon my soul. . . . II Cor. 1:23.

And ye shall not swear by my name falsely. . . .
Lev. 19:12.

155.   WHEN ARE WE PERMITTED AND EVEN REQUIRED TO TAKE AN OATH?

We are permitted to take an oath when:

A. We are called upon by the government; for example, when witnesses are asked to testify in a court of law.

Let every soul be subject unto the higher powers. . . .
Rom. 13:1.

BIBLE NARRATIVE: Jesus permitted himself to be put under oath by the government, Matt. 26:63,64.

B. An oath is necessary for the glory of God or the welfare of our neighbor.

Thou shalt fear the Lord, thy God, and serve him, and shalt swear by his name. Deut. 6:13.

Men verily swear by the greater; and an oath for confirmation is to them an end of all strife. Heb. 6:16.

BIBLE NARRATIVES: Abraham put his servant under oath, Gen. 24:3. Paul made an oath, II Cor. 1:23.

156.   WHAT THREE THINGS ARE NECESSARY TO MAKE AN OATH LAWFUL?

There must be good reason for taking the oath. There must be no doubt that what we say under oath is true. An oath must never be taken to do what is wrong.

157. WHAT IS A VOW?

A vow is a solemn promise made to God in which we dedicate ourselves to a certain act, service, or way of life; for example, a marriage vow.

> *Moreover I call God for a record upon my soul, that to spare you I came not as yet unto Corinth. II Cor. 1:23.*

158. WHEN DOES AN OATH BECOME SINFUL?

An oath becomes sinful when it is taken falsely, thoughtlessly, or in sinful, uncertain or unimportant matters.

BIBLE NARRATIVES: Peter swore falsely, Matt. 26:72; certain Jews swore to commit murder, Acts 23:12; Herod swore in an uncertain and unimportant matter, Mark 6:23.

159. WHAT IS CURSING?

Cursing is the calling down of some evil on a person, place or thing. To wish someone bodily harm is against the love we owe our neighbor.

> *(With the tongue) bless we God, even the Father: and therewith curse we men, which are made after the similitude of God. Out of the same mouth proceedeth blessing and cursing. My brethren, these things ought not to be. James 3:9,10.*

BIBLE NARRATIVES: The Jews cursed themselves and their children, Matt. 27:25; Goliath cursed David, I Sam. 17:43; Peter cursed, Matt. 26:74.

160. WHAT IS BLASPHEMY?

Blasphemy is insulting language which expresses contempt for God. When a knowledgeable person willfully attributes to the devil those works which could only be wrought by God, this is blasphemy against the Holy Spirit. Blasphemy against the Holy Spirit is the unpardonable sin.

> *Verily I say unto you, All sins shall be forgiven unto the sons of men, and blasphemies wherewith soever they shall blaspheme: But he that shall blaspheme against the Holy Ghost hath never forgiveness, but is in danger of eternal*

damnation: Because they said, he hath an unclean spirit. Mark 3:28–30.

Whosoever curseth his God shall bear his sin. Lev. 24:15.

BIBLE NARRATIVES: The Jews reviled Jesus when He was hanging on the cross, Matt. 27:39–43; Rabshakeh blasphemed the God of Israel, II Kings, 18:25–35, 19:21,22.

161. WHAT IS USING WITCHCRAFT BY GOD'S NAME?

It is using God's name in order to perform some supernatural act with the help of the devil; (for example, conjuring magic, sorcery, etc., fortunetelling, or consulting the dead.)

There shall not be found among you any one that maketh his son or his daughter to pass through fire, or that useth divination, or an observer of times, or an enchanter, or a witch, or a charmer, or a consulter with familiar spirits, or a wizard, or a necromancer. For all that do these things are an abomination unto the Lord; and because of these abominations the Lord thy God doth drive them out from before thee. Deut. 18:10–12.

BIBLE NARRATIVE: The Egyptian sorcerers performed supernatural acts with the help of the devil, Exod. 7 and 8.

162. WHAT IS LYING AND DECEIVING BY GOD'S NAME?

It is:

A. Teaching false doctrine and saying that it is God's word or revelation. (False prophets.)

But in vain do they worship me, teaching for doctrines the commandments of men. Matt. 15:9.

Behold, I am against the prophets, saith the Lord, that use their tongues, and say, He saith. Jer. 23:31.

What thing soever I command you, observe to do it: thou shalt not add thereto, nor diminish from it. Deut. 12:32.

BIBLE NARRATIVE: The lie of a false prophet caused a prophet of God to be deceived and killed, I Kings 13:11–19.

B. Covering up an unbelieving heart or a sinful life by a show of piety. (hypocrisy.)

This people draweth nigh unto me with their mouth, and honoreth me with their lips; but their heart is far from me. Matt. 15:8.

Not everyone that saith unto me, Lord, Lord, shall enter into the kingdom of heaven; but he that doeth the will of my father which is in heaven. Matt. 7:21.

BIBLE NARRATIVES: The scribes and the Pharisees were hypocrites, Matt. 23:13–16; Ananias and Sapphira were hypocrites, Acts 5:1–11.

163. HOW CAN WE BEST KEEP THE THIRD COMMANDMENT?

By calling upon God's name in every need, by praying, praising and giving thanks.

STUDY QUESTIONS—Chapter 19

1. What is the third commandment?
2. What is meant by taking God's name in vain?
3. What are we commanded by the third commandment?
4. What does the third commandment forbid?
5. What is an oath?
6. When are we to take an oath?
7. What is a vow?
8. Write Deut. 6:13; Heb. 6:16.

Chapter 20

THE FOURTH COMMANDMENT

164. WHAT IS THE FOURTH COMMANDMENT?

Remember the sabbath day, to keep it holy. Exod. 20:8.

165. WHAT IS THE SABBATH DAY?

The Hebrew word for "Sabbath" means "rest". God rested and hallowed the seventh day. By the law given at Sinai, the seventh day was to be a day of rest in which no secular work was to be done and which was to be kept holy unto God.

166. HOW DID JESUS OBSERVE THE SABBATH?

Jesus Christ fulfilled the Sabbath law by completely ceasing from His own labors and resting absolutely in *God's* will. By performing God's will and purposes on earth and permitting the Holy Spirit to direct Him, Jesus became the Master of the Sabbath.

> *For the Son of Man is Lord even of the sabbath day.* Matt. 12:8.

167. ARE CHRISTIANS OF THE NEW TESTAMENT REQUIRED TO OBSERVE THE SABBATH AND OTHER HOLY DAYS OF THE OLD TESTAMENT?

No. The Sabbath and many of the Jewish holy days were given their true meaning in Jesus Christ. When we come to God, through the redemption provided by Jesus Christ, the redemptive price which is the precious blood of Jesus, has already been paid for our souls. There is nothing more we can do to make ourselves more acceptable to God. We can now rest from our own labors. Jesus Christ is our Sabbath. When we accept Him as our salvation, we cease from our works and rest in His grace. The Sabbath now is no longer a day, but a spiritual experience.

> *Come unto me all ye that labor and are heavy laden and I will give you rest. Matt. 11:28.*

> *For by grace are ye saved through faith; and that not of yourselves: it is the gift of God: Not of works, lest any man should boast. Eph. 2:8,9.*

> *Let no man therefore judge you in meat, or in drink, or in respect of an holyday, or of a new moon, or of the sabbath days: Which are a shadow of things to come; but the body is of Christ. Col. 2:16,17.*

168. WHY IS THE SABBATH REFERRED TO AS A "SHADOW OF THINGS TO COME"?

Because it encourages us to enter into the Sabbath "rest" by letting the Spirit of God within us direct us in performing the will of God on earth.

> *For what the law could not do, in that it was weak through the flesh, God sending his own Son in the likeness of sinful flesh, and for sin, condemned sin in the flesh: That the righteousness of the law might be fulfilled in us, who walk not after the flesh, but after the Spirit. Rom 8:3,4.*

> *There remaineth therefore a rest to the people of God. For he that is entered into his rest, he also hath ceased from his own works, as God did from his. Heb. 4:9,10.*

169. DID GOD COMMAND CHRISTIANS TO OBSERVE ANY DAY?

No, Christians are not commanded by God to observe any day.

> *One man esteemeth one day above another; another esteemeth every day alike. Let every man be fully persuaded in his own mind. He that regardeth the day regardeth it unto the Lord; and he that regardeth not the day, to the Lord he doth not regard it. Rom. 14:5,6.*

> *Ye observe days, and months, and times, and years. I am afraid of you lest I have bestowed upon you labor in vain. Gal. 4:10,11.*

170. DO WE OBSERVE SUNDAY AND OTHER CHURCH FESTIVITIES AS HOLY DAYS?

No. We observe these days in order to have time and opportunity for public worship and fellowship.

> *Not forsaking the assembling of ourselves together, as the manner of some is. . . . Heb. 10:25.*

> *They continued steadfastly in the apostles' doctrine and fellowship and in breaking of bread and in prayers. Acts 2:42.*

BIBLE NARRATIVE: The early Christians observed the first day of the week. (Sunday), Acts 20:7, I Cor. 16:2.

171. WHY DO WE WORSHIP TOGETHER ON SUNDAY?

We worship together on Sunday because it is the most convenient day for us to get together and worship. In most areas of the world, Sunday has been set aside for this purpose. Sunday, the first day of the week, was celebrated by the early church in memory of Christ's resurrection.

> *And upon the first day of the week, when the disciples came together to break bread, Paul preached unto them, ready to depart on the morrow; and continued his speech until midnight. Acts 20:7.*

> *Upon the first day of the week let every one of you lay by him in store, as God hath prospered him, that there be no gatherings when I come. I Cor. 16:2.*

172. WHEN DO WE SIN AGAINST THE FOURTH COMMANDMENT?

We sin against the fourth commandment when, because of unbelief, we fail to enter into the rest that is found in the Lord Jesus Christ.

> *Let us therefore fear, lest, a promise being left us of entering into his rest, any of you should seem to come short of it. . . . Let us labour therefore to enter into that rest, lest any man fall after the same example of unbelief. Heb. 4:1,11.*

STUDY QUESTIONS—Chapter 20

1. What is the Fourth Commandment?
2. What is the meaning of the word "Sabbath"?
3. How did Jesus observe the Sabbath?
4. Are Christians commanded to observe the Sabbath as a Holy Day?
5. How do we obey the Fourth Commandment?
6. Why do we worship together on Sunday?
7. When do we sin against the Fourth Commandment?
8. What day of the week did the early Christians meet? Why?
9. Write Matt. 12:8; Matt. 11:28; Heb. 4:9,10; Col. 2:16,17.

Chapter 21

THE FIFTH COMMANDMENT

173. WHAT IS THE FIFTH COMMANDMENT?

> *Honour thy father and mother: that thy days may be long upon the land which the Lord thy God giveth thee. Exod. 20:12.*

174. WHY DOES GOD ADD THE PROMISE "THAT IT MAY BE WELL WITH THEE AND THOU MAYEST LIVE LONG UPON THE EARTH"?

By this promise, God impresses upon us the importance and benefit of honoring our parents and superiors and urges us to obey this commandment willingly.

175. WHAT DOES GOD REQUIRE OF US IN THE FIFTH COMMANDMENT?

God requires us to:

A. Honor our parents through love and respect and to regard them as God's representatives.

> *Honor thy father and mother; which is the first commandment with promise; that it may be well with thee, and thou mayest live long on the earth. Eph. 6:2,3.*

> *Thou shalt rise up before the hoary head and honor the face of the old man, and fear thy God: . . . Lev. 19:32.*

BIBLE NARRATIVES: Joseph honored his father, Gen. 46:29; King Solomon honored his mother, I Kings 2:19; Elisha honored his teacher, II Kings 2:12.

B. Serve our parents by gladly doing what we can for them and helping them when they are in need.

> *But if any widow have children or nephews, let them learn first to show piety at home and to requite (repay) their parents; for that is good and acceptable before God.*
> *I Tim. 5:4.*

BIBLE NARRATIVES: Joseph provided for his father, Gen. 47:11,12; Jesus provided for His mother, John 19:26.

C. Obey our parents in all things that are not sinful.

> *Children, obey your parents in the Lord: for this is right. Eph. 6:1.*

> *Hearken unto thy father that begat thee, and despise not thy mother when she is old. Prov. 23:22.*

BIBLE NARRATIVES: Jesus was subject to Mary and Joseph, Luke 2:41; Jonathan disobeyed his father in order to spare David's life and thus obeyed God rather than man, I Sam. 20:31–33.

D. Respect and obey all our lawful superiors. All authority comes from God. When God places people in authority over us, He expects us to obey them. If we refuse to obey lawful superiors such as parents, teachers, government officials, etc., we refuse to obey God.

> *Submit yourselves to every ordinance of man for the Lord's sake: whether it be to the king, as supreme: Or unto governors, as unto them that are sent by Him for the punishment of evildoers, and for the praise of them that do well. I Peter 2:13,14.*

> *Servants, be subject to your masters with all fear; not only to the good and gentle, but also to the froward. I Peter 2:18.*

176. **WHEN ARE WE NOT REQUIRED TO OBEY PARENTS OR SUPERIORS?**

When someone in authority over us attempts to use that authority to have us do something sinful or forbids us to follow God.

> *... We ought to obey God rather than men. Acts 5:29.*

177.   **WHAT ARE THE DUTIES OF PARENTS TOWARD THEIR CHILDREN?**

Parents are required to care especially for the spiritual needs of their children, since these are the most important. They should teach them to pray and praise God and should work to develop in their children the virtues of obedience, truthfulness, respect, cleanliness, etc. Parents are also required to care for the physical, mental and emotional needs of their children.

> *And, ye fathers, provoke not your children to wrath: but bring them up in the nurture and admonition of the Lord. Eph. 6:4.*

> *Withhold not correction from the child; for if thou beatest him with the rod, he shall not die. Thou shalt beat him with the rod, and shall deliver his soul from hell. Prov. 23:13,14.*

178.   **WHAT ARE OUR DUTIES TOWARD OUR COUNTRY?**

We must love our country, be sincerely interested in its welfare, and respect and obey its laws.

179.   **WHY MUST WE OBEY THE LAWS OF OUR COUNTRY?**

The lawful authority of our country comes from God, the source of all authority, and we must be obedient to Him. If certain laws are contrary to God's word, we are duty bound to disobey them.

BIBLE NARRATIVES: The Three Hebrew Children—Daniel 3. Daniel in the Lion's Den—Daniel 6.

180.   **WHAT DOES GOD FORBID IN THE FIFTH COMMANDMENT?**

God forbids disobedience, disrespect and unkindness toward our parents and superiors.

> *The eye that mocketh at his father and despiseth to obey his mother, the ravens of the valley shall pick it out, and the young eagles shall eat it. Prov. 30:17.*

BIBLE NARRATIVES: The sons of Eli grieved their father by their wickedness, I Sam. 2:12,23,25; Absolom rebelled against his father and king, II Sam. 15.

STUDY QUESTIONS—Chapter 21

1. What is the fifth commandment?
2. What is required of us by the fifth commandment?
3. When are we not required to be obedient to parents or superiors?
4. What is required of parents?
5. Why must we obey the laws of our country?
6. If we do not obey our country's laws, are we being obedient to God?
7. What is forbidden by the fifth commandment?
8. What does it mean to honor our parents?
9. Write Colossians 3:20; Eph. 6:2,3; I Pet. 2:13,14.
10. What does God promise if we honor our parents?

Chapter 22

THE SIXTH COMMANDMENT

181. **WHAT IS THE SIXTH COMMANDMENT?**

   Thou shalt not kill. Exod. 20:13.

182. **WHAT ARE WE COMMANDED BY THE SIXTH COMMANDMENT?**

   We are commanded to properly care for our spiritual and bodily welfare and to show love for our neighbor by respecting his person and not injuring him in any way.

183. **WHAT DOES GOD FORBID IN THE SIXTH COMMANDMENT?**

   A. God forbids us to kill or to injure our neighbor by murder, fighting, etc., or to take our own life by suicide or neglect of health.

   Whoso sheddeth man's blood, by man shall his blood be shed; for in the image of God made he man. Gen. 9:6.

   . . . All they that take the sword shall perish with the sword. Matt. 26:52.

   He (the government) beareth not the sword in vain; for he is the minister of God, a revenger to execute wrath upon him that doeth evil. Rom. 13:4 (The government has the right to inflict the death penalty and to wage just wars).

   B. God forbids us to do or say anything which may destroy, shorten or embitter our neighbor's life.

   Dearly beloved, avenge not yourselves, but rather give

place unto wrath: for it is written, Vengeance is mine; I will repay, saith the Lord. Rom. 12:19.

C. God forbids anger, hatred, revenge, reckless driving and bad example.

... I say unto you, that whosoever is angry with his brother without a cause shall be in danger of the judgment. ... Matt. 5:22.

Whosoever hateth his brother is a murderer: and ye know that no murderer hath eternal life abiding in him. I John 3:15.

For out of the heart proceed evil thoughts, murders, adulteries, fornications, thefts, false witness, blasphemies. Matt. 15:19.

Be ye angry, and sin not: let not the sun go down upon your wrath. Eph. 4:26.

184. WHAT DOES GOD REQUIRE OF US IN THE SIXTH COMMANDMENT?

A. We should be merciful, kind and forgiving towards our neighbor.

Blessed are the merciful: for they shall obtain mercy. ... Blessed are the peacemakers: for they shall be called the children of God. Matt. 5:7,9.

But if he forgive not men their trespasses, neither will your Father forgive your trespasses. Matt. 6:15.

And be ye kind one to another, tenderhearted, forgiving one another, even as God for Christ's sake hath forgiven you. Eph. 4:32.

B. We should help and befriend our neighbor whenever we can.

But a certain Samaritan, as he journeyed, came where he was: and when he saw him, he had compassion on him. And went to him, and bound up his wounds, pouring in oil and wine, and set him on his own beast, and brought him to an inn, and took care of him. And on the morrow when he departed, he took out two pence, and gave them to the host, and said unto him, Take care of him: and whatsoever

> *thou spendest more, when I come again, I will repay thee.*
> *Which now of these three, thinkest thou was neighbour*
> *unto him that fell among the thieves? Luke 10:33–35.*

BIBLE NARRATIVES: Abraham rescued Lot from his enemies, Gen. 14:12–16; David protected the life of Saul, I Sam.
26:1–12.

STUDY QUESTIONS—Chapter 22

1. What is the Sixth Commandment?
2. What are we commanded by the Sixth Commandment?
3. What does God forbid in the Sixth Commandment?
4. How should we treat our neighbor?
5. Write Eph. 4:32; Rom. 12:19; Matt. 5:7.

Chapter 23

THE SEVENTH COMMANDMENT

185. WHAT IS THE SEVENTH COMMANDMENT?

Thou shalt not commit adultery. Exod. 20:14.

186. WHAT IS ADULTERY?

Adultery is having sexual relations with someone other than the marriage partner.

187. WHAT IS COMMANDED BY THE SEVENTH COMMAND-MENT?

The seventh commandment requires married couples to love and honor each other unselfishly, to be faithful to each other, to provide for the welfare of their children and to surrender themselves to the service of God. By following God's plan for marriage, the love between husband and wife should become a reflection of the love of Jesus Christ for His bride, the Church.

> *. . . As the church is subject unto Christ, so let the wives be to their own husbands in everything. Husbands, love your wives, even as Christ loved the church and gave himself for it. Eph. 5:24,25.*

188. WHAT IS MARRIAGE?

Marriage is the lifelong union of one man and one woman. It was instituted by God and therefore, should not be entered into carelessly.

> *. . . They are no more twain, but one flesh. What therefore God hath joined together let no man put asunder.*
> *Matt. 19:6.*

BIBLE NARRATIVES: The institution of marriage, Gen. 2:18–24; The angel addresses Mary, who was engaged to Joseph, as his wife and calls Joseph her husband. Matt. 1:19,20,24.

189. **WHAT DOES GOD FORBID IN THE SEVENTH COMMANDMENT?**

A. God forbids the breaking of the marriage vows by unfaithfulness or desertion. He permits the innocent party to procure a divorce when the other party is guilty of fornication. (See chapter 59—Matrimony.)

> *. . . Whosoever shall put away his wife, except it be for fornication, and shall marry another, committeth adultery. . . . Matt. 19:9.*

> *. . . Whoremongers and adulterers God will judge.* Heb. 13:4.

BIBLE NARRATIVES: David committed adultery with the wife of Uriah, II Sam. 11; Herod took his brother's wife, Mark 6:18.

B. God forbids all impurity and immodesty, in words, actions and looks, whether it be alone or with others. Examples of this would be impure thoughts or desires, immodest dress or behavior, immodest actions, impure conversations, indecent literature, movies or plays, fornication and adultery.

> *Out of the heart proceed evil thoughts, murders, adulteries, fornications, thefts, false witness, blasphemies. Matt. 15:19.*

> *. . . Whosoever looketh on a woman to lust after her hath committed adultery with her already in his heart.* Matt. 5:28.

> *But fornication and all uncleanness or covetousness, let it not be ONCE named among you, as becometh saints; neither filthiness nor foolish talking or jesting, which are not convenient, but rather giving of thanks. Eph. 5:3,4.*

> *For it is a shame even to speak of those things which are done of them in secret. Eph. 5:12.*

BIBLE NARRATIVES: Potiphar's wife, with lust in heart, cast her eyes upon Joseph, Gen. 39:7–12; Samson committed fornication, Judges 16:1.

90. **WHAT DOES GOD REQUIRE OF EVERYONE IN THE SEVENTH COMMANDMENT?**

He requires us to lead chaste and decent lives and to be pure in our thoughts, desires, words and deeds.

> ... *Abstain from fleshly lusts, which war against the soul.* I Pet. 2:11.

> *Whatsoever things are true ... lovely ... whatsoever things are of good report; if there be any virtue, and if there be any praise, think on these things. Phil. 4:8.*

> *Let no corrupt communication proceed out of your mouth, but that which is good to the use of edifying ... that it may minister grace unto the hearers. Eph. 4:29.*

191. **WHY DOES GOD COMMAND US TO BE PURE AND MODEST IN ALL OUR ACTIONS?**

God commands us to be pure and modest because as Christians, our bodies are the temples of the Holy Spirit.

> *What? know ye not that your body is the temple of the Holy Ghost which is in you, which ye have of God, and ye are not your own? For ye are bought with a price: therefore glorify God in your body, and in your spirit, which are God's. I Cor. 6:19,20.*

192. **WHAT ARE THE CHIEF DANGERS TO PURITY?**

The chief dangers to purity are idleness, bad companions, immodest dress, drinking, indecent books, plays and movies.

193. **WHAT MUST WE DO TO LEAD A CHASTE AND DECENT LIFE?**

To lead a chaste and decent life, we must:

A. Fight to overcome all impure thoughts and desires by seeking God's help through prayer, by keeping ourselves busy and by practicing temperance.

> ... *How, then, can I do this great wickedness and sin against God? Gen. 39:9.*

> *Create in me a clean heart, O God. ... Ps. 51:10.*

Look not thou upon the wine when it is red, when it giveth his color in the cup, when it moveth itself aright. At the last it biteth like a serpent and stingeth like an adder. Thine eyes shall behold strange women, and thine heart shall utter perverse things. Prov. 23:31–33.

B. Flee and avoid every temptation. Many fall because they do not avoid dangers. Human nature is very weak, especially where purity is concerned and we must avoid all occasions that may lead us into sin.

Flee fornication. . . . I Cor. 6:18.

Flee also youthful lusts. . . . II Tim. 2:22.

My son, if sinners entice thee, consent thou not. Prov. 1:10.

STUDY QUESTIONS—CHAPTER 23

1. What is the Seventh Commandment?
2. What is commanded by the Seventh Commandment?
3. What is marriage?
4. What does God forbid in the Seventh Commandment?
5. Does the Seventh Commandment forbid outward or inward impurity?
6. What does God require of everyone in the Seventh Commandment?
7. What are the chief dangers to purity?
8. How can we lead a chaste and decent life?
9. Write Matt. 15:19; Eph. 5:3,4; Phil. 4:8.

Chapter 24

THE EIGHTH COMMANDMENT

94. WHAT IS THE EIGHTH COMMANDMENT?

Thou shalt not steal. Exod. 20:15.

95. WHAT ARE WE COMMANDED BY THE EIGHTH COMMANDMENT?

We are commanded to respect the property of others, to pay our debts, live up to business agreements and to be honest in all our dealings.

96. WHAT IS FORBIDDEN BY THE EIGHTH COMMANDMENT?

A. Every kind of stealing and fraud, as well as sinful longing for anything that belongs to our neighbor.

Let him that stole steal no more: but rather let him labor, working with his hands the thing which is good, that he may have to give to him that needeth. Eph. 4:28.

Woe unto him that buildeth his house by unrighteousness, and his chambers by wrong; that useth his neighbor's service without wages and giveth him not for his work. Jer. 22:13.

. . . If any would not work, neither should he eat. II Thess. 3:10.

B. Cheating, damaging the property of others, accepting bribes, accepting or buying stolen property, etc., is also forbidden by the eighth commandment.

Ye shall do no unrighteousness in judgment, in meteyard, in weight, or in measure. Lev. 19:35.

The wicked borroweth and payeth not again. Ps. 37:21.

Whoso is partner with a thief hateth his own soul. . . . Prov. 29:24.

197. WHAT DOES GOD REQUIRE OF US IN THE EIGHTH COMMANDMENT?

God requires us to:

A. Respect the property of our neighbor.

> *If thou meet thine enemy's ox or his ass going astray, thou shalt surely bring it back to him again. Exod. 23:4.*

> *Whatsoever ye would that men should do to you do ye even so to them. Matt. 7:12.*

B. Help our neighbor whenever we can.

> *Give to him that asketh thee, and from him that would borrow of thee turn not thou away. Matt. 5:42.*

> *He that hath pity upon the poor lendeth unto the Lord; and that which he hath given will He pay him again. Prov. 19:17.*

> *To do good and to communicate forget not; for with such sacrifices God is well pleased. Heb. 13:16.*

C. Rejoice when we see our neighbor prosper.

> *Charity envieth not . . . seeketh not her own. I Cor. 13:4,5.*

STUDY QUESTIONS—Chapter 24

1. What is the eighth commandment?
2. What does the eighth commandment tell us to do?
3. What is forbidden by the eighth commandment?
4. What is required of us by this commandment?

Chapter 25

THE NINTH COMMANDMENT

198. **WHAT IS THE NINTH COMMANDMENT?**

Thou shalt not bear false witness against thy neighbor. Exod. 20:16.

199. **WHAT ARE WE COMMANDED BY THE NINTH COMMANDMENT?**

We are commanded to be truthful in all things, especially in matters that concern the good name or honor of our neighbor.

200. **WHAT DOES GOD FORBID IN THE NINTH COMMANDMENT?**

God forbids us to judge others, to lie, to make rash judgments, to commit slander, detraction, perjury, or to reveal secrets we have promised to keep.

201. **WHAT IS THE SIN OF RASH JUDGMENT?**

The sin of rash judgment is committed when we deliberately, and without sufficient reason, believe something harmful about another's character.

Let none of you imagine evil in your hearts against his neighbor. . . . Zech. 8:17.

. . . If thy brother shall trespass against thee, go and tell him his fault between thee and him alone . . . Matt. 18:15.

202. **WHAT IS THE SIN OF DETRACTION?**

The sin of detraction is making known the hidden faults of another without a good reason.

A talebearer revealeth secrets: but he that is of a faithful spirit concealeth the matter. Prov. 11:13.

203. WHAT IS THE SIN OF SLANDER?

The sin of slander is deliberate lying to injure the good name of another.

Speak not evil one of another, brethren. . . . James 4:11.

*(Unto the wicked God saith:) Thou givest thy mouth to evil, and thy tongue frameth deceit. Thou sittest and speakest against thy brother; thou slanderest thine own mother's son. These things hast thou done, and I kept silence; thou thoughtest that I was altogether such an one as thyself: but I will reprove thee and set them in order before thine eyes. Now consider this, ye that forget God, lest I tear you in pieces, and there be none to deliver.
Ps. 50: 19–22.*

204. WHAT IS PERJURY?

Perjury is the willful telling of a lie, against our neighbor, while under oath in a court of law.

A false witness shall not be unpunished . . . Prov. 19:5.

BIBLE NARRATIVES: False witnesses testified against Jesus, Matt. 26:59–61; False witnesses arose against Naboth, I Kings 21:13.

205. WHAT KIND OF LYING IS ESPECIALLY FORBIDDEN BY THE NINTH COMMANDMENT?

Jesus said, "I am . . . the truth," and in the ninth commandment, God tells us to love truth and to show love for others by respecting their reputation. It especially forbids us to lie about our neighbor or to lie to our neighbor.

. . . He that speaketh lies shall not escape. Prov. 19:5.

. . . Putting away lying, speak every man truth with his neighbor, for we are members one of another. Eph. 4:25.

06. WHEN ARE WE OBLIGATED TO KEEP SOMETHING SECRET?

When we have promised not to reveal a secret, when something is told to us in confidence, or when the good of another is at stake.

07. WHY ARE WE FORBIDDEN TO JUDGE OTHERS?

We are forbidden to judge others because God has commanded it and He will pardon us only as we pardon those who have offended us.

> *Judge not, and ye shall not be judged: condemn not, and ye shall not be condemned . . . Luke 6:37.*

08. WHAT DOES GOD REQUIRE OF US IN THE NINTH COMMANDMENT?

God requires us to:

A. Defend our neighbor, that is, to take his part and shield him against false accusations.

> *Open thy mouth for the dumb in the cause of all such as are appointed to destruction. Open thy mouth, judge righteously, and plead the cause of the poor and needy. Prov. 31:8,9.*

B. Speak well of our neighbor, that is, praise his good qualities and deeds so far as it can be done in keeping with the truth.

C. Cover up the faults of our neighbor and explain in his favor whatever can be explained.

> *. . . Charity shall cover the multitude of sins. I Peter 4:8.*

> *. . . Charity believeth all things, hopeth all things, endureth all things. I Cor. 13:7.*

STUDY QUESTIONS—Chapter 25

1. What is the Ninth Commandment?
2. What are we commanded to do by the Ninth Commandment?
3. What does God forbid in the Ninth Commandment?
4. What is the sin of rash judgment?
5. What is the sin of detraction?
6. What is the sin of slander?
7. What is perjury?
8. What kind of lying is especially forbidden by the Ninth Commandment?
9. When are we obligated to keep something secret?
10. Why are we forbidden to judge others?
11. What does the Ninth Commandment require of us toward our neighbor?

Chapter 26

THE TENTH COMMANDMENT

09. **WHAT IS THE TENTH COMMANDMENT?**

> *Thou shalt not covet thy neighbor's house, thou shalt not covet thy neighbor's wife, nor his manservant, nor his maidservant, nor his ox, nor his ass, nor anything that is thy neighbor's. Exod. 20:17.*

10. **WHAT DOES COVET MEAN?**

To covet means to desire or long for something so strongly that a feeling of discontentment overcomes us. This is usually accompanied by ill will at seeing another's superiority or advantages of success. It is a gross form of selfishness that is highly offensive to God.

> *And he said unto them, Take heed, and beware of covetousness: for a man's life consisteth not in the abundance of things which he possesseth. And he spake a parable unto them, saying, The ground of a certain rich man brought forth plentifully: And he thought within himself, saying, What shall I do, because I have no room where to bestow my fruits? And he said, This will I do: I will pull down my barns, and build greater; and there will I bestow all my fruits and my goods. And I will say to my soul, Soul, thou hast much goods laid up for many years; take thine ease, eat, drink, and be merry. But God said unto him, Thou fool, this night thy soul shall be required of thee: then whose shall those things be, which thou hast provided? So is he that layeth up treasure for himself, and is not rich toward God. Luke 12:15–21.*

BIBLE NARRATIVE: Ahab coveted Naboth's vineyard and obtained it by deceit. I Kings 21:1–16.

211. WHAT ARE WE COMMANDED BY THE TENTH COMMANDMENT?

We are commanded to trust God to direct our lives according to His choosing.

> *Trust in the Lord with all thine heart; and lean not unto thine own understanding. In all thy ways acknowledge him, and he shall direct thy paths. Prov. 3:5,6.*

212. WHAT DOES THE TENTH COMMANDMENT FORBID

It forbids all desire to take or to keep unjustly anything that belongs to another.

> *Woe unto them that join house to house, that lay field to field, till there be no place, that they may be placed alone in the midst of the earth! Isa. 5:8.*

> *Woe unto you, scribes and Pharisees, hypocrites! for ye devour widow's houses, and for a pretence make long prayer: therefore ye shall receive the greater damnation. Matt. 23:14.*

> *And having food and raiment let us be therewith content. But they that will be rich fall into temptation and a snare, and into many foolish and hurtful lusts, which drown men in destruction and perdition. For the love of money is the root of all evil: which while some coveted after, they have erred from the faith, and pierced themselves through with many sorrows. I Tim. 6:8–10.*

BIBLE NARRATIVES: David coveted the wife of Uriah and took her, II Sam. 11:2–4; Absalom estranged the hearts of the people from David, II Sam. 15:1–6; because Judas coveted money, he betrayed Jesus, Mark 14:10,11.

213. WHY DOES GOD FORBID COVETOUSNESS IN CHURCH LEADERS?

Covetous people will not work within the limits of their calling and as a result, will bring division within the Church and will stop the flow of God's blessing.

> *For this ye know, that no whoremonger, nor unclean person, nor covetous man, who is an idolater, hath any inheritance in the kingdom of Christ and of God. Eph. 5:5.*

A bishop then must be blameless, the husband of one wife, vigilant, sober, of good behavior, given to hospitality, apt to teach; Not given to wine, no striker, not greedy of filthy lucre; but patient, not a brawler, not covetous.
I Tim. 3:2,3.

Wherefore, brethren, look ye out among you seven men of honest report, full of the Holy Ghost and wisdom, whom we may appoint over this business. Acts 6:3.

Let every man abide in the same calling wherein he was called. I Cor. 7:20.

BIBLE NARRATIVES: Uzziah's intrusion into the priest's office: his punishment, II Chron. 26; The sin of Korah, Num. 16.

214. WHAT DOES GOD REQUIRE OF US IN THE TENTH COMMANDMENT?

God requires that we seek the kingdom of God and His righteousness.

But seek ye first the kingdom of God, and his righteousness; and all these things shall be added unto you.
Matt. 6:33.

But godliness with contentment is great gain. I Tim. 6:6.

215. WHAT ARE THE BENEFITS OF AVOIDING COVETOUSNESS?

We are given an inward peace and security knowing that our heavenly Father is aware of our needs and will take care of us.

Therefore I say unto you, Take no thought for your life, what ye shall eat, or what ye shall drink; nor yet for your body, what ye shall put on. Is not the life more than meat, and the body more than raiment? Behold the fowls of the air: for they sow not, neither do they reap, nor gather into barns; yet your heavenly Father feedeth them. Are ye not much better than they? Which of you by taking thought can add one cubit unto his stature? And why take ye thought for raiment? Consider the lilies of the field, how they grow; they toil not, neither do they spin: And yet I say unto you, that even Solomon in all his glory was not arrayed like one of these. Wherefore, if God so clothe the grass of the field, which today is, and tomorrow is cast into the oven, shall he not much more clothe you, O ye of little faith? Therefore take no thought, saying, What shall we eat? or, What shall we drink? or, Wherewithal shall we be clothed? (For all these things do the Gentiles seek:) for your heavenly Father knoweth that ye have need of all these things. Matt. 6:25–32.

216. WHAT ARE SOME EXAMPLES OF COVETOUSNESS?

Examples of covetousness are gambling (greed), jealousy, envy, lust and selfishness.

217. WHY IS GAMBLING A BREAKING OF THE TENTH COMMANDMENT?

Coveting another man's goods and securing them by unlawful means and not by honest labor is breaking the tenth commandment.

STUDY QUESTIONS—Chapter 26

1. What is the Tenth Commandment?
2. What is covetousness?
3. What does this commandment require us to do instead of coveting?
4. What does this commandment forbid?
5. Why is covetousness a special problem among church leaders?
6. How may we avoid covetousness?
7. Why is gambling a breaking of the Tenth Commandment?
8. Write I Tim. 6:8–10; Eph. 5:5; I Cor. 7:20.

THE LIFE AND MINISTRY OF JESUS CHRIST

Chapter 27

THE DISPENSATION OF GRACE

218. WHAT IS THE DISPENSATION OF GRACE?

The Dispensation of Grace is the present period of time during which God is crediting His righteousness to man through faith in Jesus Christ. This dispensation began when the Son of God gave His life for the sins of the world.

> *For what the law could not do, in that it was weak through the flesh, God sending his Son in the likeness of sinful flesh, and for sin, condemned sin in the flesh: That the righteousness of the law might be fulfilled in us, who walk not after the flesh, but after the Spirit. Rom. 8:3,4.*

> *For Christ is the end of the law for righteousness to everyone that believeth. Rom. 10:4.*

> *And be found in him, not having mine own righteousness, which is of the law, but that which is through the faith of Christ, the righteousness which is of God by faith. Phil. 3:9.*

219. WHAT IS GRACE?

Grace is the unmerited love and favor of God toward man.

> *For by grace are ye saved through faith; and that not of yourselves: it is the gift of God: Not of works, lest any man should boast. Eph. 2:8,9.*

220.   HOW DOES THE DISPENSATION OF GRACE DIFFER FROM THE DISPENSATION OF LAW

A.   Law is connected with Moses and works; grace with Christ and faith.

> *For the law was given by Moses, but grace and truth came by Jesus Christ. John 1:17.*

> *For Christ is the end of the law for righteousness to every one that believeth. For Moses describeth the righteousness which is of the law, That the man which doeth those things shall live by them. But the righteousness which is of faith speaketh on this wise, Say not in thine heart, Who shall ascend into heaven? (that is, to bring Christ down from above. Or, Who shall descend into the deep? (that is, to bring up Christ again from the dead.) But what saith it? The word is nigh thee, even in thy mouth, and in thy heart: that is, the word of faith, which we preach; That if thou shalt confess with thy mouth the Lord Jesus, and shalt believe in thine heart that God hath raised him from the dead, thou shalt be saved. For with the heart man believeth unto righteousness; and with the mouth confession is made unto salvation. Rom. 10:4–10.*

B.   Law demands that blessings be earned; grace is a free gift.

> *And it shall come to pass, if thou shalt hearken diligently unto the voice of the Lord thy God, to observe and to do all his commandments which I command thee this day, that the Lord, thy God, will set thee on high above all nations of the earth: And all these blessings shall come on thee, and overtake thee, if thou shalt hearken unto the voice of the Lord thy God. Blessed shalt thou be in the city, blessed shalt thou be in the field, blessed shall be the fruit of thy body, and the fruit of thy ground, and the fruit of thy cattle, the increase of thy kine, and the flocks of thy sheep. Blessed shall be thy basket and thy store. Blessed shalt thou be when thou comest in, and blessed shalt thou be when thou goest out. Deut. 28:1–6.*

> *Now to him that worketh is the reward not reckoned of grace, but of debt. But to him that worketh not, but believeth on him that justifieth the ungodly, his faith is counted for righteousness. Rom. 4:4,5.*

221. **HOW DOES GOD TEST US DURING THIS DISPENSATION?**

God tests us through His Son, Jesus Christ—whether we accept Him or reject Him.

> *He that believeth and is baptized shall be saved; but he that believeth not shall be damned. Mark 16:16.*

222. **HOW WILL THE DISPENSATION OF GRACE END?**

It will end with the return of Jesus Christ to the earth.

> *When the Son of man shall come in his glory, and all the holy angels with him, then shall he sit upon the throne of his glory: And before him shall be gathered all nations: and he shall separate them one from another, as a shepherd divideth his sheep from the goats. Matt. 25:31,32.*

> *And the Lord shall be king over all the earth: in that day shall there be one Lord, and his name one. Zech. 14:9.*

STUDY QUESTIONS—Chapter 27

1. What is the Dispensation of Grace?
2. What is Grace?
3. How does Grace differ from Law?
4. How does God test us during this dispensation?
5. How will the Dispensation of Grace end?
6. Write Eph. 2:8,9; John 1:17; Mark 16:16.

Chapter 28

THE INCARNATION

223.   WHO IS JESUS CHRIST?

Jesus Christ, the Savior of all mankind, is true God and true man.

224.   WHY DO WE BELIEVE THAT JESUS CHRIST IS TRUE GOD?

We believe that Jesus Christ is true God because the Scriptures ascribe to Him—

A. Divine Names:

> . . . *This is the TRUE GOD and eternal LIFE.*
> *I John 5:20.*

> *And Thomas answered and said unto him, MY LORD*
> *AND MY GOD. John 20:28.*

> . . . *Behold, a voice out of the cloud, which said, This is*
> *MY BELOVED SON, in whom I am well pleased; hear*
> *ye him. Matt. 17:5.*

> . . . *Christ came, who is over all, God blessed forever.*
> *Rom. 9:5.*

B. Divine Attributes:

> *In the beginning was the Word, and the Word was with*
> *God, and the Word was God. The same was in the begin-*
> *ning with God. John 1:1,2 (Eternal).*

> *Jesus Christ the same yesterday, and to day, and for ever.*
> *Heb. 13:8 (Unchangeable).*

. . . Lo, I am with you alway, even unto the end of the world. Matt. 28:20 (Ever-present).

. . . Lord, thou knowest all things. . . . John 21:17 (All knowing).

. . . All power is given unto me in heaven and in earth. Matt. 28:18 (All powerful).

BIBLE NARRATIVES: Jesus knows the name and character of Nathanael, John 1:48; Jesus knows the woman at Jacob's well, John 4:17,18; The miraculous draught of fishes, Luke 5:4–6, John 21:6.

C. Divine Works:

All things were made by him; and without him was not any thing made that was made. John 1:3 (Creation).

(He upholds) all things by the word of his power. . . . Heb. 1:3 (Preservation).

. . . The Son of man hath power on earth to forgive sins. . . . Matt. 9:6.

(The Father) hath given him authority to execute judgment. . . . John 5:27.

BIBLE NARRATIVES: At the marriage feast in Cana, Jesus manifested His glory by turning water into wine, John 2:1–11; He rebuked the storm, Luke 8:22–25; He healed the man sick of the palsy, Matt. 9:1–8; He called Lazarus back to life, John 11:38–44; He rose from the dead, Matt. 28:6,7.

D. Divine Honor and Glory:

That all men should honor the Son even as they honor the Father. He that honoreth not the Son honoreth not the Father, which hath sent him. John 5:23.

. . . Let all the angels of God worship him. Heb. 1:6.

225. **WHY DO WE BELIEVE THAT JESUS CHRIST IS ALSO TRUE MAN?**

We believe that Jesus Christ is also true man because He is the son of a woman, and while He was on earth, He had a body and soul like ours. The Scriptures—

A. Expressly call Him man.

> *For there is one God, and one mediator between God and men, the man Christ Jesus. I Tim. 2:5.*

B. Ascribe to Him a human body and soul.

> *Behold my hands and my feet, that it is I myself: handle me, and see; for a spirit hath not flesh and bones, as ye see me have. Luke 24:39.*

C. Ascribe to Him human feelings and actions.

BIBLE NARRATIVES: Jesus slept, Mark 4:38; Jesus hungered, Matt. 4:2; Jesus thirsted, John 19:28; Jesus wept, John 11:35; Jesus suffered and died, Matt. 26 and 27.

226. WAS JESUS THE CHRIST ALWAYS MAN?

No, He became man at the time of the Incarnation.

227. WHAT IS MEANT BY THE INCARNATION?

By the Incarnation is meant that Jesus, the Son of God, while retaining His divine nature, took upon Himself the nature of man.

> *The Word (the Son of God) was made flesh, and dwelt (the Greek word means "pitched His tent") among us (and we beheld his glory, the glory as of the only begotten of the Father,) full of grace and truth. John 1:14.*

228. HOW WAS JESUS MADE MAN?

Jesus was conceived and made man by the power of the Holy Spirit in the womb of a virgin called Mary.

> *Now the birth of Jesus Christ was on this wise: When as his mother Mary was espoused to Joseph, before they came together, she was found with child of the Holy Ghost. Then Joseph her husband, being a just man, and not willing to make a publick example, was minded to put her away privily. But while he thought on these things, behold, the angel of the Lord appeared unto him in a dream, saying, Joseph, thou son of David, fear not to take unto thee Mary thy wife: for that which is conceived in her is of the Holy Ghost. And she shall bring forth a son, and thou shalt call his name JESUS: for he shall save his people*

from their sins. Now all this was done, that it might be fulfilled which was spoken of the Lord by the prophet, saying, Behold, a virgin shall be with child, and shall bring forth a son, and they shall call his name Emmanuel, which being interpreted is, God with us. Then Joseph being raised from sleep did as the angel of the Lord had bidden him, and took unto him his wife: And knew her not till she brought forth her firstborn son: and he called his name JESUS. Matt. 1:18–25.

And the angel answered and said unto her, The Holy Ghost shall come upon thee, and the power of the Highest shall overshadow thee: therefore also that holy thing which shall be born of thee shall be called the Son of God. Luke 1:35.

But when the fulness of the time was come, God sent forth his Son, made of a woman, made under the law. Gal. 4:4.

229. WAS JOSEPH THE FATHER OF JESUS?

No, Jesus had no human father.

230. HOW MANY NATURES ARE UNITED IN CHRIST?

There are two natures united in Christ, divine and human.

For unto us a child is born, unto us a son is given: and the government shall be upon his shoulder: and his name shall be called Wonderful, Counselor, The mighty God, The everlasting Father, The Prince of Peace. Isa. 9:6.

And Jesus came and spake unto them, saying, All power is given unto me in heaven and in earth. Matt. 28:18.

For in him dwelleth all the fulness of the Godhead bodily. Col. 2:9.

But if we walk in the light, as he is in the light, we have fellowship one with another, and the blood of Jesus Christ his Son cleanseth us from all sin. I John 1:7.

231. WHY WAS IT NECESSARY FOR OUR SAVIOR TO BE TRUE MAN?

It was necessary for our Savior to be true man so that—

A. He might take our place under the law.

But when the fulness of the time was come, God sent forth his Son, made of a woman, made under the law, To redeem them that were under the law, that we might receive the adoption of sons. Gal. 4:4,5.

B. He might be able to suffer and die in our stead.

Forasmuch then as the children are partakers of flesh and blood, he also himself likewise took part of the same; that through death he might destroy him that had the power of death, that is, the devil. Heb. 2:14.

232. **WHY WAS IT NECESSARY FOR OUR SAVIOR TO BE TRUE GOD?**

It was necessary for our Savior to be true God so that—

A. His fulfilling of the Law might be sufficient for all men.

None of them can by any means redeem his brother nor give to God a ransom for him. For the redemption of their soul is precious. Ps. 49:7.8.

. . . By the obedience of one shall many be made righteous. Rom. 5:19.

B. His *life* and *death* might be sufficient ransom for our redemption.

. . . The Son of man came, not to be ministered unto, but to minister and to give His life a ransom for many. Mark 10:45.

C. He might be able to overcome death and the devil for us.

. . . (Christ) abolished death. II Tim. 1:10.

Forasmuch then as the children are partakers of flesh and blood, he also himself likewise took part of the same; that through death he might destroy him that had the power of death, that is, the devil. Heb. 2:14.

But thanks be to God, which giveth us the victory through our Lord Jesus Christ. I Cor. 15:57.

233. FOR WHAT THREEFOLD PURPOSE WAS CHRIST ANOINTED?

Christ was anointed (consecrated) to be Prophet, Priest, and King.

A. As my Prophet, He revealed Himself by word and deed, and by the preaching of the Gospel still reveals Himself as the Son of God and the Redeemer of the world.

The Lord thy God, will raise up unto thee a Prophet from the midst of thee, of thy brethren, like unto me; unto him ye shall hearken. Deut. 18:15.

. . . This is my beloved Son, in whom I am well pleased; hear ye him. Matt. 17:5.

For the law was given by Moses, but grace and truth came by Jesus Christ. No man hath seen God at any time; the only begotten Son, which is in the bosom of the Father, he hath declared him. John 1:17,18.

He that heareth you heareth me; and he that despiseth you despiseth me; and he that despiseth me despiseth him that sent me. Luke 10:16.

B. As my Priest, Christ fulfilled the Law in my stead perfectly, sacrificed Himself for me and still intercedes for me with His heavenly Father.

But when the fulness of the time was come, God sent forth his Son, made of a woman, made under the law, To redeem them that were under the law that we might receive the adoption of sons. Gal. 4:4,5.

. . . Christ died for our sins according to the Scriptures. I Cor. 15:3.

For such an high priest became us, who is holy, harmless, undefiled, separate from sinners, and made higher than the heavens; Who needeth not daily, as those high priests, to offer up sacrifice, first for his own sins, and then for the people's; for this he did once, when he offered up himself. Heb. 7:26,27.

. . . If any man sin, we have an advocate with the Father, Jesus Christ, the righteous; and he is the propitiation for

our sins: and not for ours only, but also for the sins of the whole world. I John 2:1,2.

C. As my King, Christ with His mighty power rules over all creation, governs and protects His Church, and will finally lead it to glory.

... All power is given unto me in heaven and in earth. Matt. 28:18.

Jesus answered, My kingdom is not of this world; if my kingdom were of this world, then would my servants fight, that I should not be delivered to the Jews: but now is my kingdom not from hence. Pilate therefore said unto him, Art thou a king then? Jesus answered, Thou sayest that I am a King. To this end was I born, and for this cause came I into the world, that I should bear witness unto the truth. Every one that is of the truth heareth my voice. John 18:36,37.

And the Lord shall deliver me from every evil work and will preserve me unto his heavenly kingdom: to whom be glory forever and ever. Amen. II Tim. 4:18.

234. WHERE WAS JESUS BORN?

He was born in Bethlehem of Judaea, the city of David.

And Joseph also went up from Galilee, out of the city of Nazareth, into Judaea, unto the city of David, which is called Bethlehem; (because he was of the house and lineage of David:) Luke 2:4.

235. HOW LONG DID HE LIVE UPON THIS EARTH?

Approximately 33 years.

STUDY QUESTIONS—Chapter 28

1. Who is Jesus Christ?
2. Give four reasons why we know Jesus Christ is true God.
3. Give three reasons why we know Jesus Christ was true man.
4. What is meant by the Incarnation?
5. What two natures are united in Christ?
6. Write out I John 1:7.
7. Give two reasons why Christ had to be true man.
8. Give three reasons why Christ had to be true God.
9. For what threefold purpose was Christ anointed?
10. Where was Christ born?

Chapter 29

THE REDEMPTION

236. WHAT IS MEANT BY THE REDEMPTION?

By the Redemption is meant that Christ died for our sins. As the redeemer of all mankind, He offered to God His life, sufferings and death as a fitting sacrifice for our sins. As a result, He regained for us the right to be called children of God and heirs of the Kingdom of God.

237. WHAT DO THE SCRIPTURES TEACH OF THE SUFFERING AND DEATH OF CHRIST?

The Scriptures teach that—

A. In His early life, Christ suffered poverty, contempt and persecution.

> *. . . Though he was rich, yet for your sakes he became poor, that ye through his poverty might be rich. II Cor. 8:9.*

> *. . . The foxes have holes, and the birds of the air have nests; but the Son of man hath not where to lay his head. Matt. 8:20.*

> *He is despised and rejected of men; a man of sorrows and acquainted with grief: and we hid, as it were our faces from him; he was despised, and we esteemed him not. Isa. 53:3.*

> *. . . Ye seek to kill me, a man that hath told you the truth, which I have heard of God. . . . John 8:40.*

BIBLE NARRATIVES: At His birth, Jesus had only swaddling

clothes and a manger, Luke 2:7; Herod sought to destroy Him, Matt. 2:13; In Nazareth, the Jews tried to cast Him down from the brow of the hill, Luke 4:29. In the temple, the Jews took up stones to throw at Him, John 8:59.

B. Under Pontius Pilate Christ suffered extreme agony of body and soul, a cruel scourging, being crowned with thorns, the crucifixion; and finally, death upon the cross.

> *Who his own self bare our sins in his own body on the tree, that we, being dead to sins, should live unto righteousness: by whose stripes ye were healed. I Peter 2:24.*

> *Then Pilate therefore took Jesus and scourged him. And the soldiers platted a crown of thorns, and put it on his head, and they put on him a purple robe, And said, Hail, King of the Jews! and they smote him with their hands. John 19:1–3.*

> *Then delivered he him therefore unto them to be crucified. And they took Jesus and led him away. And he bearing his cross went forth into a place called the place of a skull, which is called in the Hebrew Golgotha: where they crucified him. . . . John 19:16–18.*

C. Christ died on the accursed tree of the cross.

> *. . . It is written, Cursed is everyone that hangeth on a tree. Gal. 3:13.*

238. WHAT DO THE SCRIPTURES TEACH CONCERNING THE BURIAL OF CHRIST?

Christ's body was laid in the grave and remained there for three days without seeing corruption or decay.

> *But he, whom God raised again, saw no corruption. Acts 13:37.*

> *For thou wilt not leave my soul in hell: neither wilt thou suffer thine Holy One to see corruption. Ps. 16:10.*

BIBLE NARRATIVES: The Resurrection story, Matt. 28; Mark 16:1–14; Luke 24:1–49; John 20:1–23.

239. WHAT WAS CHRIST'S STATE OF HUMILIATION?

Jesus Christ, in His everyday life, did not use the divine power that was given Him by His Father but rather subjected Himself to the weaknesses and limitations of man.

> *Let this mind be in you, which was also in Christ Jesus: who, being in the form of God, thought it not robbery to be equal with God: but made himself of no reputation, and took upon him the form of a servant, and was made in the likeness of man: and being found in fashion as a man, he humbled himself, and became obedient unto death, even the death of the cross. Phil. 2:5–8.*

240.   WHAT WAS THE FULL EXTENT OF CHRIST'S HUMILIATION?

He was conceived (God became man) by the Holy Ghost.
He was born (of a woman) of the Virgin Mary.
He suffered under Pontius Pilate.
He was crucified.
He died.
He was buried.

241.   FOR WHAT PURPOSE DID CHRIST SO HUMBLE HIMSELF?

Christ humbled Himself to redeem us lost and condemned creatures.

> *For God so loved the world, that he gave his only begotten Son, that whosoever believeth in him should not perish, but have everlasting life. For God sent not his Son into the world to condemn the world; but that the world through him might be saved. John 3:16,17.*

242.   FROM WHAT HAS CHRIST REDEEMED US?

Christ has redeemed us from all our sins, from death and from the power of the devil.

243.   HOW HAS CHRIST REDEEMED US FROM OUR SINS?

Through loving obedience to the Father, even to the extreme point of dying on the cross, Christ expressed His great love for us by offering Himself as a sacrifice for our sins.

A. Christ has taken away all our guilt and suffered all our punishment.

> ... *Behold the Lamb of God, which taketh away the sins of the world. John 1:29.*

> ... *By the obedience of one shall many be made righteous. Rom. 5:19.*

> *For he hath made him to be sin for us who knew no sin, that we might be made the righteousness of God in him. II Cor. 5:21.*

> *Christ hath redeemed us from the curse of the law, being made a curse for us; for it is written, Cursed is everyone that hangeth on a tree. Gal. 3:13.*

B. Christ has freed us from the slavery of sin.

> *(Christ) his own self bare our sins in his own body on the tree, that we, being dead to sins, should live unto righteousness; by whose stripes ye were healed. I Peter 2:24.*

> ... *Verily, verily, I say unto you, Whosoever committeth sins is the servant of sin. If the Son therefore shall make you free ye shall be free indeed. John 8:34,36.*

244. HOW HAS CHRIST REDEEMED US FROM DEATH?

Through His own death on the cross, Christ abolished eternal death. We need not fear physical death.

> *Forasmuch then as the children are partakers of flesh and blood, he also himself likewise took part of the same; that through death he might destroy him that had the power of death, that is, the devil; And deliver them who through fear of death were all their lifetime subject to bondage. Heb. 2:14,15.*

> *O death, where is thy sting? O grave, where is thy victory? The sting of death is sin; and the strength of sin is the law. But thanks be to God, which giveth us the victory through our Lord Jesus Christ. I Cor. 15:55-57.*

> ... *Our Saviour Jesus Christ, who hath abolished death, and hath brought life and immortality to light through the gospel. II Tim. 1:10.*

245. HOW HAS CHRIST REDEEMED US FROM THE POWER OF THE DEVIL?

When Christ descended into hell, He overcame and conquered the devil taking away his power to enslave men and to accuse and condemn us before the Lord; At the same time, Christ gave us power to resist the temptations of the devil.

BIBLE NARRATIVES: Christ's descent into hell (sheol), Eph. 4:9,10; Isa. 44:23; Rom. 10:6; Ps. 16:10; Matt. 12:40; Acts 2:27; I Peter 3:10-21.

> *For this purpose the Son of God was manifested, that he might destroy the works of the devil. I John 3:8.*

> *There is therefore now no condemnation to them which are in Christ Jesus, who walk not after the flesh, but after the Spirit. Rom. 8:1.*

> *And I heard a loud voice saying in heaven, Now is come salvation, and strength, and the kingdom of our God, and the power of his Christ: for the accuser of our brethren is cast down, which accused them before our God day and night. Rev. 12:10.*

> *Resist the devil, and he will flee from you. James 4:7.*

246. WITH WHAT HAS CHRIST REDEEMED US?

Christ has redeemed us not with silver or gold but with His holy, precious blood and with His innocent suffering and death.

> *. . . The blood of Jesus Christ, his Son cleanseth us from all sin. I John 1:7.*

> *Forasmuch as ye know that ye were not redeemed with corruptible things, as silver and gold, from your vain conversation received by tradition from your fathers; But with the precious blood of Christ, as of a lamb without blemish and without spot. I Peter 1:18,19.*

> *With his stripes are we healed. Isa. 53:5.*

247. HOW DOES THIS WORK OF REDEMPTION BENEFIT YOU?

As my substitute, Christ has made satisfaction for my sins by paying for my guilt.

For he hath made him to be sin for us, who knew no sin; that we might be made the righteousness of God in him II Cor. 5:21.

Surely he hath borne our griefs, and carried our sorrows: yet we did esteem him stricken, smitten of God, and afflicted. But he was wounded for our transgressions, he was bruised for our iniquities: the chastisement of our peace was upon him; and with his stripes we are healed. Isa. 53:4,5.

248.   HAS CHRIST REDEEMED, PURCHASED AND WON ONLY YOU?

Christ has redeemed me, as well as all of mankind.

For the Son of man is come to save that which was lost. Matt. 18:11.

Behold the Lamb of God, which taketh away the sin of the world. John 1:29.

. . . he died for all . . . II Cor. 5:15.

This is a faithful saying, and worthy of all acceptation, that Christ Jesus came into the world to save sinners; of whom I am chief. I Tim. 1:15.

(They deny) the Lord that bought them and bring upon themselves swift destruction. II Peter 2:1.

And he is the propitiation for our sins: and not for ours only, but also for the sins of the whole world. I John 2:2.

STUDY QUESTIONS—Chapter 29

1. What is meant by the Redemption?
2. What did Christ suffer in the early part of His life?
3. What did Christ suffer under Pontius Pilate?
4. Where did Christ die?
5. What was the full extent of Christ's humiliation?
6. What do the Scriptures teach concerning the burial of Christ?
7. From what has Christ redeemed us?
8. Name two things from which Christ has redeemed you.
9. With what has Christ redeemed you?
10. Who has Christ redeemed?

Chapter 30

THE RESURRECTION AND ASCENSION

249. **WHAT DO THE SCRIPTURES TEACH CONCERNING CHRIST'S RESURRECTION?**

The Scriptures teach that after three days in the grave, Christ victoriously arose from the dead.

> *For as Jonas was three days and three nights in the whale's belly; so shall the Son of man be three days and three nights in the heart of the earth. Matt. 12:40.*

> *Him God raised up the third day, and shewed him openly; Not to all the people, but unto witnesses chosen before of God, even to us, who did eat and drink with him after he rose from the dead. Acts 10:40,41.*

BIBLE NARRATIVES: Christ's Resurrection, Matt. 27:62–66; Matt. 28; Mark 16; Luke 24; John 20 and 21.

250. **WHERE WERE THE SOUL AND SPIRIT OF CHRIST DURING THE THREE DAYS HIS BODY WAS IN THE GRAVE?**

The soul and spirit of Christ descended into hell (sheol), which was the temporary abode of the dead.

> *Thou wilt not leave my soul in hell, neither wilt thou suffer thine Holy One to see corruption. Acts 2:27.*

> *(Christ was) put to death in the flesh, but quickened by the Spirit: By which also he went and preached unto the spirits in prison. I Peter 3:18,19.*

> *He that descended is the same also that ascended up far above all heavens. Eph. 4:10.*

251. WHY DID CHRIST DESCEND INTO HELL?

Christ descended into hell (Sheol) to accomplish two things:

1. He released the souls of the righteous dead that they might go into the presence of God.

   Wherefore he saith, When he ascended up on high, he led captivity captive, and gave gifts unto men. (Now that he ascended, what is it but that he also descended first into the lower parts of the earth? He that descended is the same also that ascended up far above all heavens, that he might fill all things.) Eph. 4:8–10.

   I am he that liveth, and was dead; and, behold, I am alive for evermore, Amen; and have the keys of hell and death. Rev. 1:18.

2. He proclaimed everlasting defeat to the angels that sinned in Noah's day and showed them that he, as the seed of the woman, had spoiled Satan's plan and overthrew the power of death, hell and the grave.

   And I will put enmity between thee and the woman, and between thy seed and her seed; it shall bruise thy head, and thou shalt bruise his heel. Gen. 3:15.

   For Christ also hath once suffered for sins, the just for the unjust, that he might bring us to God, being put to death in the flesh, but quickened by the Spirit: By which also he went and preached unto the spirits in prison; Which sometime were disobedient, when once the longsuffering of God waited in the days of Noah, while the ark was a preparing, wherein few, that is, eight souls were saved by water. I Peter 3:18–20.

   For if God spared not the angels that sinned, but cast them down to hell and delivered them into chains of darkness, to be reserved unto judgment. II Peter 2:4.

   Forasmuch then as the children are partakers of flesh and blood, he also himself took part of the same; that through death he might destroy him that had the power of death, that is, the devil. Heb. 2:14.

252. HOW LONG DID CHRIST REMAIN ON EARTH AFTER HIS RESURRECTION?

Christ remained on earth for forty days.

> To whom also he shewed himself alive after his passion by many infallible proofs, being seen of them forty days, and speaking of the things pertaining to the kingdom of God. Acts 1:3.

253. HOW DO WE KNOW THAT CHRIST WAS REALLY ALIVE?

We know that Christ was alive because He showed Himself in bodily form to His disciples and to others as well.

> And as they thus spake, Jesus himself stood in the midst of them, and saith unto them, Peace be unto you. But they were terrified and affrighted, and supposed that they had seen a spirit. And he said unto them, Why are ye troubled? and why do thoughts arise in your hearts? Behold my hands and my feet, that it is I myself: handle me, and see: for a spirit hath not flesh and bones, as ye see me have. And when he had thus spoken, he shewed them his hands and his feet. And while they yet believed not for joy, and wondered, he said unto them, Have ye here any meat? And they gave him a piece of broiled fish, and of an honeycomb, And he took it, and did eat before them. Luke 24:36–43.

> Then the same day at evening, being the first day of the week, when the doors were shut where the disciples were assembled for fear of the Jews, came Jesus and stood in the midst, and saith unto them, Peace be unto you. And when he had so said, he shewed them his hands and his side. Then were the disciples glad, when they saw the Lord. John 20:19,20.

> And after eight days again his disciples were within, and Thomas with them: then came Jesus, the doors being shut, and stood in the midst, and said, Peace be unto you. Then saith he to Thomas, Reach hither thy finger, and behold my hands; and reach hither thy hand, and thrust it into my side: and be not faithless, but believing. And Thomas answered and said unto him, My Lord and my God. Jesus

saith unto him, Thomas, because thou hast seen me, thou hast believed: blessed are they that have not seen, and yet have believed. John 20:26–29.

And that he was seen of Cephas, then of the twelve: After that, he was seen of above five hundred brethren at once; of whom the greater part remain unto this present, but some are fallen asleep. After that, he was seen of James; then of all the apostles. And last of all he was seen of me also, as of one born out of due time. I Cor. 15:5–8.

254.　WHAT KIND OF BODY DID CHRIST HAVE?

He appeared to Mary and to His disciples in a resurrected body.

Jesus saith unto her, Touch me not; for I am not yet ascended to my Father: but go to my brethren, and say unto them, I ascend unto my Father, and your Father; and to my God, and your God. John 20:17.

Behold my hands and my feet, that it is I myself: handle me, and see; for a spirit hath not flesh and bones, as ye see me have. Luke 24:39.

255.　WAS HIS RESURRECTED BODY THE SAME AS THE ONE HE HAD BEFORE HE DIED?

No, in His resurrected body, Christ was able to appear at will in any place at any time, and He was freed from material limitations.

And after eight days again his disciples were within, and Thomas with them: then came Jesus, the doors being shut, and stood in the midst, and said, Peace be unto you. John 20:26.

256.　WHY DID JESUS APPEAR IN VARIOUS FORMS?

Jesus appeared in various forms so that men would not remember Him as a man but as the glorified Christ—a new man.

After that he appeared in another form unto two of them, as they walked, and went into the country. Mark 16:12.

God is a Spirit: and they that worship him must worship him in spirit and in truth. John 4:24.

Jesus saith unto them, Come and dine. And none of the disciples durst ask him, Who art thou? knowing that it was the Lord. Jesus then cometh, and taketh bread, and giveth them, and fish likewise. This is now the third time that Jesus shewed himself to his disciples, after that he was risen from the dead. John 21:12–14.

And that he died for all, that they which live should not henceforth live unto themselves, but unto him which died for them, and rose again. II Cor. 5:15.

Thou shalt not make unto thee any graven image, or any likeness of anything that is in heaven above, or that is in the earth beneath, or that is in the water under the earth. Exod. 20:4.

257.   WHY IS THE RESURRECTION OF CHRIST OF SUCH IMPORTANCE AND COMFORT TO US?

Christ's Resurrection definitely proves—

A. That Christ is the Son of God.

(He was) declared to be the Son of God with power, according to the spirit of holiness, by the resurrection from the dead. Rom. 1:4.

B. That His doctrine is the truth.

. . . Destroy this temple, and in three days I will raise it up. John 2:19.

C. That God the Father has accepted the sacrifice of His Son for the reconciliation of the world.

And if Christ be not raised, your faith is vain; ye are yet in your sins. I Cor. 15:17.

(Christ) was delivered for our offenses, and was raised again for our justification. Rom. 4:25.

D. That all believers shall rise unto eternal life.

. . . Because I live, ye shall live also. John 14:19.

. . . I am the resurrection and the life: he that believeth in me, though he were dead, yet shall he live; And whosoever liveth and believeth in me shall never die. . . . John 11:25,26.

258.   WHAT DO THE SCRIPTURES TEACH CONCERNING CHRIST'S ASCENSION?

The Scriptures teach that forty days after His Resurrection from the dead, Christ visibly ascended to heaven and entered into the glory of His Father. The proof of His acceptance into the presence of God is His shedding forth upon the earth the gift of the Holy Spirit.

> *This Jesus hath God raised up, whereof we all are witnesses. Therefore being by the right hand of God exalted, and having received of the Father the promise of the Holy Ghost, he hath shed forth this, which ye now see and hear. Acts 2:32,33.*

> *He that descended is the same also that ascended up far above all heavens. . . . Eph. 4:10.*

> *Father, I will that they also whom thou hast given me, be with me where I am; that they may behold my glory. . . . John 17:24.*

> *. . . I will come again and receive you unto myself, that where I am, there ye may be also. John 14:3.*

BIBLE NARRATIVES: Christ's Ascension, Luke 24:50,51; Acts 1:9–11.

259.   WHERE IS CHRIST NOW?

He is seated at the right hand of God the Father Almighty.

> *. . . (God) set him (Christ) at his own right hand in the heavenly places, Far above all principality, and power, and might, and dominion, and every name that is named, not only in this world, but also in that which is to come: And hath put all things under his feet, and gave him to be the head over all things to the church, Which is his body, the fulness of him that filleth all in all. Eph. 1:20–23.*

260.   WHAT IS MEANT BY THE EXPRESSION "SEATED AT THE RIGHT HAND OF GOD"?

It means that Christ occupies the throne of all authority and power. The authority and power possessed by the rulers of the earth comes from Him.

Let every soul be subject unto the higher powers. For there is no power but of God: the powers that be are ordained of God. Whosoever therefore resisteth the power, resisteth the ordinance of God: and they that resist shall receive to themselves damnation. Rom. 13:1,2.

261. WHAT COMFORT CAN WE DERIVE FROM CHRIST'S SEAT OF AUTHORITY?

We are comforted by knowing that it is the exalted Christ who—

A. As our Prophet, sends men to preach the Gospel of Redemption.

> *(He) ascended up far above all heavens that he might fill all things. And he gave some, apostles; and some, prophets; and some, evangelists; and some, pastors and teachers; for the perfecting of the saints, for the work of the ministry, for the edifying of the body of Christ. Eph. 4:10–12.*

> *He that heareth you heareth me; and he that despiseth you despiseth me; and he that despiseth me despiseth him that sent me. Luke 10:16.*

B. As our Priest, intercedes (pleads) for us before God.

> *If any man sin, we have an advocate with the Father, Jesus Christ the righteous. I John 2:1.*

> *(Christ) is even at the right hand of God, who also maketh intercession for us. Rom. 8:34.*

C. As our King, controls all circumstances, is the Source of all authority, is the Head of the Church, and will bring all things into fulfillment of His eternal purposes.

> *And we know that all things work together for good to them that love God, to them who are the called according to his purpose. For whom he did foreknow, he also did predestinate to be conformed to the image of his Son, that he might be the firstborn among many brethren. Moreover whom he did predestinate, them he also called: and whom he called, them he also justified: and whom he justified, them he also glorified. Rom. 8:28–30.*

> *(Christ) shall change our vile body, that it may be fash-*

ioned like unto his glorious body, according to the working whereby he is able even to subdue all things unto himself. Phil. 3:21.

Having made known unto us the mystery of his will, according to his good pleasure which he hath purposed in himself: That in the dispensation of the fulness of times he might gather together in one all things in Christ, both which are in heaven, and which are on earth; even in him. Eph. 1:9,10.

. . . The kingdoms of this world are become the kingdoms of our Lord, and of his Christ; and he shall reign for ever and ever. Rev. 11:15.

The Lord said unto my Lord, Sit thou on my right hand, till I make thine enemies thy footstool. Matt. 22:44.

Note: See Eph. 1:20–23.

262. WHAT DO THE SCRIPTURES TEACH CONCERNING THE SECOND COMING OF CHRIST?

The Scriptures teach that—

A. Christ shall return visibly and in glory with His angels.

. . . This same Jesus, which is taken up from you into heaven, shall so come in like manner as ye have seen him go into heaven. Acts 1:11.

Behold, he cometh with clouds; and every eye shall see him, and they also which pierced him. . . . Rev. 1:7.

When the Son of man shall come in his glory, and all the holy angels with him, then shall he sit upon the throne of his glory. Matt. 25:31.

B. He will judge the living and the dead.

. . . It is he which was ordained of God to be the Judge of quick and dead. Acts 10:42.

For we must all appear before the judgment seat of Christ; that every one may receive the things done in his body, according to that he hath done, whether it be good or bad. II Cor. 5:10.

Because he hath appointed a day, in the which he will judge the world in righteousness by that man whom he hath ordained. . . . Acts 17:31.

He that rejecteth me, and receiveth not my words, hath one that judgeth him: the word that I have spoken, the same shall judge him in the last day. John 12:48.

C. He will come on the Last Day which is appointed by God but unknown to man.

(God) hath appointed a day in the which he will judge the world. Acts 17:31.

But of that day and that hour knoweth no man, no, not the angels which are in heaven, neither the Son, but the Father. Mark 13:32.

But the day of the Lord will come as a thief in the night; in the which the heavens shall pass away with a great noise, and the elements shall melt with fervent heat, the earth also and the works that are therein shall be burned up. II Peter 3:10.

For as the lightning cometh out of the east, and shineth even unto the west; so shall also the coming of the Son of man be. Matt. 24:27.

But the end of all things is at hand. . . . I Peter 4:7.

BIBLE NARRATIVES: The final judgment, Matt. 25:31–46; Signs preceding Christ's coming, Matt. 24 and II Thess. 2.

263. WHAT IS THE ENTIRE PURPOSE OF CHRIST'S DEATH, BURIAL AND RESURRECTION?

The purpose of Christ's entire work of Redemption is—

A. That we may be His own and be made righteous and blameless in the sight of God.

. . . for thou wast slain, and hast redeemed us to God by the blood. . . . Rev. 5:9.

. . . and ye are not your own? I Cor. 6:19.

For he hath made him to be sin for us, who knew no sin; that we might be made the righteousness of God in him. II Cor. 5:21.

B. That we may live under Him in His kingdom and serve Him in everlasting righteousness, innocence and blessedness. We willingly serve Him by an active Christian life and enjoy His blessings, now on earth and hereafter, in heaven.

I am crucified with Christ; nevertheless I live; yet not I, but Christ liveth in me; and the life which I now live in the flesh I live by the faith of the Son of God, who loved me and gave himself for me. Gal. 2:20.

. . . That we, being delivered out of the hand of our enemies, might serve him without fear, in holiness and righteousness before him, all the days of our life. Luke I: 74, 75.

. . . He died for all that they which live should not henceforth live unto themselves, but unto him which died for them and rose again. II Cor. 5:15.

For we are his workmanship, created in Christ Jesus unto good works, which God hath before ordained that we should walk in them. Eph. 2:10.

Note: See Rom. 12:4–16.

STUDY QUESTIONS—Chapter 30

1. What do the Scriptures teach concerning Christ's resurrection?
2. Where were the soul and spirit of Christ during the three days His body was in the grave?
3. What is sheol?
4. Why did Christ descend into sheol?
5. How do we know that Christ was really alive?
6. What kind of body did Christ have after His resurrection?
7. Why is the resurrection of Christ of such importance to us?
8. What do the Scriptures teach concerning Christ's ascension?
9. Where is Christ now?
10. What is meant by the expression "seated at the right hand of God"?
11. What does the exalted Christ do for us from His seat of authority?
12. What do the Scriptures teach concerning the second coming of Christ?
13. What was the purpose of Christ's entire work of redemption?
14. Write Eph. 4:8–10; Acts 1:3; I Cor. 15:17.

Chapter 31

THE APOSTLES' CREED

264. WHAT IS THE APOSTLES' CREED?

I believe in God, the Father Almighty, Creator of heaven and earth; and in Jesus Christ, His only Son, our Lord; who was conceived by the Holy Ghost, born of the Virgin Mary, suffered under Pontius Pilate, was crucified, died, and was buried. He descended into hell, the third day He arose again from the dead; He ascended into heaven, sitteth at the right hand of God, the Father Almighty; from thence He shall come to judge the living and the dead. I believe in the Holy Ghost, the holy Christian Church, the communion of saints, the forgiveness of sins, the resurrection of the body, and the life everlasting. Amen.

265. WHAT IS A CREED?

A creed is a statement of what we believe and teach.

BIBLE NARRATIVE: Peter's statement of what the disciples believed, Matt. 16:13–16.

266. WHY IS THIS STATEMENT OF BELIEFS CALLED THE APOSTLES' CREED?

It is called the Apostles' Creed because it is a statement of the teachings, or doctrines, of the Apostles as found in the Bible.

267. WHY SHOULD I MEMORIZE THE APOSTLES' CREED?

If anyone asks, I should know by memory what I believe.

> *But sanctify the Lord God in your hearts: and be ready always to give an answer to every man that asketh you a*

reason of the hope that is in you with meekness and fear.
I Peter 3:15.

STUDY QUESTIONS—Chapter 31

1. What is a creed?
2. Why is it called the Apostles' Creed?
3. Write the Apostles' Creed.

THE BENEFITS OF THE CROSS

Chapter 32

WOUNDED FOR OUR TRANSGRESSIONS

268.   WHAT IS MEANT BY THE BENEFITS OF THE CROSS?

The benefits of the cross are the gifts which Jesus Christ purchased for us when He died upon the cross of Calvary.

269.   WHAT ARE THESE BENEFITS?

A. Forgiveness of sins and eternal life.
B. Deliverance from iniquities.
C. Peace for the mind and heart.
D. Healing for the body.

> But he was wounded for our transgressions, he was bruised for our iniquities: the chastisement of our peace was upon him; and with his stripes we are healed. Isa. 53:5.

270.   WHAT IS MEANT BY FORGIVENESS OF SINS AND ETERNAL LIFE?

The forgiveness of sins is the cleansing of the soul by the blood of Jesus Christ. Eternal life means to live forever.

> And almost all things are by the law purged with blood; and without shedding of blood is no remission. Heb. 9:22.

> Verily, verily, I say unto you, He that heareth my word, and believeth on him that sent me, hath everlasting life,

and shall not come into condemnation; but is passed from death unto life. John 5:24.

For this is my blood of the new testament, which is shed for many for the remission of sins. Matt. 26:28.

271.   WHY WAS CHRIST WOUNDED FOR OUR SINS?

The law of God demanded the shedding of blood in order to forgive the sins of man. Jesus Christ became that sacrifice. He took our place before God and suffered the punishment for our sins.

For God so loved the world that he gave his only begotten Son, that whosoever believeth in him should not perish but have everlasting life. John 3:16.

Who his own self bare our sins in his own body on the tree, that we, being dead to sins, should live unto righteousness: by whose stripes ye were healed. I Peter 2:24.

272.   HOW DO WE RECEIVE FORGIVENESS FOR OUR SINS?

Our sins are forgiven and forgotten by God when we confess them to Jesus Christ and ask His forgiveness for them.

If we confess our sins, he is faithful and just to forgive us our sins, and to cleanse us from all unrighteousness. I John 1:9.

Come now, let us reason together, saith the Lord: though your sins be as scarlet, they shall be as white as snow; though they be red like crimson, they shall be as wool. Isa. 1:18.

As far as the east is from the west, so far hath he removed our transgressions from us. Ps. 103:12.

273.   HOW CAN WE KNOW OUR SINS ARE FORGIVEN?

A. The Word of God tells us so.

If we confess our sins, he is faithful and just to forgive us our sins, and to cleanse us from all unrighteousness. I John 1:9.

B. We have the witness of the Spirit that we have been forgiven.

The Spirit itself beareth witness with our spirit, that we are the children of God. Rom. 8:16.

274. WHAT IS THE WITNESS OF THE SPIRIT?

The witness of the Spirit is an inward assurance that we are the children of God and no longer the enemies of God.

The Spirit itself beareth witness with our spirit, that we are the children of God: And if children, then heirs; heirs of God, and joint-heirs with Christ; if so be that we suffer with him, that we may be also glorified together. Rom. 8:16,17.

275. HOW CAN WE OBTAIN ASSURANCE OF ETERNAL LIFE?

A. To have well-grounded assurance of eternal life, we must *believe* on the name of the Son of God.

Verily, verily, I say unto you, He that believeth on me hath everlasting life. Your fathers did eat manna in the wilderness, and are dead. Whoso eateth my flesh, and drinketh my blood, hath eternal life; and I will raise him up at the last day. John 6:47,49,54.

These things have I written unto you that believe on the name of the Son of God; that ye may know that ye have eternal life, *and that ye may believe on the name of the Son of God. I John 5:13.*

B. We obtain assurance of eternal life through what is written in the Word of God. Therefore, we should study the Scriptures.

He that believeth on the Son of God hath the witness in himself: he that believeth not God hath made him a liar; because he believeth not the record *that God gave of his Son.* And this is the record, that God hath given to us eternal life, and this life is in his Son. *He that hath the Son hath life; and he that hath not the Son of God hath not life. I John 5:10–12.*

C. We obtain assurance by loving our brethren.

We know that we have passed from death unto life, because we love the brethren. *He that loveth not his brother abideth in death. Whosoever hateth his brother is a mur-*

derer: and ye know that no murderer hath eternal life abiding in him. Hereby perceive we the love of God, because he laid down his life for us: and we ought to lay down our lives for the brethren. But whoso hath this world's good, and seeth his brother have need, and shutteth up his bowels of compassion from him, how dwelleth the love of God in him? My little children, let us not love in word, neither in tongue; but in deed *and in* truth. *And hereby* we know *that we are of the truth, and shall assure our hearts before him. I John 3:14–19.*

D. We allow ourselves to be led by the Spirit of God.

For as many as are led *by the Spirit of God, they* are *the sons of God. Rom. 8:14.*

E. We come out of darkness into light.

Then spake Jesus again unto them, saying, I am the light of the world: he that followeth me shall not walk in darkness, but shall have the light of life. *John 8:12.*

STUDY QUESTIONS—Chapter 32

1. What is meant by the benefits of the cross?
2. List the four benefits of the cross.
3. What is meant by forgiveness of sins?
4. Why was Christ wounded for us?
5. How do we receive forgiveness for our sins?
6. How can we know that our sins are forgiven?
7. What is the witness of the Spirit?
8. How can we obtain assurance of eternal life?
9. Write Isa. 53:5; Ps. 103:2–6.

Chapter 33

BRUISED FOR OUR INIQUITIES

276.   WHAT IS MEANT BY BRUISED FOR OUR INIQUITIES?

It means Jesus Christ endured physical pain caused by the weight of our iniquities. He did it that we might be freed from the curse of having the same weakness toward sin as our fathers had.

> *All we like sheep have gone astray; we have turned everyone to his own way; and the Lord hath laid on him the iniquity of us all. Isa. 53:6.*

> *... For I the Lord thy God, am a jealous God, visiting the iniquity of the fathers upon the children, unto the third and fourth generation of them that hate me. Exod. 20:5.*

> *Yet it pleased the Lord to bruise him; he hath put him to grief ... Isa. 53:10.*

277.   WHAT IS INIQUITY?

Iniquity is a weakness in a particular area of our nature that is born in us as a result of the sins of our forefathers.

> *Among whom also we all had our conversation in times past in the lusts of our flesh fulfilling the desires of the flesh and of the mind; and were by nature the children of wrath, even as others. Eph. 2:3.*

> *Wherefore, as by one man sin entered into the world, and death by sin; and so death passed upon all men, for that all have sinned. Rom. 5:12.*

278. HOW IS INIQUITY BORN IN US?

Iniquity is born in us through our parents.

> *Behold, I was* shapen in iniquity; *and in sin did my mother conceive me.* Ps. 51:5.

279. WHAT DOES GOD MEAN WHEN HE THREATENS TO VISIT THE INIQUITY OF THE FATHERS UPON THE CHILDREN UNTO THE THIRD AND FOURTH GENERATIONS?

If we fail to recognize and confess our iniquities to Jesus Christ, we become prone to the weaknesses found in our ancestors and in turn, our children, grandchildren, etc., will manifest these same weaknesses.

> *The Lord is longsuffering, and of great mercy, forgiving iniquity and transgression, and by no means clearing the guilty, visiting the iniquity of the fathers upon the children unto the third and fourth generation.* Num. 14:18.

280. HOW DO INIQUITOUS TRAITS AND HABITS DEVELOP IN US?

Iniquitous traits and habits develop in us by the continuous and willful breaking of any commandment. For example:

THE COMMANDMENT	THE INIQUITY
1. No other gods.	Rebellion.
2. No graven images.	Idolatry and stubbornness.
3. Using God's Name in vain.	Cursing.
4. Keeping the Sabbath holy.	No rest or peace.
5. Honoring parents.	Disobedience to parents.
6. Not to kill.	Murder.
7. Not to commit adultery.	All sexual uncleanness.
8. Not to steal.	Stealing.
9. Not to lie.	Deception, dishonesty.
10. Not to covet.	Jealousy, envy, greed.

281. WHY DOES GOD THREATEN TO VISIT INIQUITY UPON FUTURE GENERATIONS?

God threatens to visit iniquity upon future generations to make us fear His wrath that we do not act contrary to His commandments.

> *... Repent, and turn yourselves from all your transgressions; so iniquity shall not be your ruin. Ezek. 18:30.*

282.   HOW DOES INIQUITY DIFFER FROM SIN?

Iniquity is the weakness in us that is the breeding ground for sin and it is in this area that Satan tempts us to transgress against God's laws. Sin is the willful and actual transgression of God's laws.

> *Behold, I was shapen in iniquity; and in sin did my mother conceive me. Ps. 51:5.*

> *Whosoever committeth sin transgresseth also the law: for sin is the transgression of the law. I John 3:4.*

283.   IF INIQUITY IS ONLY THE BREEDING PLACE FOR SIN, WHY MUST WE BE FORGIVEN FOR SINS WE HAVE NEVER COMMITTED?

Because God looks at the heart, He knows our inward thoughts and secret desires. Our heart must be *pure* before God for it is the heart that condemns us.

> *If I regard iniquity in my heart, the Lord will not hear me. Ps. 66:18.*

> *... For the Lord seeth not as man seeth; for man looketh on the outward appearance, but the Lord looketh on the heart. I Sam. 16:7.*

> *But I say unto you, that whosoever looketh on a woman to lust after her hath committed adultery with her already in his heart. Matt. 5:28.*

> *For if our heart condemn us, God is greater than our heart, and knoweth all things. Beloved, if our heart condemn us not, then have we confidence toward God. I John 3:20,21.*

284.   HOW DOES INIQUITY DIFFER FROM ORIGINAL SIN?

Iniquity is the weakness in us in a particular area of life because of the sins of our forefathers. Original sin is the total corruption of our nature because of the enmity (hostility against God) that is in us as the result of the sin of Adam and Eve.

Note: See Chapter 55 on Water Baptism.

> *Then said I, Woe is me! for I am undone; because I am a man of unclean lips, and I dwell in the midst of a people of unclean lips: for mine eyes have seen the King, the Lord of hosts. Isa. 6:5.*

> *For that which I do I allow not: for what I would, that do I not; but what I hate, that do I. If then I do that which I would not, I consent unto the law that it is good. Now then it is no more I that do it, but sin that dwelleth in me. Rom. 7:15–17.*

285. CAN WE BE DELIVERED FROM THE CURSE OF INIQUITY?

Yes, Jesus Christ gave His body to be bruised at Calvary to deliver us from the curse of iniquity.

> *He was bruised for our iniquities. Isa. 53:5.*

> *Who forgiveth all thine iniquities; who healeth all thy diseases. Ps. 103:3.*

> *Blessed is the man unto whom the Lord imputeth not iniquity, and in whose spirit there is no guile. Ps. 32:2.*

> *Speak ye comfortably to Jerusalem, and cry unto her, that her warfare is accomplished, that her iniquity is pardoned: for she hath received of the Lord's hand double for all her sins. Isa. 40:2.*

286. HOW CAN WE BE DELIVERED FROM THE CURSE OF INIQUITY?

Iniquity is purged when we recognize it as such, acknowledge it and ask God for His mercy.

> *In meekness instructing those that oppose themselves; if God peradventure will give them repentance to the acknowledging of the truth; And that they may recover themselves out of the snare of the devil, who are taken captive by him at his will. II Tim. 2:25,26.*

Therefore I will judge you, O house of Israel, every one according to his ways, saith the Lord God. Repent, and turn yourselves from all your transgressions; so iniquity shall not be your ruin. Ezek. 18:30.

287. WHAT ASSURANCE DO WE HAVE THAT OUR INIQUITIES WILL BE TAKEN AWAY?

The deliverance from iniquity is a part of the atonement which Jesus Christ purchased for us at Calvary. If we ask for deliverance from iniquity and believe He will grant it, deliverance is ours.

If ye shall ask anything in my name, I will do it. John 14:14.

If we confess our sins he is faithful and just to forgive us our sins; and to cleanse us from all unrighteousness. I John 1:9.

He shall see of the travail of his soul, and shall be satisfied: by his knowledge shall my righteous servant justify many; for he shall bear their iniquities. Isa. 53:11.

288. WILL OUR INIQUITIES BE VISITED ON OUR CHILDREN AFTER WE ARE DELIVERED FROM THEM?

No, when God pardons our iniquities, He casts them into the depths of the sea never to be remembered against us or our seed.

Who is a God like unto thee, that pardoneth iniquity, and passeth by the transgression of the remnant of his heritage? he retaineth not his anger for ever, because he delighteth in mercy. He will turn again, he will have compassion upon us; he will subdue our iniquities; and thou wilt cast all their sins into the depths of the sea. Micah 7:18,19.

In those days, and in that time, saith the Lord, the iniquity of Israel shall be sought for, and there shall be none; and the sins of Judah, and they shall not be found: for I will pardon them whom I reserve. Jer. 50:20.

. . . For I the Lord thy God am a jealous God, visiting the iniquity of the fathers upon the children unto the third and fourth generation of them that hate me; And shewing

mercy unto thousands of them that love me, and keep my commandments. Exod. 20:5,6.

STUDY QUESTIONS—Chapter 33

1. What is meant by bruised for our iniquities?
2. What is iniquity?
3. How does iniquity differ from sin?
4. How does iniquity begin in us?
5. How are iniquities related to the Ten Commandments?
6. Why must iniquity be forgiven?
7. How can we be delivered from iniquity?
8. What assurance do we have that our iniquities will be taken away?
9. Will our iniquities be visited on our children after we are delivered from them?
10. Write I John 1:9.

Chapter 34

CHASTISED FOR OUR PEACE

289. WHY DID JESUS CHRIST SUBMIT TO THE SUF-FERINGS AND DEATH UPON THE CROSS?

Jesus Christ submitted Himself to the sufferings and death upon the cross to reconcile us to God.

290. WHAT DOES IT MEAN TO BE RECONCILED TO GOD?

To be reconciled to God means to receive divine pardon for our sins and peace with God.

> *For if, when we were enemies, we were reconciled to God by the death of his son, much more, being reconciled, we shall be saved by his life. Rom. 5:10.*

291. WHAT IS PEACE WITH GOD?

Knowing that we have received pardon for our sins, we are free from guilt and have the assurance that we are no longer the enemies of God.

> *Therefore being justified by faith, we have peace with God through our Lord Jesus Christ. Rom. 5:1.*

292. WHAT DOES THIS PEACE DO FOR US?

A. It gives us an inner serenity that can come to us through no other means.

> *And the peace of God, which passeth all understanding, shall keep your hearts and minds through Christ Jesus. Phil. 4:7.*

B. It frees us from the haunting sense of sin.

Let us draw near with a true heart in full assurance of faith, having our hearts sprinkled from an evil conscience, and our bodies washed with pure water. Heb. 10:22.

C. It cleanses us from all feeling of self-condemnation and unfitness.

There is therefore now no condemnation to them which are in Christ Jesus who walk not after the flesh, but after the Spirit. Rom. 8:1.

D. It keeps our mind sound in the hour of grief, distress or trouble.

For God hath not given us the spirit of fear; but of power, and of love, and of a sound mind. II Tim. 1:7.

E. It enables us to stand before God in the hour of our death with this same feeling of peace and security.

Yea, though I walk through the valley of the shadow of death, I will fear no evil: for thou art with me; thy rod and thy staff they comfort me. Ps. 23:4.

293. HOW CAN WE KEEP THIS PEACE?

The Lord will keep us in perfect peace if our mind is kept on Him and we trust Him to help us in every circumstance of life.

Thou wilt keep him in perfect peace, whose mind is stayed on thee: because he trusteth in thee. Isa. 26:3.

294. CAN WE HAVE PEACE OF MIND IN THE MIDST OF TROUBLE?

We can have peace of mind in every situation if we rigidly adhere to the promises God gives us.

Peace I leave with you, my peace I give unto you: not as the world giveth, give I unto you. Let not your heart be troubled, neither let it be afraid. John 14:27.

295. HOW DO WE RECEIVE PEACE THROUGH THE PROMISES OF GOD?

When we earnestly seek the Lord, God through the Holy Spirit will inspire a certain Scripture to us. Only the promises that are given directly to us by the inspiration of the Holy Spirit can we claim for ourselves.

All scripture is given by inspiration of God . . .
II Tim. 3:16.

It is the spirit that quickeneth; the flesh profiteth nothing: the words that I speak unto you, they are spirit, and they are life. John 6:63.

296. HOW ARE WE MADE TO BELIEVE THE PROMISES OF GOD?

As a direct result of receiving an inspired promise from God, we receive the gift of faith.

So then faith cometh by hearing, and hearing by the word of God. Rom. 10:17.

297. WHAT IS FAITH IN GOD?

Faith in God is believing God unquestionably even when all reason tells us a situation is impossible.

Now faith is the substance of things hoped for, the evidence of things not seen. Heb. 11:1.

STUDY QUESTIONS—Chapter 34

1. Why did Jesus Christ suffer and die upon the cross?
2. What does it mean to be reconciled to God?
3. What is peace with God?
4. What does God's peace do for us?
5. How do we receive the promises of God?
6. How are we enabled to believe the promises of God?
7. What is faith in God?
8. Write II Tim. 1:7; Isa. 26:3; John 14:27.

Chapter 35

HEALED BY HIS STRIPES

298. **WHAT DOES "BY HIS STRIPES WE ARE HEALED" MEAN?**

It means that at the cross Jesus Christ bore all the sicknesses, infirmities and diseases of the world. He was beaten for our healing.

> *That it might be fulfilled which was spoken by Esaias the prophet, saying, Himself took our infirmities, and bare our sicknesses. Matt. 8:17.*

> *. . . And with his stripes we are healed. Isa. 53:5.*

> *He took on him our sickness and bore our pains. My righteous servant shall justify many for he will bear their iniquities. He shall divide the spoil with the strong, because . . . he bore the sins of many. Isa. 53:4,11,12 RSV.*

299. **WHERE DOES SICKNESS AND DISEASE ORIGINATE?**

Sickness and disease originates with sin. Sin is the cause of all our misery and sorrow, of our diseases and pain, of death itself.

> *Wherefore, as by one man sin entered into the world, and death by sin; so death passed upon all men, for that all have sinned. Rom. 5:12.*

300. **HOW IS HEALING ADMINISTERED?**

Healing is administered through:

A. Personal prayer and praise.

> *In those days was Hezekiah sick unto death. And the*

prophet Isaiah the son of Amoz came to him, and said unto him, Thus saith the Lord, Set thine house in order; for thou shalt die, and not live. Then he turned his face to the wall, and prayed unto the Lord, saying . . . Thus saith the Lord, the God of David thy father, I have heard thy prayer, I have seen thy tears: behold, I will heal thee . . . II Kings 20:1,2,5.

And, behold, there came a leper and worshipped him, saying, Lord, if thou wilt, thou canst make me clean. And Jesus put forth his hand, and touched him, saying, I will; be thou clean. And immediately his leprosy was cleansed. Matt. 8:2,3.

B. Laying on of hands. By the laying on of the believer's hands, healing is imparted to the sick.

And these signs shall follow them that believe; in my name shall they cast out devils; they shall speak with new tongues; they shall take up serpents; and if they drink any deadly thing, it shall not hurt them; they shall lay hands on the sick, and they shall recover. Mark 16:17,18.

C. The Word of the Lord. By God's Word coming from the mouth of an anointed believer, the strongest hold of Satan can be broken.

. . . speak the word only, and my servant shall be healed. Matt. 8:8.

He sent his word, and healed them, and delivered them from their destructions. Ps. 107:20.

D. Anointed cloths.

And God wrought special miracles by the hands of Paul: So that from his body were brought unto the sick handkerchiefs or aprons, and the diseases departed from them, and the evil spirits went out of them. Acts 19:12.

E. Gifts of Healing.

To another faith by the same Spirit; to another the gifts of healing by the same Spirit; And God hath set some in the church, first apostles, secondarily prophets, thirdly teachers, after that miracles, then gifts of healings, helps, governments, diversities of tongues. I Cor. 12:9,28.

F. Prayer of Faith.

And the prayer of faith shall save the sick, and the Lord shall raise him up and if he have committed sins, they shall be forgiven him. James 5:15.

G. Anointing with Oil.

And they cast out many devils, and anointed with oil many that were sick, and healed them. Mark 6:13.

301.   CAN EVERYONE BE HEALED?

The provision for healing that was made at Calvary is for all men.

. . . God is no respecter of persons. Acts 10:34.

Who his own self bare our sins in his own body on the tree, that we, being dead to sins, should live unto righteousness: by whose stripes ye were healed. I Peter 2:24.

Bless the Lord, O my soul: and all that is within me, bless his holy name. Bless the Lord, O my soul, and forget not all his benefits: Who forgiveth all thine iniquities; who healeth all thy diseases. Ps. 103:1–3.

302.   IS FAITH IN THE LORD NECESSARY FOR HEALING?

Yes. Without faith we receive nothing from God. Faith must be exercised either in the one who prays for the sick or in the one who is sick.

But without faith it is impossible to please him: for he that cometh to God must believe that he is, and that he is a rewarder of them that diligently seek him. Heb. 11:6.

And he did not many mighty works there because of their unbelief. Matt. 13:58.

303.   HOW DO WE RECEIVE THIS FAITH?

When we earnestly seek the Lord for healing, the Holy Spirit allows us to hear the Word of God. This inspired "Word of God" that is sent into our heart creates faith in us. In that instant we are able to grasp hold of the promise of God that brings healing.

So then faith cometh by hearing, and hearing by the word of God. Rom. 10:17.

He sent his word, and healed them, and delivered them from their destructions. Ps. 107:20.

304. WHY ISN'T ALL HEALING INSTANTANEOUS?

All healing is not instantaneous because:

A. The purpose for our affliction has not yet been accomplished.

For a small moment have I forsaken thee; but with great mercies will I gather thee. In a little wrath I hid my face from thee for a moment; but with everlasting kindness will I have mercy on thee, saith the Lord thy Redeemer. Isa. 54:7,8.

B. Sin or unbelief blocks our way to Christ.

But your iniquities have separated between you and your God, and your sins have hid his face from you, and he will not hear. Isa. 59:2.

Then shall they call upon me, but I will not answer; they shall seek me early, but they shall not find me: For that they hated knowledge, and did not choose the fear of the Lord: Prov. 1:28,29.

For this people's heart is waxed gross, and their ears are dull of hearing, and their eyes they have closed; lest at any time they would see with their eyes, and hear with their ears, and should understand with their hearts, and should be converted, and I should heal them. Matt. 13:15.

305. WHAT CAN PREVENT US FROM RECEIVING HEALING?

Unconfessed sin, an unforgiving spirit and enmity against a brother can prevent us from receiving healing. (See Sacrament of Anointing with Oil, Ch. 61.)

But your iniquities have separated between you and your God, and your sins have hid his face from you, and he will not hear. Isa. 59:2.

But if ye forgive not men their trespasses, neither will your Father forgive your trespasses. Matt. 6:15.

Therefore if thou bring thy gift to the altar, and there rememberest that thy brother hath ought against thee; leave there thy gift before the altar and go thy way; first be reconciled to thy brother, and then come and offer thy gift. Matt. 5:23,24. (See Sacrament of the Lord's Supper, Ch. 52.)

306. WHILE AWAITING HEALING, WHAT SHOULD WE DO?

We should pray and patiently await direction from God concerning the lesson He is teaching us in our sickness.

And not only so, but we glory in tribulations also: knowing that tribulation worketh patience; and patience, experience; and experience, hope; And hope maketh not ashamed; because the love of God is shed abroad in our hearts by the Holy Ghost which is given unto us. Rom. 5:3–5.

Though he were a Son, yet learned he obedience by the things which he suffered. Heb. 5:8.

He staggered not at the promise of God through unbelief; but was strong in faith, giving glory to God; And being fully persuaded that, what he had promised, he was able to perform. Rom. 4:20,21.

307. WHEN DOES HEALING BEGIN?

The recovery from our illness is progressive at times. When we receive a healing touch from Christ, the healing process begins immediately.

And Jesus went about all Galilee, teaching in their synagogues, and preaching the gospel of the kingdom, and healing all manner of sickness and all manner of disease among the people. Matt. 4:23.

And when he saw them, he said unto them, Go shew yourselves unto the priests. And it came to pass, that, as they went, they were cleansed. And one of them, when he saw that he was healed, turned back, and with a loud voice glorified God. Luke 17:14,15.

How God anointed Jesus of Nazareth with the Holy Ghost and with power: who went about doing good, and healing all that were oppressed of the devil; for God was with him. Acts 10:38.

But that ye may know that the Son of man hath power on earth to forgive sins, (he saith to the sick of the palsy,) I say unto thee, Arise, and take up thy bed, and go thy way into thine house. Mark 2:10,11.

308. WHEN WE ARE HEALED, DO WE RECEIVE SPIRITUAL AS WELL AS A PHYSICAL HEALING?

When we receive a healing touch from Christ for our body, we are quickened in spirit as well. Christ's healing touch affects our spiritual relationship with God.

And when ye stand praying, forgive, if ye have ought against any: that your Father also which is in heaven may forgive you your trespasses. But if ye do not forgive, neither will your Father which is in heaven forgive your trespasses. Mark 11:25,26.

309. WHAT DOES GOD COMMAND US TO DO AFTER WE HAVE BEEN HEALED? WHY?

God commands us to sin no more lest a worse thing come upon us.

Afterward Jesus findeth him in the temple, and said unto him, Behold, thou art made whole; sin no more, lest a worse thing come unto thee. John 5:14.

Then goeth he, and taketh with himself seven other spirits more wicked than himself, and they enter in and dwell there: and the last state of that man is worse than the first. Matt. 12:45.

For it had been better for them not to have known the way of righteousness, than, after they have known it, to turn from the holy commandment delivered unto them. II Peter 2:21.

STUDY QUESTIONS—Chapter 35

1. What does "by His stripes we are healed" mean?
2. Where did sickness and disease originate?
3. List five ways by which healing is administered.
4. Does God heal everyone?
5. Why is faith necessary for healing?
6. What two things hinder us from receiving healing?
7. When does healing begin?
8. What does God command us to do after we have been healed? Why?
9. Write Acts 10:38; Ps. 103:2–4; I Peter 2:24.

THE FOUNDATION STONES

Chapter 36

THE DOCTRINES OF CHRIST

310. WHAT ARE THE DOCTRINES OF CHRIST?

The doctrines of Christ are the six basic principles (foundation stones) upon which our Christian faith is built.

> *And are built upon the foundation of the apostles and prophets. Jesus Christ himself being the chief corner stone. Eph. 2:20.*

311. WHAT ARE THE SIX PRINCIPLES OF CHRIST?

The six principles (foundation stones) are the foundations we must personally experience before we can go on to maturity in Christ. They are:

1. Repentance from dead works.
2. Faith toward God. (Justification.)
3. Doctrine of Baptisms.
   a. Water Baptism.
   b. Baptism of the Holy Spirit and Fire.
4. Laying on of Hands.
5. Resurrection of the Dead.
6. Eternal Judgment.

> *Therefore leaving the principles of the doctrine of Christ, let us go on to perfection; not laying again the foundation of repentance from dead works, and of faith toward God, Of the doctrine of baptisms, and of laying on of hands, and*

*of resurrection of the dead, and of eternal judgment.
Heb. 6:1,2.*

312. HOW DO WE LAY THE FOUNDATIONS?

We lay the foundations by obediently setting the principles into place in our lives as they are revealed and experienced by us.

And they continued steadfastly in the apostles' doctrine and fellowship, and in breaking of bread, and in prayers. Acts 2:42.

Then Peter said unto them, Repent, and be baptized every one of you in the name of Jesus Christ for the remission of sins, and ye shall receive the gift of the Holy Ghost. Acts 2:38.

313. WHY MUST WE BE SURE THAT THE DOCTRINES OF CHRIST (FOUNDATION STONES) ARE CAREFULLY PLACED IN OUR LIVES?

If the foundation of a building is not sound, the building will collapse under pressure. Likewise, if our spiritual foundation is weak, we cannot add more truth and experience without causing the fall of the whole building. We are only permitted to go on to perfection after these doctrines of Christ have become a part of our lives.

Therefore whosoever heareth these sayings of mine, and doeth them, I will liken him unto a wise man, which built his house upon a rock: And the rain descended, and the floods came, and the winds blew, and beat upon that house; and it fell not: for it was founded upon a rock. And every one that heareth these sayings of mine, and doeth them not, shall be likened unto a foolish man, which built his house upon the sand: And the rain descended, and the floods came, and the winds blew, and beat upon that house; and it fell: and great was the fall of it. Matt. 7:24-27.

Therefore leaving the principles of the doctrine of Christ, let us go on unto perfection; . . . And this will we do, if God permit. Heb. 6:1,3.

STUDY QUESTIONS—Chapter 36

1. What are the doctrines of Christ?
2. What are the six foundation stones?
3. How do we lay the foundations?
4. Why must we be sure that the doctrines of Christ are carefully placed in our lives?
5. Write Hebrews 6:1,2; Eph. 2:20.

Chapter 37

REPENTANCE FROM DEAD WORKS

314. WHAT IS THE DOCTRINE OF REPENTANCE FROM DEAD WORKS?

Repentance from dead works is turning from man-made laws and practices (traditions) to the commandments of God.

> *Therefore leaving the principles of the doctrine of Christ, let us go on unto perfection, not laying again the foundation of* repentance from dead works. *Heb. 6:1.*

315. WHAT ARE MAN-MADE LAWS AND PRACTICES?

Man-made laws and practices are religious observances or ceremonies based upon tradition. They appear to have great spiritual meaning but there is no spiritual life in them.

> *Having a form of godliness, but denying the power thereof: from such turn away. II Tim. 3:5.*

316. WHAT ARE "DEAD WORKS"?

Dead works are the man-made rites, customs, beliefs and good works that we perform believing they will earn us the favor of God and an entrance into His Kingdom. They are based on the traditions of the elders rather than on Scripture and are futile attempts to work out our own salvation hoping that God will approve.

> *Beware lest any man spoil you through philosophy and vain deceit, after the tradition of men, after the rudiments of the world, and not after Christ. Col. 2:8.*

> *Not by works of righteousness which we have done, but ac-*

cording to his mercy he saved us, by the washing of regeneration, and renewing of the Holy Ghost. Titus 3:5.

317. WHAT IS MEANT BY THE "TRADITIONS OF THE ELDERS"?

"Traditions of the elders" are a mixture of the commandments of God and the commandments of men passed down to us from previous generations.

> *Howbeit in vain do they worship me, teaching for doctrines the commandments of men. For laying aside the commandments of God, ye hold the traditions of men ... Full well ye reject the commandment of God, that ye may keep your own tradition. Mark 7:7,8,9.*

318. WHY MUST WE TURN FROM DEAD WORKS?

Unless we turn from dead works, our worship of God is in vain. God wants us to be totally dependent upon Him. When we emphasize our works, we are trying to make ourselves more acceptable and presentable to God. The only thing that makes us worthy to come into the presence of God is the blood of Jesus Christ.

> *... why do ye also transgress the commandment of God by your tradition? ... thus have ye made the commandment of God of none effect by your tradition. Matt. 15:3,6.*

> *But we are all as an unclean thing, and all our righteousnesses are as filthy rags; and we all do fade as a leaf; and our iniquities, like the wind, have taken us away. Isa. 64:6.*

> *Forasmuch as ye know that ye were not redeemed with corruptible things, as silver and gold, from your vain conversation received by tradition from your fathers; But with the precious blood of Christ, as of a lamb without blemish and without spot. I Peter 1:18,19.*

319. HOW DO WE RECEIVE REPENTANCE FROM DEAD WORKS?

We receive repentance from dead works when the Holy Spirit causes us:

1. To become dissatisfied with our spiritual life (we don't know why).
2. To wonder if our own efforts to earn salvation through works can possibly justify us in the eyes of God.
3. To hear or read the Word of God revealing truth to us by showing us what is contrary to God's commandments.
4. To repent ... to turn from the laws of men to Christ.

320.   WHY IS REPENTANCE FROM DEAD WORKS SO IMPORTANT?

Before we can build a sure foundation of Christian faith, we must tear down everything we have built that is contrary to the teachings of Christ.

> *According to the grace of God which is given unto me, as a wise masterbuilder, I have laid the foundation, and another buildeth thereon. But let every man take heed how he buildeth thereupon. For other foundation can no man lay than that is laid, which is Jesus Christ. I Cor. 3:10,11.*

STUDY QUESTIONS—Chapter 37

1. What is repentance from dead works?
2. What are "dead works"?
3. What are the "traditions of the elders"?
4. Why must we turn from dead works?
5. How do we receive repentance from dead works?
6. Why is repentance from dead works important?
7. Write Col. 2:8; II Tim. 3:5; Isa. 64:6.

Chapter 38

THE DOCTRINE OF JUSTIFICATION
or
FAITH TOWARD GOD

WHAT IS THE DOCTRINE OF FAITH TOWARD GOD?

Faith toward God is the teaching of the apostles that faith is the gift of God which enables us to believe Him for justification and all other benefits.

For by grace are ye saved through faith; and that not of yourselves: it is the gift of God. Eph. 2:8.

WHAT IS JUSTIFICATION?

Justification is an act of God which frees believing sinners from the guilt and penalty of sin. God transfers our guilt and punishment onto Jesus Christ and His righteousness to those who believe Him. In God's eyes we stand justified (just-as-if-I-never-did-it).

Therefore being justified by faith, we have peace with God through our Lord Jesus Christ: By whom also we have access by faith into this grace wherein we stand, and rejoice in hope of the glory of God. Rom. 5:1,2.

If we confess our sins, he is faithful and just to forgive us our sins, and to cleanse us from all unrighteousness. I John 1:9.

HOW DO WE OBTAIN JUSTIFICATION?

We obtain justification through repentance from sin and faith toward God. To be justified we must:

A. Repent of our sins by admitting that we have sinned ag
God, asking Him for forgiveness and forsaking our sin.

If we confess our sins, He is faithful and just to forg
us our sins and to cleanse us from all unrighteousne.
I John 1:9.

Against thee, thee only, have I sinned, and done this evil
thy sight: that thou mightest be justified when thou spea
est and be clear when thou judgest. Behold, I was shape
in iniquity; and in sin did my mother conceive m
Ps. 51:4,5.

He that covereth his sins shall not prosper, but whoso co
fesseth and forsaketh them shall have mercy. Prov. 28:1.

B. Accept Jesus Christ as our sacrifice for sin so that thro
faith in His blood we are cleansed from all sin.

(Jesus Christ) God hath set forth to be a propitiatio
(sacrifice) through faith in his blood, to declare his righ
eousness for the remission of sins that are past, throug
the forbearance of God; To declare, I say, at this time h
righteousness: that he might be just, and the justifier o
him which believeth in Jesus. Rom. 3:25,26.

Much more then, being now justified by his blood, we sha
be saved from wrath through him. Rom. 5:9.

C. Believe that God has accepted our repentance and faith
Christ Jesus, making us His child.

For ye are all the children of God by faith in Christ Jesus.
Gal. 3:26.

And this is the confidence that we have in him, that, if we
ask anything according to his will, he heareth us: And
if we know that he hear us, whatsoever we ask, we know
that we have the petitions that we desired of him.
I John 5:14,15.

324. WHY DO WE NEED TO BE JUSTIFIED?

We are all sinners under condemnation by a holy God. There
no good in any of us.

For all have sinned, and come short of the glory of God.
Rom. 3:23.

They are all gone out of the way, they are together become unprofitable; there is none that doeth good, no, not one. Rom. 3:12.

WHAT IS SIN?

Sin is the willful breaking of God's law (The Ten Commandments).

> *Whosoever committeth sin transgresseth also the law: for sin is the transgression of the law. I John 3:4.*

HOW MANY KINDS OF SIN ARE THERE?

There are two kinds of sin: original sin (See Chapter 55) and actual sin.

WHAT IS ORIGINAL SIN?

Original Sin is the total corruption of our nature because of the enmity that is in us as the result of the sin of Adam and Eve.

WHAT IS ACTUAL SIN?

Actual sin is every act committed against a commandment of God in thought, desire, word or deed.

> *Whosoever committeth sin transgresseth also the law: for sin is the transgression of the law. I John 3:4.*

> *For out of the heart proceed evil thoughts, murders, adulteries, fornications, thefts, false witness, blasphemies. Matt. 15:19.*

> *Then when lust hath conceived, it bringeth forth sin ... James 1:15.*

> *Therefore to him that knoweth to do good, and doeth it not, to him it is sin. James 4:17 (sin of omission).*

WHAT IS THE PUNISHMENT FOR ACTUAL SIN?

Actual sin separates us from God.

> *But your iniquities have separated between you and your God, and your sins have hid his face from you, that he will not hear. Isa. 59:2.*

330. HOW CAN WE BE REUNITED WITH GOD?

We are reunited with God when the blood of Jesus cleanses us from all sin and unrighteousness.

> *To the praise of the glory of his grace, wherein he*
> *made us accepted in the beloved. In whom we have*
> *demption through his blood, the forgiveness of sins,*
> *cording to the riches of his grace. Eph. 1:6,7.*

> *But now in Christ Jesus ye who sometimes were far off*
> *made nigh by the blood of Christ. Eph. 2:13.*

> *For he hath made him to be sin for us, who knew no*
> *that we might be made the righteousness of God in h*
> *II Cor. 5:21.*

331. HOW CAN A JUST AND HOLY GOD JUSTIFY SINN

God provided Jesus Christ as our substitute to have our
placed upon Him and to suffer the punishment for us.

> *(All) are justified and made upright and in right stand*
> *with God, freely and gratuitously by His grace (His u*
> *merited favor and mercy) through the redemption which*
> *(provided) in Christ Jesus. Whom God put forward (befo*
> *the eyes of all) as a mercy seat and propitiation by h*
> *blood—the cleansing and life-giving sacrifice of atoneme*
> *and reconciliation—(to be renewed) through faith. T*
> *was to show God's righteousness, because in His divi*
> *forbearance He had passed over and ignored former si*
> *without punishment. It was to demonstrate and prove*
> *the present time (in the now season) that He Himself*
> *righteous and that He justifies and accepts as righteo*
> *him who has (true) faith in Jesus. Rom. 3:24-26 AM*

332. WHAT IS MEANT BY BEING JUSTIFIED BY GRACE?

It means we are justified apart from any works. It is an unr
ited gift of God to those who believe in Christ.

> *For by grace are ye saved, through faith; and that not*
> *yourselves: it is the gift of God: Not of works, lest an*
> *man should boast. Eph. 2:8,9.*

> *Being justified freely by his grace through the redemptio*
> *that is in Christ Jesus. Rom. 3:24.*

33. WHAT MUST WE DO TO RECEIVE THIS GRACE?

We must believe that God's offer of justification through Christ is true, then admit our need and ask for repentance.

> *For God so loved the world, that he gave his only begotten Son, that whosoever believeth in him should not perish, but have everlasting life. John 3:16.*

334. WHAT IS REPENTANCE?

Repentance, a gift from God, is godly sorrow for our sins. We admit that we have sinned against God, ask Him for forgiveness and cleansing, and ask His help to change our ways.

> *In meekness instructing those that oppose themselves; if God peradventure will give them repentance to the acknowledging of the truth, and that they may recover themselves out of the snare of the devil, who are taken captive by him at his will. II Tim. 2:25,26.*

> *When they heard these things, they held their peace, and glorified God, saying Then hath God also to the Gentiles granted repentance unto life. Acts 11:18.*

335. HOW DO WE RECEIVE REPENTANCE?

We receive repentance by:

A. Telling God that we are sorry that we have sinned against Him.

> *Against thee, thee only, have I sinned, and done this evil in thy sight: that thou mightest be justified when thou speakest, and be clear when thou judgest. Ps. 51:4.*

B. Being specific in confessing all sins that He brings to our remembrance.

> *He that covereth his sins shall not prosper; but whoso confesseth and forsaketh them shall have mercy. Prov. 28:13.*

> *If we confess our sins, he is faithful and just to forgive us our sins, and to cleanse us from all unrighteousness. I John 1:9.*

C. Telling God we can do no better without His help because we are sinners by nature.

> *Behold, I was shapen in iniquity; and in sin did my mother conceive me. Ps. 51:5.*

> *... God be merciful to me a sinner. Luke 18:13.*

D. Telling God that we need and want Him in mercy to save us from our sins through Jesus Christ and believing Him for it.

> *... the word is nigh thee even in thy mouth, and in thy heart: that is, the word of faith which we preach; That if thou shalt confess with thy mouth the Lord Jesus, and shalt believe in thine heart that God hath raised him from the dead, thou shalt be saved. For with the heart man believeth unto righteousness; and with the mouth confession is made unto salvation ... For whosoever shall call upon the name of the Lord shall be saved. Rom. 10:8–10,13.*

336. HOW DO WE KNOW WHEN WE HAVE TRULY REPENTED?

True repentance comes from God and is demonstrated by the fruit of change in our lives. We are sincerely sorry that we have offended God not simply regretful that we have been caught in sin. We have been turned away from sin and show it by our obedience to Him in water baptism, the next step in coming to Christ.

> *Bring forth therefore fruits meet for repentance. Matt. 3:8.*

> *Even so faith, if it hath not works, is dead, being alone ... But wilt thou know, O vain man, that faith without works is dead? James 2:17,20.*

> *Now when they heard this they were pricked in their heart, and said unto Peter and to the rest of the apostles, Men and brethren, what shall we do? Then Peter said unto them, Repent, and be baptized every one of you in the name of Jesus Christ for the remission of sins, and ye shall receive the gift of the Holy Ghost. Acts 2:37,38.*

337. IS FAITH NECESSARY FOR US TO ACCEPT JUSTIFICATION?

Yes. We must believe Jesus' death, burial and resurrection was sufficient payment for our sins.

. . . how that Christ died for our sins according to the scriptures; And that he was buried, and that he rose again the third day according to the scriptures. I Cor. 15:3,4.

(Christ) was delivered for our offenses, and was raised again for our justification. Rom. 4:25.

If Christ be not raised, your faith is vain; ye are yet in your sins. I Cor. 15:17.

338. HOW DO WE RECEIVE FAITH?

We receive faith by hearing the inspired Word of God.

So then faith cometh by hearing, and hearing by the word of God. Rom. 10:17.

339. WHAT IS MEANT BY GOD'S INSPIRED WORD?

God's inspired word is the word that the Holy Spirit uses to enlighten us in a particular matter. We can always confirm this word by the Scriptures.

All scripture is given by inspiration of God, and is profitable for doctrine, for reproof, for correction, for instruction in righteousness. II Tim. 3:16.

. . . In the mouth of two or three witnesses shall every word be established. II Cor. 13:1.

340. IN WHAT WAYS DOES THE INSPIRED WORD OF GOD COME TO US?

The inspired word of God can come to us by:

1. The preaching of the Gospel.

(God) . . . hath in due times manifested his word through preaching, which is committed unto me (Paul) according to the commandment of God our Savior. Titus 1:3.

2. Searching the Scriptures.

For whatsoever things were written aforetime were written for our learning, that we through patience and comfort of the scriptures might have hope. Rom. 15:4.

3. In a vision or a dream.

And it shall come to pass in the last days, saith God, I will pour out of my Spirit upon all flesh: and your sons and your daughters shall prophesy, and your young men shall see visions, and your old men shall dream dreams. Acts 2:17.

4. In times of prayer.

He will be very gracious unto thee at the voice of thy cry; when he shall hear it, he will answer thee ... And thine ears shall hear a word behind thee saying, This is the way, walk ye in it, when ye turn to the right hand and when ye turn to the left. Isa. 30:19,21.

341. WHY MUST WE FIRMLY MAINTAIN THE DOCTRINE OF JUSTIFICATION BY FAITH?

We must maintain firmly this doctrine because:

A. It is the chief doctrine of the Christian religion.
B. It distinguishes the Christian religion from false religions, all of which teach salvation by works.
C. It gives enduring comfort to penitent sinners.
D. It gives all glory to God.
E. It is the means by which we are led into the full knowledge of redemption through Jesus Christ.

Christ is become of no effect unto you, whosoever of you are justified by the law; ye are fallen from grace. For we through the Spirit wait for the hope of righteousness by faith. Gal. 5:4,5.

342. HOW CAN WE CONTINUE IN RIGHT STANDING WITH GOD?

By daily confessing our sins and asking Him to cleanse us with His precious blood.

If we say that we have no sin, we deceive ourselves, and the truth is not in us. If we confess our sins, he is faithful and just to forgive us our sins, and to cleanse us from all unrighteousness. I John 1:8,9.

STUDY QUESTIONS—Chapter 38

1. What is faith toward God?
2. What is justification?
3. How do we obtain justification?
4. Why do we need to be justified?
5. What is sin?
6. How can a just and holy God justify sinners?
7. What is meant by being justified by grace?
8. What is repentance?
9. How do we receive repentance?
10. How do we know when we have truly repented?
11. Is faith necessary for us to accept justification?
12. How do we receive faith?
13. How can we continue in right standing with God?
14. Write Eph. 2:8,9; II Cor. 5:21; Rom. 10:8-10.

Chapter 39

THE DOCTRINE OF BAPTISMS

343.   WHAT IS THE DOCTRINE OF BAPTISMS?

It is the teaching of the apostles that all believers must experience three distinct but related baptisms as an entrance into the new covenant.

> *Therefore leaving the principles of the doctrine of Christ, let us go on unto perfection; not laying again the foundation of repentance from dead works, and of faith toward God, of* the doctrine of baptisms . . . Heb. 6:1,2.

344.   WHAT IS THE NEW COVENANT?

The new covenant is God's agreement to fulfill all of His promises to those who enter into covenant with Him. It is guaranteed by an oath and purchased by the blood of Jesus Christ.

> *I the Lord have called thee (Jesus) in righteousness, and will hold thine hand, and will keep thee, and give thee for a covenant of the people, for a light of the Gentiles; To open the blind eyes, to bring out the prisoners from the prison, and them that sit in darkness out of the prison house. Isa. 42:6,7.*

> *For this is the covenant that I will make with the house of Israel after those days, saith the Lord; I will put my laws into their mind, and write them in their hearts: and I will be to them a God, and they shall be to me a people: And they shall not teach every man his neighbour, and every man his brother, saying, Know the Lord: for all shall know me, from the least to the greatest. For I will be merciful to their unrighteousness, and their sins and their iniquities will I remember no more. Heb. 8:10–12.*

345. WHAT ARE THE PROVISIONS OF THE NEW COVENANT?

In the New Covenant, God gives us promises along with their conditions and fulfills these conditions in us by His Holy Spirit. These provisions include:

A. He will be our God and take us to be His people. He gives Himself fully to us in all that He is and takes possession of us to make us His peculiar treasure.

B. He puts His laws into our inner man. He works within us to will and to do His good pleasure by putting His law into our minds and hearts. His ways are no longer foreign to us but become a very part of our life-style.

C. He will be known in first-hand experience by all who are in covenant fellowship with Him. All are made priests and kings with free access even into His Holy Presence by the blood of the Covenant.

D. He will continue to be merciful to forgive us our sins and to change our nature from unrighteousness to His righteousness. He, in mercy, not only takes the cost of our sin Himself but changes us so that we do not have to continue in bondage to sin.

E. His presence shall dwell within our bodies as individuals and in our local churches so that we may all enjoy Him without any veils or restrictions. Fellowship with God is freely available without condemnation or partiality.

> *What? know ye not that your body is the temple of the Holy Ghost which is in you, which ye have of God, and ye are not your own? I Cor. 6:19.*

> *. . . for ye are the temple of the living God; as God hath said, I will dwell in them, and walk in them; and I will be their God, and they shall be my people. II Cor. 6:16.*

346. HOW DO WE ENTER INTO COVENANT WITH GOD?

We enter into covenant with God by becoming partakers of the death (repentance), burial (water baptism) and resurrection (Holy Spirit baptism) of His son, the Lord Jesus Christ.

347. WHAT ARE THE THREE BAPTISMS?

They are Water Baptism, Holy Spirit Baptism and the Baptism of Fire.

348.   WHAT IS THE PURPOSE FOR THREE BAPTISMS?

In each baptism, when it is entered into by faith, the Holy Spirit produces a distinct spiritual change in us.

> *. . . Except a man be born of water and of the Spirit, he cannot enter into the kingdom of God. John 3:5.*

349.   WHAT IS THE FIRST BAPTISM WE MUST EXPERIENCE?

We must be baptized into Christ through water baptism after we have repented of our sins.

> *Then Peter said unto them, Repent, and be baptized every one of you in the name of Jesus Christ for the remission of sins, and ye shall receive the gift of the Holy Ghost. Acts 2:38.*

> *John answered, saying unto them all, I indeed baptize you with water; but one mightier than I cometh, the latchet of whose shoes I am not worthy to unloose: he shall baptize you with the Holy Ghost and with fire: Whose fan is in his hand, and he will throughly purge his floor, and will gather the wheat into his garner; but the chaff he will burn with fire unquenchable. Luke 3:16,17. (See Chapter 55 on Sacrament of Baptism.)*

350.   HOW ARE WE BAPTIZED INTO CHRIST?

The Scriptures teach that through water baptism, the Holy Spirit immerses us into Christ causing us to put on His nature and making us members of His body, the church.

> *For by one Spirit are we all baptized into one body, whether we be Jews or Gentiles, whether we be bond or free; and have been all made to drink into one Spirit. I Cor. 12:13.*

> *Know ye not, that so many of us as were baptized into Jesus Christ were baptized into his death? Rom. 6:3.*

> *For as many of you as have been baptized into Christ have put on Christ. Gal. 3:27.*

351. HOW DOES WATER BAPTISM PREPARE US FOR THE BAPTISM IN THE HOLY SPIRIT?

In water baptism, the Holy Spirit prepares our hearts by cutting away the enmity (hostility) that is in us and frees us to love God so much that we welcome the Presence of the Holy Spirit into our lives.

> *Therefore we are buried with him by baptism into death: that like as Christ was raised up from the dead by the glory of the Father, even so we also should walk in newness of life. Rom. 6:4.*

> *In Him also you were circumcised with a circumcision not made with hands, but in a (spiritual) circumcision (performed by) Christ by stripping off the body of the flesh (the whole corrupt, carnal nature with its passions and lusts). (Thus you were circumcised when) you were buried with Him in (your) baptism, in which you were also raised with Him (to a new life) through (your) faith in the working of God (as displayed) when He raised Him up from the dead. Col. 2:11,12 AMP.*

352. ARE WATER BAPTISM AND THE HOLY SPIRIT BAPTISM CONNECTED TOGETHER?

The Scriptures speak of water baptism and Holy Spirit baptism with fire as *one* doctrine. The early Christians who received "circumcision of heart" through water baptism were filled with the Holy Spirit. Those who were not were questioned about how and in whose name they were baptized.

> *And it came to pass, that, while Apollos was at Corinth, Paul having passed through the upper coasts came to Ephesus: and finding certain disciples, He said unto them, Have ye received the Holy Ghost since ye believed? And they said unto him, We have not so much as heard whether there be any Holy Ghost. And he said unto them, Unto what then were ye baptized? And they said, Unto John's baptism. Then said Paul, John verily baptized with the baptism of repentance, saying unto the people, that they should believe on him which should come after him, that is, on Christ Jesus. When they heard this, they were baptized in the name of the Lord Jesus. And when Paul had laid his*

hands upon them, the Holy Ghost came on them; and they spake with tongues, and prophesied. And all the men were about twelve. Acts 19:1–7.

353.   DOES WATER BAPTISM ALWAYS PRECEDE THE HOLY SPIRIT BAPTISM?

No. The order that the apostles taught was water baptism first and then the baptism of the Holy Spirit. However, God sovereignly baptized some in the Spirit before they had been water baptized.

> *. . . Repent, and be baptized every one of you in the name of Jesus Christ for the remission of sins, and ye shall receive the gift of the Holy Ghost. Acts 2:38.*

> *While Peter yet spake these words, the Holy Ghost fell on all them which heard the word. And they of the circumcision which believed were astonished, as many as came with Peter, because that on the Gentiles also was poured out the gift of the Holy Ghost. For they heard them speak with tongues, and magnify God. Then answered Peter, Can any man forbid water, that these should not be baptized, which have received the Holy Ghost as well as we? And he commanded them to be baptized in the name of the Lord. Then prayed they him to tarry certain days. Acts 10:44–48.*

354.   IF A BELIEVER RECEIVES THE HOLY SPIRIT BAPTISM FIRST, IS IT STILL NECESSARY TO BE WATER BAPTIZED?

Yes. In every instance where God sovereignly baptized believers in the Holy Spirit, they were immediately water baptized. The enmity (hostility) in the heart against God can only be removed by having the heart circumcised in water baptism.

> *Can any man forbid water, that these should not be baptized, which have received the Holy Ghost as well as we? And he commanded them to be baptized in the name of the Lord . . . Acts 10:47,48.*

355.   HOW ARE WE BAPTIZED INTO THE HOLY SPIRIT?

Jesus Christ baptizes us with the Holy Spirit either by a sovereign act or through the laying on of hands by anointed believers.

> *As for me, I baptize you in water for repentance; but He who is coming after me is mightier than I, and I am not even fit to remove His sandals; He Himself will baptize you with the Holy Spirit and fire. Matt. 3:11 NASV.*

356. HOW DO WE EXPERIENCE THE BAPTISM OF FIRE?

God uses chastening and pruning to purify us from the sins and weaknesses of the flesh which hinder our spiritual growth.

> *For whom the Lord loveth he chasteneth, and scourgeth every son whom he receiveth. Heb. 12:6.*

> *Every branch in me that beareth not fruit he taketh away: and every branch that beareth fruit, he purgeth it, that it may bring forth more fruit. John 15:2.*

> *Blessed is the man whom thou chastenest, O Lord, and teachest him out of thy law. Ps. 94:12.*

357. HOW SHOULD THE DOCTRINE OF BAPTISM BE UNDERSTOOD?

It should be regarded as one doctrine . . . as a whole with three necessary and related parts. We should understand that one experience prepares us for the next one and that the three combined equip us to live an overcoming Christian life.

> *One Lord, one faith, one baptism. Eph. 4:5.*

> *Therefore leaving the principles of the doctrine of Christ, let us go on unto perfection; not laying again the foundation of repentance from dead works, and of faith toward God, Of the doctrine of baptisms, and of laying on of hands, and of resurrection of the dead, and of eternal judgment. Heb. 6:1,2.*

STUDY QUESTIONS—Chapter 39

1. What is the Doctrine of Baptisms?
2. What is the New Covenant?
3. What are the provisions of the New Covenant?
4. How do we enter into covenant with God?
5. What are the three baptisms?
6. How are we baptized into Christ?
7. How does water baptism prepare us for the baptism in the Holy Spirit?
8. How are water baptism and the Holy Spirit baptism connected?
9. How should the doctrine of baptisms be understood?
10. Write Heb. 8:10–13; Eph. 4:4–6; Acts 2:38.

Chapter 40

THE BAPTISM IN THE HOLY SPIRIT

8. WHAT IS THE DOCTRINE OF THE BAPTISM IN THE HOLY SPIRIT?

It is a baptism (immersing, dipping or plunging) of the believer into the Holy Spirit and an entrance into the realm of supernatural spiritual power.

> *But ye shall receive power, after that the Holy Ghost is come upon you: and ye shall be witnesses unto me both in Jerusalem, and in all Judaea, and in Samaria, and unto the uttermost part of the earth. Acts 1:8.*

9. WHAT IS THE PURPOSE OF THE BAPTISM IN THE HOLY SPIRIT?

The purpose of the baptism in the Holy Spirit is to endue (clothe) us with power.

> *And, behold, I send the promise of my Father upon you: but tarry ye in the city of Jerusalem, until ye be endued with power from on high. Luke 24:49.*

0. WHY IS THIS POWER GIVEN TO US?

This power is given to us to seal us, give us understanding and make us effective witnesses for Christ.

> *And with great power gave the apostles witness of the resurrection of the Lord Jesus ... Acts 4:33.*

> *And these signs shall follow them that believe; In my name shall they cast out devils; they shall speak with new tongues; they shall take up serpents; and if they drink any*

deadly thing, it shall not hurt them; they shall lay hand on the sick, and they shall recover. Mark 16:17,18.

. . . in whom also after that ye believed, ye were sealed with that holy Spirit of promise, Eph. 1:13.

361. WHAT IS A WITNESS?

A witness is one who tells and shows others what Christ has done for him.

We speak only of what we know—we know absolutely what we are talking about; we have actually seen what we are testifying to—were eyewitnesses of it.
John 3:11 AMP.

For we cannot but speak the things which we have seen and heard. Acts 4:20.

For thou shalt be his witness unto all men of what thou hast seen and heard. Acts 22:15.

362. IS THE BAPTISM IN THE HOLY SPIRIT FOR EVERY ONE?

The Bible says,

. . . I will pour out of my Spirit upon all flesh . . . Acts 2:17.

For the promise is unto you, and to your children, and to all that are afar off, even as many as the Lord our God shall call. Acts 2:39.

363. WHAT ARE THE BLESSINGS OF THE BAPTISM IN THE HOLY SPIRIT?

The blessings of the baptism in the Holy Spirit are:

A. We are enabled to pray in the Spirit.

Likewise the Spirit also helpeth our infirmities: for we know not what we should pray for as we ought: but the Spirit itself maketh intercession for us with groanings which cannot be uttered. And he that searcheth the hearts knoweth what is the mind of the Spirit, because he maketh intercession for the saints according to the will of God. Rom. 8:26,27.

B. We are enabled to praise God in the Spirit.

> . . . *I will sing with the spirit, and I will sing with the understanding also. I Cor. 14:15.*

> *Saying, I will declare thy name unto my brethren, in the midst of the church will I sing praise unto thee. Heb. 2:12.*

C. Through spiritual ears, we can hear the voice of God.

> *As they ministered to the Lord, and fasted, the Holy Ghost said, Separate me Barnabas and Saul for the work whereunto I have called them. Acts 13:2.*

> *But when they shall lead you, and deliver you up, take no thought beforehand what ye shall speak, neither do ye premeditate: but whatsoever shall be given you in that hour, that speak ye: for it is not ye that speak, but the Holy Ghost. Mark 13:11.*

> . . . *after that he through the Holy Ghost, had given commandments unto the apostles whom he had chosen. Acts 1:2.*

D. We are made eligible for the gifts of the Spirit and the power of God.

> *Follow after charity, and desire spiritual gifts . . . I Cor. 14:1.*

> *That in everything ye are enriched by him, in all utterance and in all knowledge; Even as the testimony of Christ was confirmed in you: So that ye come behind in no gift; waiting for the coming of our Lord Jesus Christ. I Cor. 1:5–7.*

> . . . *ye shall receive power, after that the Holy Ghost is come upon you . . . Acts 1:8.*

E. We begin to walk in the Spirit, thereby, producing the fruits and graces of the Spirit.

> . . . *Walk in the Spirit, and ye shall not fulfill the lust of the flesh. For the flesh lusteth against the Spirit, and the Spirit against the flesh: and these are contrary the one to the other: so that ye cannot do the things that ye would. But if ye be led of the Spirit, ye are not under the law. Now the works of the flesh are manifest, which are these; Adultery, fornication, uncleanness, lasciviousness, Idola-*

*try, witchcraft, hatred, variance, emulations, wrath, stri,
seditions, heresies, Envyings, murders, drunkenness, reve
ings, and such like: of the which I tell you before, as
have also told you in time past, that they which do suc
things shall not inherit the kingdom of God. But the fru
of the Spirit is love, joy, peace, longsuffering, gentlenes
goodness, faith, Meekness, temperance: against such the
is no law. Gal. 5:16–23.*

*If we live in the Spirit, let us also walk in the Spiri
Gal. 5:25.*

364. WHAT MUST WE DO TO RECEIVE THE BAPTISM THE HOLY SPIRIT?

We must obey Christ's command to repent and be baptized.

*. . . Repent, and be baptized every one of you in the nam
of Jesus Christ for the remission of sins, and ye shall re
ceive the gift of the Holy Ghost. Acts 2:38.*

*If ye then, being evil, know how to give good gifts unt
your children: how much more shall your heavenly Father
give the Holy Spirit to them that ask him? Luke 11:13.*

*And we are his witnesses of these things; and so is also the
Holy Ghost, whom God hath given to them that obey him.
Acts 5:32.*

365.. HOW DO WE RECEIVE THE BAPTISM IN THE HOL SPIRIT?

The Lord employs two distinct methods of baptizing believers
the Holy Spirit.

1. By the sovereign act of God.

*And suddenly there came a sound from heaven as of a
rushing mighty wind, and it filled all the house where they
were sitting. And there appeared unto them cloven tongues
like as of fire, and it sat upon each of them. And they were
all filled with the Holy Ghost, and began to speak
with other tongues, as the Spirit gave them utterance.
Acts 2:2–4.*

While Peter yet spake these words, the Holy Ghost fell on

all them which heard the word. And they of the circumcision which believed were astonished, as many as came with Peter, because that on the Gentiles also was poured out the gift of the Holy Ghost. For they heard them speak with tongues, and magnify God ... Acts 10:44–46.

2. By the laying on of hands.

Now when the apostles which were at Jerusalem heard that Samaria had received the word of God, they sent unto them Peter and John: Who, when they were come down, prayed for them, that they might receive the Holy Ghost: (For as yet he was fallen upon none of them: only they were baptized in the name of the Lord Jesus.) Then laid they their hands on them, and they received the Holy Ghost. And when Simon saw that through laying on of the apostles' hands the Holy Ghost was given, he offered them money, Saying, Give me also this power, that on whomsoever I lay hands, he may receive the Holy Ghost. Acts 8:14–19.

366. **WHAT INSTRUCTIONS ARE TO BE FOLLOWED TO RECEIVE THE BAPTISM IN THE HOLY SPIRIT?**

A. We pray to the Lord Jesus for forgiveness of sin and cleansing of the mind and spirit so that we may approach Him with confidence.

Who shall ascend into the hill of the Lord? or who shall stand in his holy place? He that hath clean hands, and a pure heart; who hath not lifted up his soul unto vanity, nor sworn deceitfully. He shall receive the blessing from the Lord, and righteousness from the God of his salvation. Ps. 24:3–5.

B. Pray to the Lord Jesus Christ for the gift of the Holy Ghost.

If ye then, being evil, know how to give good gifts unto your children: how much more shall your heavenly Father give the Holy Spirit to them that ask him? Luke 11:13.

C. Believing that God has heard our prayer, we enter into praise, thanksgiving and worship through psalms and hymns until an atmosphere is created for the presence of the Spirit of God.

Lift up your hands in the sanctuary, and bless the Lord. Ps. 134:2.

Enter into his gates with thanksgiving, and into his courts with praise: be thankful unto him, and bless his name. Ps. 100:4.

Note: See Chapter 50—Worship and Praise.

D. When we become aware of the presence of the Holy Spirit, there is a breaking within us and our spirit springs up to respond to the Spirit of God.

Draw nigh to God, and he will draw nigh to you . . . James 4:8.

My soul longeth, yea, even fainteth for the courts of the Lord; my heart and my flesh crieth out for the living God. Ps. 84:2.

The Lord is nigh unto them that are of a broken heart; and saveth such as be of a contrite spirit. Ps. 34:18.

The sacrifices of God are a broken spirit: a broken and contrite heart, O God, thou wilt not despise. Ps. 51:17.

E. While our spirit is melted in the presence of the Lord, an anointed servant of God may lay hands upon us to impart the Holy Spirit to us.

Then laid they their hands on them, and they received the Holy Ghost. Acts 8:17.

And when Paul had laid his hands upon them, the Holy Ghost came on them; and they spake with tongues, and prophesied. Acts 19:6.

F. When the Spirit of God descends upon us, our organs of speech are quickened (stimulated) producing the stammering of lips which will form into syllables or words as we yield to the prompting of the Holy Spirit.

For with stammering lips and another tongue will he speak to this people. Isa. 28:11.

In the law it is written, With men of other tongues and other lips will I speak unto this people . . . I Cor. 14:21.

Note: Your mind has no understanding of what you are saying.

G. As the Spirit of God overwhelms us, our own words are no longer adequate to praise God. The Holy Spirit then leads us, encourages us and prompts us but does not force us to speak. However, once we begin, the language is spontaneous and fluent.

For he that speaketh in an unknown tongue speaketh not unto men, but unto God: for no man understandeth him; howbeit, in the spirit he speaketh mysteries. I Cor. 14:2.

H. We yield and speak in tongues.

... Holy men of God spake as they were moved by the Holy Ghost. II Peter 1:21.

They were all filled with the Holy Spirit, and began to speak in other tongues according as the Spirit gave them words to utter. Acts 2:4 Weymouth.

367. WHY DO WE SPEAK IN TONGUES WHEN WE RECEIVE THE BAPTISM IN THE HOLY SPIRIT?

This is our initial experience of hearing the Spirit speak divinely inspired words and repeating them.

Now we have received, not the spirit of the world, but the spirit which is of God; that we might know the things that are freely given to us of God. Which things also we speak, not in the words which man's wisdom teacheth, but which the Holy Ghost teacheth. I Cor. 2:12,13.

368. DO WE SPEAK IN TONGUES ONLY AT THE TIME OF OUR BAPTISM?

No, we speak in tongues in times of prayer as the Spirit directs us.

He that speaketh in an unknown tongue edifieth (builds up) himself. I Cor. 14:4.

But ye, beloved, building up yourselves on your most holy faith, praying in the Holy Ghost. Jude 20.

Likewise the Spirit also helpeth our infirmities: for we know not what we should pray for as we ought: but the Spirit itself maketh intercession for us with groanings which cannot be uttered. And he that searcheth the hearts knoweth what is the mind of the Spirit, because he maketh intercession for the saints according to the will of God. Rom. 8:26,27.

369. HOW OFTEN SHOULD WE PRAY IN TONGUES?

We should pray in tongues daily. As the Holy Spirit anoints us in our daily time of devotion, we receive edification and strength.

For if I pray in an unknown tongue, my spirit prayeth . . . I Cor. 14:14.

I thank my God, I speak with tongues more than ye all. I Cor. 14:18.

He that speaketh in an unknown tongue edifieth himself; . . . I Cor. 14:4.

370. WHAT IS THE ANOINTING?

It is the abiding presence of God, the Holy Spirit.

But the anointing which ye have received of him abideth in you, and ye need not that any man teach you: but as the same anointing teacheth you of all things, and is truth, and is no lie, and even as it hath taught you, ye shall abide in him. I John 2:27.

But ye have an unction from the Holy One, and ye know all things. I John 2:20.

371. IS THERE A SPECIAL (BEYOND THE ORDINARY) ANOINTING OF THE HOLY SPIRIT?

Yes! The special anointing is the presence of the Holy Spirit through which we receive divine aid for some specific task. It can be compared to the physical reaction we experience in times of danger, stress, etc., when the body begins to secrete adrenalin to give additional strength and alertness. The same holds true when we are anointed. We receive that extra surge of spiritual energy whenever it is needed.

Then Peter said, Silver and gold have I none; but such as I have give I thee: In the name of Jesus Christ of Nazareth rise up and walk. And he took him by the right hand,

and lifted him up; and immediately his feet and ankle bones received strength. And he leaping up stood, and walked, and entered with them into the temple, walking, and leaping, and praising God. Acts 3:6–8.

And God wrought special miracles by the hands of Paul: So that from his body were brought unto the sick handkerchiefs or aprons, and the diseases departed from them, and the evil spirits went out of them. Acts 19:11,12.

372.   HOW NECESSARY IS THE ANOINTING?

Without the anointing, we are totally ineffective in our service to God and man.

. . . He that abideth in me, and I in him, the same bringeth forth much fruit: for without me ye can do nothing. John 15:5.

373.   IS THE ANOINTING NECESSARY FOR SPEAKING IN TONGUES?

Yes! When we speak or pray in tongues without the anointing of the Holy Spirit, it is fruitless and completely meaningless.

And they were all filled with the Holy Ghost, and began to speak with other tongues, as the Spirit gave them utterance. Acts 2:4.

But all these worketh that one and the selfsame Spirit, dividing to every man severally as he will. I Cor. 12:11.

It is the spirit that quickeneth; the flesh profiteth nothing: the words that I speak unto you, they are spirit, and they are life. John 6:63.

Not that we are sufficient of ourselves to think anything as of ourselves; but our sufficiency is of God; Who also hath made us able ministers of the new testament; not of the letter, but of the spirit: for the letter killeth, but the spirit giveth life. II Cor. 3:5,6.

BIBLE NARRATIVE: Nadab and Abihu, the sons of Aaron, were slain by the Lord for using "strange fire" to burn incense before the Lord. It typifies the use of carnal means to kindle the fire of devotion and praise, Lev. 10:1–15.

374. HOW DO WE MAINTAIN THE ANOINTING?

By continually abiding in Jesus Christ.

> *I am the vine, ye are the branches: He that abideth in me, and I in him, the same bringeth forth much fruit: for without me ye can do nothing. John 15:5.*

STUDY QUESTIONS—Chapter 40

1. What is the baptism in the Holy Spirit?
2. Why do we need the baptism in the Holy Spirit?
3. What is a witness?
4. Who may receive the baptism in the Holy Spirit?
5. What are the blessings of the baptism in the Holy Spirit?
6. What must we do to receive the baptism in the Holy Spirit?
7. What two distinct methods does God use to baptize believers in the Holy Spirit?
8. What instructions should we follow to receive the baptism of the Holy Spirit?
9. Why do we speak in tongues when we receive the baptism in the Holy Spirit?
10. How often should we pray in tongues?
11. What is the anointing?
12. Why do we need the anointing?
13. Write Acts 2:3,39; Romans 8:26,27; Acts 5:32.

Chapter 41

THE BAPTISM OF FIRE

375. **WHAT IS THE DOCTRINE OF THE BAPTISM OF FIRE?**

The Baptism of Fire, also called sanctification, is the process of separation employed by God such as trials, tribulations, illness, trouble, persecution, to bring us into maturity and set us aside for His service ... it begins with the Holy Spirit Baptism.

> *John answered, Saying unto them all, I indeed baptize you with water; but one mightier than I cometh, the latchet of whose shoes I am not worthy to unloose; he shall baptize you with the Holy Ghost and WITH FIRE: Whose fan is in his hand, and he will thoroughly purge his floor, and will gather the wheat into his garner; but the chaff he will burn with fire unquenchable. Luke 3:16,17.*

> *I am come to send fire on the earth; and what will I, if it be already kindled: But I have a baptism to be baptized with; and how am I straightened till it be accomplished! Suppose ye that I am come to give peace on earth: I tell you, Nay; but rather division: For from henceforth there shall be five in one house divided, three against two, and two against three. Luke 12:49–52.*

> *And Jesus being full of the Holy Ghost returned from Jordan, and was led by the Spirit into the wilderness, Being forty days tempted of the devil. Luke 4:1,2a.*

376. **WHY IS IT CALLED "THE BAPTISM OF FIRE"?**

It is called the Baptism of Fire because through it the flame of God's love is fanned within the believer.

> *Whose fan is in his hand, and he will thoroughly purge his*

floor, and will gather the wheat into his garner; but the chaff he will burn with fire unquenchable. Luke 3:17.

377.   WHAT IS IDEAL CHASTENING?

Ideal chastening fits the offense in such a way that it forms and strengthens those parts of our character which are weak.

> *But he knoweth the way that I take: when he hath tried me, I shall come forth as gold. Job 23:10.*

> *For he performeth the thing that is appointed for me: and many such things are with him. Job 23:14.*

> *Behold, I have refined thee, but not with silver; I have chosen thee in the furnace of affliction. Isa. 48:10.*

378.   HOW DOES CHASTENING OVERCOME THE WEAK AREAS IN OUR CHARACTER?

Chastening draws our attention to them and when the awareness becomes great enough, we acknowledge the weakness to ourselves and to God. He then gives us power to overcome it.

> *In meekness instructing those that oppose themselves; if God peradventure will give them repentance to the acknowledging of the truth; and that they may recover themselves out of the snare of the devil who are taken captive by him at his will. II Tim. 2:25,26.*

379.   WHAT IS GOD'S PURPOSE IN CHASTENING US?

Through chastening God draws us nearer to Himself. However heavy His hand may seem, God sympathizes with our passing distress. The presence of trials and distresses are not proof of sin and God's anger but are tokens of His love.

> *Now no chastening for the present seemeth to be joyous, but grievous: nevertheless afterward it yieldeth the peaceable fruit of righteousness unto them which are exercised thereby. Heb. 12:11.*

380.   WHAT IS THE DIFFERENCE BETWEEN CHASTENING AND PUNISHMENT?

Chastening is corrective, for our good. Punishment is the expression of wrath.

> *... Furthermore we have had fathers of our flesh which corrected us, and we gave them reverence: shall we not much rather be in subjection unto the Father of spirits, and live? For they verily for a few days chastened us after their own pleasure; but he for our profit, that we might be partakers of his holiness. Heb. 12:9,10.*

381. WHAT SHOULD BE OUR ATTITUDE TOWARD CHASTENING?

We should be totally submissive to our heavenly Father, trusting in His love to do a work within us that will be for our profit and His glory and honor.

> *And we know that all things work together for good to them that love God, to them who are the called according to his purpose. For whom He did foreknow, he also did predestinate to be conformed to the image of his Son, that he might be the firstborn among many brethren. Moreover whom he did predestinate, them he also called; and whom he called, them he also justified: and whom he justified, them he also glorified. What shall we say then to these things? If God be for us, who can be against us? Rom. 8:28–31.*

> *... My son, despise not thou the chastening of the Lord, nor faint when thou art rebuked of him. Heb. 12:5.*

> *Keep thy heart with all diligence: for out of it are the issues of life. Prov. 4:23.*

> *Looking diligently lest any man fail of the grace of God; lest any root of bitterness springing up trouble you, and thereby many be defiled; Heb. 12:15.*

382. WHAT COMFORT DO WE RECEIVE THROUGH CHASTENING?

The sense of belonging to God's family through the knowledge that our Father is treating us as His own.

> *For whom the Lord loveth he chasteneth, and scourgeth every son whom he receiveth. If ye endure chastening, God dealeth with you as with sons; for what son is he whom the father chasteneth not? But if ye be without chastisement,*

whereof all are partakers, then are ye bastards, and not sons. Heb. 12:6–8.

Every branch in me that beareth not fruit he taketh away; and every branch that beareth fruit, he purgeth it, that it may bring forth more fruit. John 15:2.

383. WHAT PART OF US DOES GOD SANCTIFY THROUGH CHASTENING?

God sanctifies our will.

Though he were a Son, yet learned he obedience by the things which he suffered; And being made perfect, he became the author of eternal salvation unto all them that obey him. Heb. 5:8,9.

. . . Not as I will, but as thou wilt. Matt. 26:39b.

384. IS SANCTIFICATION PROGRESSIVE OR INSTANTANEOUS?

Sanctification is both progressive and instantaneous. Through each chastening, we learn to trust, love and yield to God.

Many are the afflictions of the righteous: but the Lord delivereth him out of them all. Ps. 34:19.

The Lord will perfect that which concerneth me . . . Ps. 138:8.

By the which will we are sanctified through the offering of the body of Jesus Christ once for all. Heb. 10:10.

385. WHY MUST WE BE CHASTENED?

If we are left without correction and discipline, we can never become partakers of God's holiness; and without holiness, we cannot see God.

For they verily for a few days chastened us after their own pleasure: but he for our profit, that we might be partakers of his holiness. Heb. 12:10.

Follow peace with all men, and holiness, without which no man shall see the Lord. Heb. 12:14.

Having therefore these promises, dearly beloved, let us

cleanse ourselves from all filthiness of the flesh and spirit, perfecting holiness in the fear of God. II Cor. 7:1.

386. CAN WE ATTAIN SANCTIFICATION AND HOLINESS?

Yes. God would not command us to strive for an unattainable goal. If our will is sanctified, we can live and move according to the dictates of the Holy Spirit.

Be ye therefore perfect, even as your Father which is in heaven is perfect. Matt. 5:48.

And ye shall be holy unto me; for I the Lord am holy, and have severed you from other people, that ye should be mine. Lev. 20:26.

Note: Our Lord's baptism of suffering (Luke 12:50) was His Baptism of Fire, teaching Him obedience to the Father's will.

STUDY QUESTIONS—Chapter 41

1. What is the Baptism of Fire?
2. Why is it called the "Baptism of Fire"?
3. How are the sins and weaknesses of the flesh purified in us?
4. What is ideal chastening?
5. Is chastening a sign of sin in our lives?
6. What do we learn through each chastening?
7. Why must we be chastened?
8. What is the difference between chastening and punishment?
9. What should our reaction be to chastening?
10. What part of us does God sanctify through chastening?

Chapter 42

THE DOCTRINE OF THE LAYING ON
OF HANDS

387. WHAT IS THE DOCTRINE OF THE LAYING ON OF HANDS?

It is the belief that divine power or qualities can be transferred from one believer to another by laying the hands upon the head of an individual.

> Then laid they their hands on them, and they received the Holy Ghost. Acts 8:17.

> And by the hands of the apostles were many signs and wonders wrought among the people; (and they were all with one accord in Solomon's porch.) Acts 5:12.

388. WAS THIS DOCTRINE PRACTICED IN THE OLD TESTAMENT?

This doctrine was practiced in the Old Testament for various reasons:

1. The priests laid their hands on the scapegoat to transfer to it the sins of the people.

> And Aaron shall lay both his hands upon the head of the live goat, and confess over him all the iniquities of the children of Israel, and all their transgressions in all their sins, putting them upon the head of the goat, and shall send him away by the hand of a fit man into the wilderness: And the goat shall bear upon him all their iniquities unto a land not inhabited: and he shall let go the goat in the wilderness. Lev. 16:21,22.

392. WHAT IS THE LIFE
SHOULD MAKE A PA

Confirmation by the Layi
by every believer so that h
made firm in the faith as

> And Judas and Silas,
> horted the brethren wit
> Acts 15:32.

393. WHAT BENEFITS DOES
US?

It gives us inner strength an
that are sent to us making
lished in God and enter into

> And when they had prea
> had taught many, they r
> Iconium, and Antioch, C
> ples, and exhorting them
> we must through much tr
> of God. Acts 14:21,22.

STUDY QUESTIONS—Chapter 4

1. What is the doctrine of the laying
2. For what reasons was the laying o
   Testament?
3. How was laying on of hands practi
4. How did the early Church use layin
5. How is laying on of hands practiced
6. How do we lay the foundation of la
7. What benefits are imparted throug
   confirmation?

---

2. Jacob placed his hands upon Joseph's children to convey
blessing.

> And Israel stretched out his right hand, and laid it upon
> Ephraim's head, who was the younger, and his left hand
> upon Manasseh's head, ... Gen. 48:14.

3. Moses conferred a portion of his wisdom and spirit up
Joshua.

> And the Lord said unto Moses, Take thee Joshua the son
> of Nun, a man in whom is the spirit, and lay thine hand
> upon him; And set him before Eleazar the priest, and be-
> fore all the congregation; and give him a charge in their
> sight. And thou shalt put some of thine honour upon him,
> that all the congregation of the children of Israel may be
> obedient. And he shall stand before Eleazar the priest,
> who shall ask counsel for him after the judgment of Urim
> before the Lord: at his word shall they go out, and at his
> word they shall come in, both he, and all the children of
> Israel with him, even all the congregation. And Moses did
> as the Lord commanded him: and he took Joshua, and set
> him before Eleazar the priest, and before all the congrega-
> tion: And he laid his hands upon him, and gave him a
> charge, as the Lord commanded by the hand of Moses.
> Num. 27:18–23.

389. WAS THE LAYING ON OF HANDS PRACTICED IN THE
NEW TESTAMENT?

Yes. The laying on of hands was practiced by Christ and His followers.

1. In healing.

> And besought him greatly, saying, My little daughter lieth
> at the point of death: I pray thee, come and lay thy hands
> on her, that she may be healed; and she may live.
> Mark 5:23.

> And they bring unto him one that was deaf, and had an
> impediment in his speech; and they beseech him to put his
> hand upon him. Mark 7:32.

2. In benediction.

And ...
and putting ...
even Jesus, t ...
camest, hath ...
and be filled ...

And it came t ...
a fever and of ...
prayed, and la ...
28:8.

2. For the reception ...

Then laid they (...
they received the ...

And when Paul h ...
the Holy Ghost ...
tongues, and prop ...

3. For the conferring ...
the Church.

Whom they set be ...
prayed, they laid th ...

And when they had ...
hands on them, they ...

391. IS THE LAYING ON O...

In the present day visitati...
to the Church, the laying ...
the Holy Spirit and His ...
confirmation, marriage, he...
dren, the sacrament of and...
blessing and protection for ...

Chapter 43

THE DOCTRINE OF RESURRECTION OF THE DEAD

394. WHAT IS THE DOCTRINE OF THE RESURRECTION OF THE DEAD?

It is the belief that God will raise the dead to life again.

> *I am the resurrection and the life: he that believeth on me, though he were dead, yet shall he live. John 11:25.*

395. HOW MANY RESURRECTIONS WILL THERE BE?

There will be two resurrections: the resurrection of the dead in Christ and the resurrection of the wicked.

> *Behold, I show you a mystery; We shall not all sleep, but we shall all be changed. In a moment, in the twinkling of an eye, at the last trump: for the trumpet shall sound, and the dead shall be raised incorruptible, and we shall be changed. I Cor. 15:51,52.*

> *But the rest of the dead lived not again until the thousand years were finished. This is the first resurrection. Blessed and holy is he that hath part in the first resurrection: on such the second death hath no power, but they shall be priests of God and of Christ, and shall reign with him a thousand years. Rev. 20:5,6.*

> *Marvel not at this: for the hour is coming, in the which all that are in the graves shall hear his voice, And shall come forth; they that have done good, unto the resurrection of life; and they that have done evil, unto the resurrection of damnation. John 5:28,29.*

396. **WHAT DO THE SCRIPTURES TEACH CONCERNING THE RESURRECTION OF THE DEAD IN CHRIST?**

The Scriptures teach that those who are dead in Christ shall be raised to life at the return of Jesus Christ to earth.

> *For this we say unto you by the word of the Lord, that we which are alive and remain unto the coming of the Lord shall not prevent (precede) them which are asleep. For the Lord himself shall descend from heaven with a shout, with the voice of the archangel, and with the trump of God: and the dead in Christ shall rise first. I Thess. 4:15,16.*

397. **WHAT WILL HAPPEN AT THE FIRST RESURRECTION?**

Jesus Christ shall descend from heaven to the earth's atmosphere. Then a shout shall be given for the dead in Christ to arise. Those who are alive in Christ and the risen dead shall then be caught up together to meet the Lord in the air.

> *For the Lord himself shall descend from heaven with a shout, with the voice of the archangel, and with the trump of God: and the dead in Christ shall rise first: Then we which are alive and remain shall be caught up together with them in the clouds, to meet the Lord in the air; and so shall we ever be with the Lord. I Thess. 4:16,17.*

398. **WHAT KIND OF A BODY WILL BELIEVERS HAVE AT THE RESURRECTION?**

Believers will have a body fashioned by God. It will be like the resurrected body of Jesus Christ ... immortal, incorruptible, spiritual and powerful.

> *God gives to it (the seed you sow) the body that he plans and sees fit, and to each kind of seed a body of it's own. I Cor. 15:38 AMP.*

> *So also is the resurrection of the dead. It is sown in corruption; it is raised in incorruption; It is sown in dishonour; it is raised in glory: it is sown in weakness; it is raised in power: It is sown a natural body; it is raised a spiritual body. I Cor. 15:42,44.*

> *For our conversation is in heaven; from whence also we look for the Savior, the Lord Jesus Christ: Who shall*

change our vile body, that it may be fashioned like unto his glorious body, according to the working whereby he is able even to subdue all things unto himself. Phil. 3:20,21.

399. WHAT DOES IT MEAN TO BE "IN CHRIST"?

To be "in Christ" is to be a born-again believer . . . one who has repented of his sins, has been baptized in water and has been filled with the Holy Spirit.

If any man be in Christ, he is a new creature . . . II Cor. 5:17.

Know ye not, that so many of us as were baptized into Jesus Christ were baptized into his death? Rom. 6:3.

. . . Except a man be born of water and of the Spirit, he cannot enter into the kingdom of God. John 3:5.

400. WHAT HAPPENS TO A MAN WHEN HE DIES?

When a man dies, the soul and spirit return to God and the body falls into the sleep of death. The flesh decays and returns to dust, but the seed of the body lies dormant (sleeps) awaiting resurrection.

If a man die, shall he live again? All the days of my appointed time will I wait, till my change come. Job 14:14.

Then shall the dust return to the earth as it was: and the spirit shall return unto God who gave it. Eccl. 12:7.

But some man will say, How are the dead raised up? and with what body do they come? Thou fool, that which thou sowest is not quickened, except it die: And that which thou sowest, thou sowest not that body that shall be, but bare grain, it may chance of wheat, or of some other grain: But God giveth it a body as it hath pleased him, and to every seed his own body. So also is the resurrection of the dead. I Cor. 15:35–38,42.

401. WHERE DOES GOD SEND THE SOUL AND SPIRIT OF THE RIGHTEOUS AT DEATH?

God sends the soul and spirit of the righteous dead to paradise.

And Jesus said unto him, Verily I say unto thee, To day shalt thou be with me in paradise. Luke 23:43.

> *Therefore, we are always confident, knowing that, whilst we are at home in the body, we are absent from the Lord: We are confident, I say, and willing rather to be absent from the body, and to be present with the Lord. II Cor. 5:6,8.*

402. WHERE IS PARADISE?

Paradise is located in the third heaven. Before the resurrection of Jesus Christ, paradise was located in the center of the earth in Sheol-hades; which was divided into two compartments—one for the wicked and one for the righteous.

> *I knew a man in Christ above fourteen years ago, (whether in the body, I cannot tell, or out of the body, I cannot tell: God knoweth;) such an one caught up to the THIRD HEAVEN. And I knew such a man, (whether in the body, or out of the body, I cannot tell: God knoweth;) How that he was caught up into PARADISE, and heard unspeakable words, which it is not lawful for a man to utter. II Cor. 12:2–4.*

403. WHY WAS PARADISE RE-LOCATED?

God does not allow anyone with unremitted sin into His holy presence. He provided a temporary dwelling place for the souls of the righteous dead in Sheol-hades until Jesus Christ paid for the sins of the world by His death on the cross. The death and resurrection of Jesus Christ gave the righteous access into the presence of God and paradise was re-located in heaven.

> *Thou art of purer eyes than to behold evil, and canst not look on iniquity. Hab. 1:13.*

> *. . . But now once in the end of the world hath (Jesus) appeared to put away sin by the sacrifice of Himself. Heb. 9:26.*

> *For it is not possible that the blood of bulls and of goats should take away sins. Heb. 10:4.*

404. WHERE ARE THE SOULS AND SPIRITS OF THE WICKED DEAD NOW?

The wicked dead are now in Sheol-hades.

When a cloud vanishes, it is gone, so he who goes down to Sheol does not come up. He will not return again to his house, nor will his place know him any more. Job 7:9,10. NASV

What man can live and not see death? Can he deliver his soul from the power of Sheol? Ps. 89:48 NASV

For Sheol cannot thank Thee, Death cannot praise Thee; Those who go down to the pit cannot hope for Thy faithfulness. Isa. 38:18 NASV.

Note: Sheol is the Hebrew word for the underworld abode of the dead. Hades is the Greek translation of this word.

405. WHAT IS SHEOL-HADES?

Sheol-hades is the temporary abode of the souls of the wicked dead.

He (David) forseeing this, spoke (by foreknowledge) of the resurrection of the Christ, the Messiah, that He was not deserted (in death) and left in Hades (the state of departed spirits), nor did his body know decay or see destruction. Acts 2:31 AMP. See also Ps. 16:10.

406. WHERE IS SHEOL-HADES?

Sheol-hades is located in the center of the earth.

Wherefore he saith, when he ascended up on high, he led captivity captive, and gave gifts unto men. (Now that he ascended, what is it but that he also descended first INTO THE LOWER PARTS OF THE EARTH? He that descended is the same also that ascended up far above all heavens, that he might fill all things.) Eph. 4:8–10.

407. IS THERE ANY WAY WE CAN HELP THE DEAD IN SHEOL-HADES TO AVOID HELL?

No. Eternity is settled in this life. Neither prayer nor baptism for the dead can help them avoid judgment and hell.

And as it is appointed unto men once to die, but after this the judgment. Heb. 9:27.

The Lord knoweth how to deliver the godly out of temptations, and to reserve the unjust unto the day of judgment to be punished. II Peter 2:9.

408. WHERE IS HELL?

It is referred to as a place of darkness which implies that it is a place far removed from God or a solar sun. The Bible does not tell us where hell is located.

And I say unto you, That many shall come from the east and west, and shall sit down with Abraham, and Isaac, and Jacob, in the kingdom of heaven. But the children of the kingdom shall be CAST INTO OUTER DARKNESS: there shall be weeping and gnashing of teeth. Matt. 8:11,12.

These are wells without water, clouds that are carried with a tempest; TO WHOM THE MIST OF DARKNESS IS RESERVED FOREVER. II Peter 2:17.

Raging waves of the sea, foaming out their own shame; wandering stars, to whom is reserved THE BLACKNESS OF DARKNESS FOREVER. Jude 13.

409. WHAT IS HELL?

Hell is a place of everlasting torment; a lake of fire that does not burn out.

And whosoever was not found written in the book of life was cast into the lake of fire. Rev. 20:15.

410. IS ANYONE IN HELL TODAY?

No. Hell will not be occupied until after the final judgment at the end of the world.

Then shall he say unto them on the left hand, Depart from me, ye cursed, into everlasting fire, prepared for the devil and his angels. Matt. 25:41.

411. WHAT DO THE SCRIPTURES TEACH CONCERNING THE RESURRECTION OF THE WICKED?

The Scriptures teach that the wicked dead will be resurrected from their graves after the reign of Christ upon the earth. They will stand before the great white throne of God and will give an account of their rejection of Jesus Christ and the deeds they have done on earth.

> *Marvel not at this: for the hour is coming, in the which all that are in the graves shall hear his voice, And shall come forth; they that have done good, unto the resurrection of life; and they that have done evil, unto the resurrection of damnation. John 5:28,29.*

> *And the sea gave up the dead which were in it; and death and hell (Sheol-hades) delivered up the dead which were in them: and they were judged every man according to their works. Rev. 20:13.*

> *But the rest of the dead lived not again until the thousand years were finished. Rev. 20:5.*

412.   WHAT WILL BE THE PUNISHMENT OF THE WICKED?

At the White Throne Judgment, they will be sentenced to a second death. There is no such thing as immortality for the wicked. Immortality is only promised to believers.

> *Blessed and holy is he that hath part in the first resurrection: on such the second death hath no power, but they shall be priests of God and of Christ, and shall reign with him a thousand years. And whosoever was not found written in the book of life was cast into the lake of fire. Rev. 20:6,15.*

413.   IS THE SOUL CONSCIOUS AFTER DEATH?

Yes. Jesus taught that Lazarus and the rich man were conscious, had memory and the faculties of expression. (See Luke 16:19–31.)

> *By which also he went and preached unto the spirits in prison; I Peter 3:19.*

414.   IS THERE RECOGNITION OF LOVED ONES AFTER DEATH?

Yes. The dead in paradise and in Sheol-hades recognized those whom they knew on earth.

And I say unto you, That many shall come from the east and west, and shall sit down with Abraham, and Isaac, and Jacob, in the kingdom of heaven. Matt. 8:11.

415. HOW DOES GOD DETERMINE MAN'S DESTINY?

God determines man's destiny according to his acceptance or rejection of His Son, Jesus Christ.

He that hath the Son hath life; and he that hath not the Son of God, hath not life. I John 5:12.

416. WHY MUST WE BELIEVE IN THE DOCTRINE OF RESURRECTION?

We must believe in the doctrine of resurrection in order to have purpose for living a God-fearing and God-centered life. If there is no resurrection then there can be no judgment, no future state of rewards and punishments, no reason to bear crosses and keep ourselves under discipline.

If after the manner of men I have fought with beasts at Ephesus, what advantageth it me, if the dead rise not? let us eat and drink; for tomorrow we die. I Cor. 15:32.

And every man that hath this hope in him purifieth himself, even as he is pure. I John 3:3.

417. WHY MUST WE BELIEVE IN THE RESURRECTION OF JESUS CHRIST?

If we do not believe in the resurrection of Jesus Christ, we do not believe that God accepted His death in payment for our sins.

And if Christ be not raised, your faith is vain; ye are yet in your sins. I Cor. 15:17.

418. CAN WE EXPERIENCE THE RESURRECTION POWER OF GOD IN THIS LIFE?

Yes. We can experience a spiritual and moral resurrection in this life.

But if the Spirit of him that raised up Jesus from the dead dwell in you, he that raised up Christ from the dead shall also quicken your mortal bodies by his Spirit that dwelleth in you. Rom. 8:11.

419. HOW DO WE EXPERIENCE SPIRITUAL AND MORTAL RESURRECTION IN THIS LIFE?

We experience the resurrection power of God when:

1. We are dead in trespasses and in sins and He forgives our sins and gives us a new life.

   And you hath he quickened who were dead in trespasses and sins; ... Even when we were dead in sins, hath quickened us together with Christ, (by grace ye are saved;) And hath raised us up together, and made us sit together in heavenly places in Christ Jesus. Eph. 2:1,5,6.

2. A physical affliction works death in our bodies and He sends His Word and heals us.

   But we had the sentence of death in ourselves, that we should not trust in ourselves, but in God which raiseth the dead: Who delivered us from so great a death, and doth deliver: in whom we trust that he will yet deliver us. II Cor. 1:9–10.

3. We are faced with an impossible situation and He manifests His life-giving power.

   (Abraham) Who against hope believed in hope, that he might become the father of many nations, according to that which was spoken, So shall thy seed be. And being not weak in faith, he considered not his own body now dead, when he was about an hundred years old, neither yet the deadness of Sarah's womb: He staggered not at the promise of God through unbelief; but was strong in faith, giving glory to God. Rom. 4:18–20.

4. We reach the end of our physical strength and find His power made perfect in our weakness.

   . . . Most gladly therefore will I rather glory in my infirmities, that the power of Christ may rest upon me. II Cor. 12:9b.

STUDY QUESTIONS—Chapter 43

1. What is the Doctrine of the Resurrection from the Dead?
2. How many resurrections will there be?
3. What will happen at the first resurrection?
4. What kind of body will believers have at the resurrection?
5. What does it mean to be "in Christ"?
6. What happens to a man when he dies?
7. Where is Paradise?
8. Where are the souls and spirits of the wicked dead now?
9. Where is Sheol-hades?
10. Is there any way we can help the dead in Sheol-hades avoid hell?
11. Where is hell?
12. Who is in hell today?
13. What will be the punishment of the wicked?
14. Why must we believe in the Doctrine of the Resurrection?
15. How do we experience spiritual and mortal resurrection in this life?

Chapter 44

THE DOCTRINE OF ETERNAL JUDGMENT

420. WHAT IS THE DOCTRINE OF ETERNAL JUDGMENT?

It is the belief that Jesus Christ will sit as judge over all the world at the end of the age.

> *God . . . hath appointed a day, in the which he will judge the world in righteousness by that men whom he hath ordained . . . Acts 17:31.*

421. WHY IS IT CALLED "ETERNAL JUDGMENT"?

It is called "eternal judgment" because the sentences that will be pronounced upon men can never be changed.

422. WHO WILL BE JUDGED?

Every man who ever lived will be judged.

> *It is appointed unto men once to die, but after this the judgment. Heb. 9:27.*

423. HOW MANY JUDGMENTS WILL THERE BE?

There will be two separate judgments.

424. WHAT ARE THEY:

They are:

1. The judgment of believers or, the Judgment Seat of Christ.

> *For we must all appear before the judgment seat of Christ; that everyone may receive the things done in his body, according to that he hath done, whether it be good or bad. II Cor. 5:10. Also see Ps. 135:14.*

2. The judgment of unbelievers, also known as the White Throne Judgment.

> *I beheld till the thrones were cast down, and the Ancient of days did sit, whose garment was white as snow, and the hair of his head like the pure wool: his throne was like the fiery flame, and his wheels as burning fire. A fiery stream issued and came forth from before him: thousand thousands ministered unto Him, and ten thousand times ten thousand stood before Him: the judgment was set, and the books were opened. Dan. 7:9,10.*

> *And I saw a great white throne, and him that sat on it, from whose face the earth and the heaven fled away; and there was found no place for them. Rev. 20:11.*

425.   WHAT IS THE JUDGMENT SEAT OF CHRIST?

The Judgment Seat of Christ is the throne of Jesus Christ in heaven. All who have been redeemed by the blood of Christ will gather there to give an account of their stewardship on earth. Christ will then determine their reward and position in His kingdom.

> *For the Father judgeth no man, but hath committed all judgment unto the Son. John 5:22.*

426.   WHEN WILL THE FIRST JUDGMENT TAKE PLACE?

The first judgment will take place when Jesus Christ returns to earth for the redeemed that are in their graves and those living on the earth. The angels will gather them together and escort them to the Judgment Seat of Christ where they will be judged.

> *And then shall appear the sign of the Son of man in heaven; and then shall all the tribes of the earth mourn, and they shall see the Son of man coming in the clouds of heaven with power and great glory. And he shall send his angels with a great sound of a trumpet, and they shall gather together his elect from the four winds from one end of heaven to the other. Matt. 24:30,31.*

427.   HOW WILL JESUS CHRIST JUDGE MEN?

All men will be judged out of the various record books that have been kept of their deeds on earth.

For we must all appear before the judgment seat of Christ; that every one may receive the things done in his body, according to that he hath done, whether it be good or bad. II Cor. 5:10.

428.   WHAT ARE THESE RECORD BOOKS?

There are four record books mentioned in the Scriptures. They are:

1. The Book of Conscience. (God's laws are written in the conscience of every man born on earth.)

   For when the Gentiles, which have not the law, do by nature the things contained in the law, these, having not the law, are a law unto themselves: Which shew the work of the law written in their hearts, their conscience also bearing witness, and their thoughts the meanwhile accusing or else excusing one another. Rom. 2:14–15.

2. The Book of Providence. (The record kept of man's response to God's guidance through his foreknowledge, loving care or intervention.)

   Or despisest thou the riches of his goodness and forebearance and longsuffering; not knowing that the goodness of God leadeth thee to repentance? But after thy hardness and impenitent heart treasurest up unto thyself wrath against the day of wrath and revelation of the righteous judgment of God; who will render to every man according to his deeds. Rom. 2:4–6.

3. The Book of Law and the Gospel. (The laws and commandments of Christ that lead us to eternal life.)

   For as many as have sinned without law shall also perish without law; and as many as have sinned in the law shall be judged by the law; ... In the day when God shall judge the secrets of men by Jesus Christ according to my gospel. Rom. 2:12,16.

4. The Book of Life. (The names of the redeemed are written in the Book of Life.)

   He that overcometh, the same shall be clothed in white raiment: and I will not blot out his name out of the book of life, but I will confess his name before my Father, and before his angels. Rev. 3:5.

And I saw the dead, small and great, stand before God; and the books were opened: and another book was opened, which is the book of life . . . Rev. 20:12.

429. WILL BELIEVERS BE JUDGED FOR EVERY SIN THEY EVER COMMITTED?

No. Only for every sin for which they have not repented.

Some men's sins are open beforehand, going before to judgment; and some men they follow after. I Tim. 5:24.

. . . for I will forgive their iniquity, and I will remember their sin no more. Jer. 31:34.

430. WHAT WILL HAPPEN AT THE JUDGMENT SEAT OF CHRIST?

Believers will be judged out of the four record books and rewarded or punished according to their deeds.

The lord of that servant will come in a day when he looketh not for him, and at an hour when he is not aware, and will cut him in sunder, and will appoint him his portion with the unbelievers. And that servant which knew his lord's will, and prepared not himself, neither did according to his will, shall be beaten with many stripes. But he that knew not and did commit things worthy of stripes, shall be beaten with few stripes. For unto whomsoever much is given, of him shall be much required: and to whom men have committed much, of him they will ask the more. Luke 12:46–48.

Every man's work shall be made manifest: for the day shall declare it, because it shall be revealed by fire; and the fire shall try every man's work of what sort it is. If any man's work abide which he hath built thereupon, he shall receive a reward. If any man's work shall be burned he shall suffer loss: but he himself shall be saved; yet so as by fire. I Cor. 3:13–15.

Then shall the King say unto them on his right hand, Come, ye blessed of my Father, inherit the kingdom pre-

pared for you from the foundation of the world: For I was an hungred, and ye gave me meat: I was thirsty, and ye gave me drink: I was a stranger, and ye took me in: Naked, and ye clothed me: I was sick, and ye visited me: I was in prison, and ye came unto me. Matt. 25:34–36.

BIBLE NARRATIVE: Parable of the talents—Matt. 25:19–30.

431. DO BELIEVERS EXPERIENCE GOD'S JUDGMENT BEFORE CHRIST RETURNS?

Yes. There are two judgments for every believer before the return of Christ:

1. The judgment of sin.
2. The judgment by fire.

432. WHAT IS THE JUDGMENT OF SIN?

The judgment of sin occurs when the Holy Spirit convicts us of sin by making us aware of our sinful state, granting us sorrow for our sins and giving us repentance for them. When we acknowledge sins of the past they are judged, forgiven and removed from His record.

And you, being dead in your sins and the uncircumcision of your flesh, hath he quickened together with him, having forgiven you all trespasses; Blotting out the handwriting of ordinances that was against us, which was contrary to us, and took it out of the way, nailing it to his cross. Col. 2:13,14.

If we confess our sins, he is faithful and just to forgive us our sins, and to cleanse us from all unrighteousness. I John 1:9.

As far as the east is from the west, so far hath he removed our transgressions from us. Ps. 103:12.

For if we would judge ourselves, we should not be judged. But when we are judged, we are chastened of the Lord, that we should not be condemned with the world. I Cor. 11:31,32.

433. WHAT IS THE JUDGMENT BY FIRE?

God sends the fire of tribulation into the lives of all believers to test the depth of their love and the strength of their faith in Him.

If they endure tribulation, their love and faith deepens, maturing them as sons of God.

> *That the trial of your faith, being much more precious than of gold that perisheth, though it be tried with fire, might be found unto praise and honour and glory at the appearing of Jesus Christ. I Peter 1:7.*

> *But he knoweth the way that I take: when he hath tried me, I shall come forth as gold. Job 23:10.*

> *And not only so, but we glory in tribulation also; knowing that tribulation worketh patience; And patience, experience; and experience, hope: And hope maketh not ashamed; because the love of God is shed abroad in our hearts by the Holy Ghost which is given unto us. Rom. 5:3–5.*

434. WHAT HAPPENS TO THE BELIEVER WHO CANNOT ENDURE THE JUDGMENT BY FIRE?

The believer whose love and faith cannot endure judgment by fire becomes offended with God and loses confidence in what he has believed to be true.

> *But he that received the seed into stony places, the same is he that heareth the word, and anon with joy receiveth it; Yet hath he not root in himself, but dureth for a while: for when tribulation or persecution ariseth because of the word, by and by he is offended. Matt. 13:20–21.*

435. WHAT SHOULD A BELIEVER DO WHO LOSES CONFIDENCE BECAUSE OF THE JUDGMENT BY FIRE?

When a believer loses confidence because of the judgment by fire, he should ask God to reveal to him what area of his faith needs to be corrected or changed.

> *That the trial of your faith, being much more precious than of gold that perisheth, though it be tried with fire, might be found unto praise and honour and glory at the appearing of Jesus Christ. I Pet. 1:7.*

> *Beloved, think it not strange concerning the fiery trial which is to try you, as though some strange thing happened unto you: I Pet. 4:12.*

436. WHY ARE THERE TIMES WHEN OUR FAITH NEEDS CORRECTING OR CHANGING?

1. The natural man has a tendency to follow the wisdom of men rather than the wisdom of God.

2. As we grow in the grace and knowledge of the Lord, our faith is being developed continually.

> *And my speech and my preaching was not with enticing words of man's wisdom, but in demonstration of the Spirit and of power: That your faith should not stand in the wisdom of men, but in the power of God. I Cor. 2:4,5.*

> *Now the Lord is that Spirit: and where the Spirit of the Lord is, there is liberty. But we all, with open face beholding as in a glass the glory of the Lord, are changed into the same image from glory to glory, even as by the Spirit of the Lord. II Cor. 3:17,18.*

437. WHAT HAPPENS WHEN WE REBEL AGAINST THE JUDGMENT OF FIRE?

We backslide.

> *Now the just shall live by faith: but if any man draw back, my soul shall have no pleasure in him. Heb. 10:38.*

Note: See Chapter 41 on Baptism of Fire.

438. WHAT IS A BACKSLIDER?

A backslider is a believer who abandons the faith and returns to his former life of sin.

> *For it had been better for them not to have known the way of righteousness, than, after they have known it, to turn from the holy commandment delivered unto them. But it is happened unto them according to the true proverb, The dog is turned to his own vomit again; and the sow that was washed to her wallowing in the mire. II Peter 2:21,22.*

439. WHAT WILL HAPPEN TO BACKSLIDERS?

Backsliders will be judged with believers at the Judgment Seat of Christ where they will be sentenced and appointed the fate of hypocrites and unbelievers.

For we must all appear before the judgment seat of Christ; that everyone may receive the things done in his body, according to that he hath done, whether it be good or bad. II Cor. 5:10.

If anyone separates from me, he is thrown away like a useless branch, withers, and is gathered into a pile with all others and burned. John 15:6 Living Bible.

But and if that evil servant shall say in his heart, My lord delayeth his coming; and shall begin to smite his fellow-servants, and to eat and drink with the drunken, the Lord of that servant shall come in a day when he looketh not for him, and in an hour that he is not aware of, And shall cut him asunder, and appoint him his portion with the hypocrites: there shall be weeping and gnashing of teeth. Matt. 24:48–51 (see also Luke 12:41–46).

For if after they have escaped the pollutions of the world through the knowledge of the Lord and Savior Jesus Christ, they are again entangled therein, and overcome, the latter end is worse with them than the beginning. For it had been better for them not to have known the way of righteousness, than, after they have known it, to turn from the holy commandment delivered unto them. II Peter 2:20,21.

440. CAN A BELIEVER LOSE HIS SALVATION?

Yes. The believer who lives to please himself and separates himself from the company of God's people will be permanently separated from the company of saints, lose all the gifts he neglected or abused and will be appointed the fate of hypocrites and unbelievers.

But and if that evil servant shall say in his heart, My Lord delayeth his coming; and shall begin to smite his fellow-servants, and to eat and drink with the drunken, the Lord of that servant shall come in a day when he looketh not for him, and in an hour that he is not aware of, And shall cut him asunder, and appoint him his portion with the hypocrites: there shall be weeping and gnashing of teeth. Matt. 24:48–51 (see also Luke 12:41–46).

For if after they have escaped the pollutions of the world through the knowledge of the Lord and Savior Jesus Christ, they are again entangled therein, and overcome, the latter end is worse with them than the beginning. For it had been better for them not to have known the way of righteousness, than, after they have known it, to turn from the holy commandment delivered unto them. II Pet. 2:20,21.

441.   IS SALVATION ALL OF GRACE?

Yes. Man cannot merit God's salvation. However, the grace of God is not a license for loose living nor does it eliminate the judgment seat where believers face the things they have done on this earth. If a man lives in sin, the grace of God is not at work in his life.

The grace of God that bringeth salvation hath appeared to all men, Teaching us that denying ungodliness and worldly lusts, we should live soberly, righteously, and godly in this present world. Titus 2:11,12.

442.   WHAT IS THE WHITE THRONE JUDGMENT?

The White Throne Judgment is the final judgment of all unbelievers as well as the fallen angels.

And I saw a Great White Throne and him that sat on it, from whose face the earth and heavens fled away: and there was found no place for them. And I saw the dead, small and great, stand before God; and the books were opened: and another book was opened, which is the book of life: and the dead were judged out of those things which were written in the books, according to their works. Rev. 20:11,12.

And the angels which kept not their first estate, but left their own habitation, he hath reserved in everlasting chains under darkness unto the judgment of the great day. Jude 6.

443.   DO BELIEVERS HAVE POWER TO JUDGE SPIRITUAL MATTERS?

Mature believers have power, given to them by the Holy Spirit, to execute the judgment of God in spiritual matters. Through prayer they are enabled to bind the forces of evil and free men from the strongholds of Satan.

> *And I will give unto thee the keys of the kingdom of heaven: and whatsoever thou shalt bind on earth shall be bound in heaven: and whatsoever thou shalt loose on earth shall be loosed in heaven. Matt. 16:19.*

> *Let the saints be joyful in glory: let them sing aloud upon their beds. Let the high praises of God be in their mouth, and a two-edged sword in their hand: To execute vengeance upon the heathen, and punishments upon the people; to bind their kings with chains, and their nobles with fetters of iron; To execute upon them the judgment written: this honour have all his saints. Praise ye the Lord. Ps. 149:5–9.*

444. WHAT DOES IT MEAN "JUDGE NOT, THAT YE BE NOT JUDGED!"?

The Lord does not judge any man by outward appearance, He judges man according to his heart. Man judges by what he sees and condemns out of the bitterness of his own heart, thereby condemning himself.

> *Judge not, that ye be not judged. For with what judgment ye judge, ye shall be judged: and with what measure ye mete, it shall be measured to you again. And why beholdest thou the mote that is in thy brother's eye, but considerest not the beam that is in thine own eye? Or how wilt thou say to thy brother, Let me pull out the mote out of thine eye: and behold, a beam is in thine own eye? Thou hypocrite, first cast out the beam out of thine own eye; and then shalt thou see clearly to cast out the mote out of thy brother's eye. Matt. 7:1–5.*

445. HOW CAN WE AVOID THE JUDGMENT OF GOD?

If we judge ourselves through self-examination, acknowledge our weaknesses or sins, and repent, we avoid the judgment or chastening of God.

> *For if we would judge ourselves, we should not be judged.*

But when we are judged, we are chastened of the Lord that we should not be condemned with the world. I Cor. 11:31,32.

. . . For if I go not away, the Comforter will not come unto you; but if I depart, I will send him unto you. And when he is come, he will reprove the world of sin, and of righteousness, and of judgment. John 16:7b–8.

446. WHAT SHOULD A BELIEVER DO WHO HAS BEEN JUDGED (CHASTENED) BY GOD?

A believer who is chastened by God should pray and confess his sins to God. If the chastening is sickness, he should call for the spiritual leaders of the Church. He should confess his faults that brought the judgment of God upon him to the elders. The fervent prayer of the elders and the anointing of oil will save him from the chastening rod of God. The Lord will forgive him his sin and restore him to health.

Is any among you afflicted? let him pray. Is any merry? let him sing psalms. Is any sick among you? let him call for the elders of the church; and let them pray over him, anointing him with oil in the name of the Lord: And the prayer of faith shall save the sick, and the Lord shall raise him up; and if he have committed sins, they shall be forgiven him. Confess your faults one to another, and pray one for another, that ye may be healed. The effectual fervent prayer of a righteous man availeth much. James 5:13–16.

447. FOR WHAT PURPOSE DOES GOD JUDGE HIS PEOPLE?

To teach us all things work together for our good if we learn to praise God in the fire. The Lord wants us to be partakers of His holiness. Without holiness we cannot see the Lord nor can we rule and reign with Him in His kingdom.

For the time is come that judgment must begin at the house of God: and if it first begin at us, what shall the end be of them that obey not the gospel of God? And if the righteous scarcely be saved, where shall the ungodly and the sinner appear? Wherefore let them that suffer according to the will of God commit the keeping of their souls to him in well doing, as unto a faithful Creator. I Peter 4:17–19.

If ye endure chastening, God dealeth with you as with sons; for what son is he whom the father chasteneth not? But if ye be without chastisement, whereof all are partakers, then are ye bastards, and not sons. Furthermore we have had fathers of our flesh which corrected us, and we gave them reverence: shall we not much rather be in subjection unto the Father of spirits, and live? For they verily for a few days chastened us after their own pleasure; but he for our profit, that we might be partakers of his holiness. Heb. 12:7–10.

448. WHAT WILL BE THE REWARD OF FAITHFUL BELIEVERS?

Believers who have been faithful will be given responsible positions in the Kingdom.

And the Lord said, who then is that faithful and wise steward, whom his lord shall make ruler over his household . . . Luke 12:42.

Note: See parable of the talents, Matt. 25:14–30. Even in this life the Lord rewards our faithfulness by giving us increased responsibility.

STUDY QUESTIONS—Chapter 44

1. What is the Doctrine of Eternal Judgment?
2. Why is it called "eternal judgment"?
3. Who will be judged?
4. What are the two separate judgments?
5. What is the judgment seat of Christ?
6. What record books will Jesus Christ use to judge men?
7. Will believers be judged for every sin they ever committed?
8. What is the judgment by fire?
9. What is a backslider?
10. What will happen to backsliders?
11. Can a believer lose his salvation?
12. What is the White Throne Judgment?
13. How can we avoid the judgment of God?
14. Why does God chasten His people?
15. What will be the reward of faithful believers?

THE CHURCH
OF JESUS CHRIST

Chapter 45

THE UNIVERSAL CHURCH
or
GOD'S NEW NATION

449. **WHAT IS THE MEANING OF THE WORD "CHURCH"?**

The word "church" is the translation of the Greek word "ecclesia" which means "called out".

> Simeon hath declared how God at the first did visit the Gentiles, to take out of them a people for his name. Acts 15:14.

> How that by revelation he made known unto me the mystery; (as I wrote afore in few words, Whereby, when ye read, ye may understand my knowledge in the mystery of Christ). Which in other ages was not made known unto the sons of men, as it is now revealed unto his holy apostles and prophets by the Spirit; That the Gentiles should be fellowheirs, and of the same body, and partakers of his promise in Christ by the gospel. Eph. 3:3–6.

Note: The word "church" comes from the Greek word meaning "the called-out ones"

450. **WHAT IS THE UNIVERSAL CHURCH?**

The Universal Church is a spiritual nation made up of the people of God.

> *But ye are a chosen generation, a royal priesthood, an holy nation, a peculiar people; that ye should shew forth the praise of him who hath called you out of darkness into his marvellous light. Which in time past were not a people, but are now the people of God: which had not obtained mercy, but now have obtained mercy. I Peter 2:9,10.*

451. WHAT IS THIS SPIRITUAL NATION CALLED?

This spiritual nation is called the New Jerusalem or the City of God.

> *But ye are come unto mount Sion, and unto the city of the living God, the heavenly Jerusalem and to an innumerable company of angels; To the general assembly and church of the firstborn, which are written in heaven, and to God the Judge of all, and to the spirits of just men made perfect. Heb. 12:22,23.*

> *. . . Come hither, I will shew thee the bride, the Lamb's wife. And he carried me away in the spirit to a great high mountain, and showed me that great city, the holy Jerusalem, descending out of heaven from God. Rev. 21:9,10.*

> *Great is the Lord, and greatly to be praised in the city of our God, in the mountain of his holiness. Beautiful for situation, the joy of the whole earth, is mount Zion on the sides of the north, the city of the great King. Ps. 48:1–2.*

452. WHAT ARE THE CITIZENS OF THIS NATION CALLED?

The citizens of this nation are called true Jews, God's covenant people, the seed of Abraham, or Christians.

> *For he is not a Jew, which is one outwardly; neither is that circumcision, which is outward in the flesh: But he is a Jew, which is one inwardly; and circumcision is that of the heart, in the spirit, and not in the letter; whose praise is not of men, but of God. Rom. 2:28,29.*

> *And if ye be Christ's, then are ye Abraham's seed, and heirs according to the promise. Gal. 3:29.*

53. WHEN DID THIS SPIRITUAL NATION COME INTO BEING?

God has always purposed to have a people of His own and began to form this nation on earth with Abraham.

54. HOW DID GOD FORM A NATION FROM ABRAHAM?

God fulfilled His promise to Abraham giving him a seed ... a son, Isaac, miraculously born to him and his wife, Sarah. Through Isaac and his son, Jacob, the nation of Israel began.

> *And I will make of thee a great nation, and I will bless thee, and make thy name great; and thou shalt be a blessing; ... and in thee shall all families of the earth be blessed. Gen. 12:2,3.*

455. WAS THE SEED GIVEN TO ABRAHAM NATURAL OR SPIRITUAL?

It was both natural and spiritual.

> *And I will make thy seed as the dust of the earth so that if a man can number the dust of the earth, then shall thy seed be numbered. Arise, walk through the land in the length of it and in the breadth of it; for I will give it unto thee. Gen. 13:16,17.*

> *... Look now toward heaven, and tell the stars, if thou be able to number them; and he said unto him, so shall thy seed be. Gen. 15:5.*

456. WHO WAS THE NATURAL SEED OF ABRAHAM AND SARAH?

The natural descendants of Abraham and Sarah were:

A. Isaac, who had a son named Jacob.

> *And God Almighty bless thee, and make thee fruitful, and multiply thee, that thou mayest be a multitude of people; And give thee the blessing of Abraham, to thee, and to thy seed with thee; that thou mayest inherit the land wherein thou art a stranger, which God gave unto Abraham. Gen. 28:3,4.*

B. Jacob, who had twelve sons who became the fathers of the tribes of Israel (Jacob's new name).

The sons of Leah; Reuben, Jacob's firstborn, and Simeon, and Levi, and Judah, and Issachar, and Zebulun: The sons of Rachel; Joseph, and Benjamin: And the sons of Bilhah, Rachel's handmaid; Dan, and Naphtali: And the sons of Zilpah, Leah's handmaid; Gad, and Asher; these are the sons of Jacob, which were born to him in Padanaram. Gen. 35:23–26.

BIBLE NARRATIVES: Jacob's name changed—Gen. 32; Prophecy of Israel's bondage in Egypt—Gen. 15.

457. WHO IS THE SPIRITUAL SEED OF ABRAHAM?

Jesus Christ is the fulfillment of the promises concerning the seed of Abraham and through Him many other sons are born.

Now to Abraham and his seed were the promises made. He saith not, And to seeds, as of many; but as of one, And to thy seed, which is Christ. Gal. 3:16.

458. HOW DID GOD CREATE A NEW NATION THROUGH CHRIST?

He gathered together in Christ as one all who became children of God through the new birth.

For ye are all the children of God by faith in Christ Jesus. For as many of you as have been baptized into Christ have put on Christ. There is neither Jew nor Greek, there is neither bond nor free, there is neither male nor female: for ye are all one in Christ Jesus. Gal. 3:26–28.

459. HOW DO WE BECOME A PART OF THIS NEW NATION?

We relinquish (give up) our earthly citizenship and all that is identified with it. When we become citizens of the new nation, we identify with it, accept its government and give our allegiance to it.

For by one Spirit are we all baptized into one body, whether we be Jews or Gentiles, whether we be bond or free; and have been all made to drink into one spirit. I Cor. 12:13.

460. HOW ARE GOD AND HIS PEOPLE JOINED TOGETHER IN THIS NEW NATION?

This union of God and His people is a mystery which has always been hidden in the heart of God. It was hidden from men in other ages but is now revealed to us by the Holy Spirit.

> *Whereby, when ye read, ye may understand my knowledge in the mystery of Christ. Which in other ages was not made known unto the sons of men, as it is now revealed unto his holy apostles and prophets by the Spirit. Eph. 3:4,5.*

461. WHAT DO WE MEAN BY "MYSTERY"?

A mystery is a truth which has been hidden from man until a time appointed and chosen by God when He reveals it and makes it plain.

> *Blessed are the eyes which see the things that ye see: For I tell you, that many prophets and kings have desired to see those things which ye see, and have not seen them; and to hear those things which ye hear, and have not heard them. Luke 10:23,24.*

462. WHAT MYSTERIES HAVE BEEN REVEALED TO US ABOUT THE UNION OF CHRIST AND HIS CHURCH?

Several mysteries were unfolded in the New Testament to show us the purpose of God for His church. These include:

A. The mystery that the Church is the Body of Christ of which Christ is the Head and His people are the members.

> *And he is the head of the body, the church: Who is the beginning, the firstborn from the dead; that in all things he might have the preeminance. Col. 1:18.*

> *But speaking the truth in love, may grow up into him in all things, which is the head, even Christ, From whom the whole body fitly joined together and compacted by that which every joint supplieth, according to the effectual working in the measure of every part maketh increase of the body unto the edifying of itself in love. Eph. 4:15,16.*

B. The mystery that the Church is the Bride of Christ and that to be joined to Him we must forsake all other ties.

So ought men to love their wives as their own bodies. He that loveth his wife loveth himself. For no man ever yet hated his own flesh; but nourisheth and cherisheth it, even as the Lord the church. For we are members of his body, of his flesh, and of his bones. For this cause shall a man leave his father and mother, and shall be joined unto his wife, and they two shall be one flesh. Eph. 5:28–32.

C. The mystery that Christ indwells each member of the Church and makes us temples for His spiritual habitation.

I am crucified with Christ; nevertheless I live; yet not I, but Christ liveth in me: and the life which I now live in the flesh I live by the faith of the Son of God, who loved me, and gave himself for me. Gal. 2:20.

Even the mystery which hath been hid from ages and from generations but now is made manifest to his saints: To whom God would make known what is the riches of the glory of this mystery among the Gentiles: which is Christ in you, the hope of glory. Col. 1:26,27.

D. The mystery that in Christ dwells the fullness of the Godhead and that we are only made complete in Him.

For in him dwelleth all the fulness of the Godhead bodily. Col. 2:9.

E. The mystery that godliness is restored to man through experiencing the doctrines God has set in the Church for the perfecting of the saints.

And without controversy great is the mystery of godliness: God was manifest in the flesh, justified in the Spirit, seen of angels, preached unto the Gentiles, believed on in the world, received up into glory. I Tim. 3:16.

For the perfecting of the saints, for the work of the ministry, for the edifying of the body of Christ. Till we all come in the unity of the faith, and of the knowledge of the Son of God, unto a perfect man, unto the measure of the stature of the fulness of Christ. Eph. 4:12,13.

F. The mystery that God supernaturally appoints messengers to bring each Local Church under His direct supervision.

The mystery of the seven stars which thou sawest in my

right hand, and the seven golden candlesticks, The seven stars are the angels of the seven churches: and the seven candlesticks which thou sawest are the seven churches. Rev. 1:20.

G. The mystery that there is a counterfeit man-made church (Babylon) which opposes the true Church and that all who belong to God must come out of it.

And upon her forehead was a name written, MYSTERY, BABYLON THE GREAT, THE MOTHER OF HAR-LOTS AND ABOMINATIONS OF THE EARTH. And the angel said unto me, Wherefore didst thou marvel? I will tell thee the mystery of the woman, and of the beast that carrieth her, which hath the seven heads and ten horns. Rev. 17:5.7.

463. HOW DOES GOD BRING US TO THE PLACE WHERE WE SURRENDER OUR LIVES AND ALL THAT IS DEAR TO US IN ORDER TO BECOME A PART OF CHRIST?

The Father draws us to His Son by giving us the revelation of who Christ is and creating within us the desire to belong to Him. As the revelation of who Jesus Christ is shines into our hearts, it begins to shake us loose from all other loyalties and treasures.

And I will shake all nations, and the desire of all nations shall come: and I will fill this house with glory, saith the Lord of hosts. Hag. 2:7.

He that loveth father or mother more than me is not worthy of me: and he that loveth son or daughter more than me is not worthy of me. And he that taketh not his cross, and followeth after me, is not worthy of me. He that findeth his life shall lose it: and he that loseth his life for my sake shall find it. Matt. 10:37–39.

464. IS EVERYONE WILLING TO RECEIVE THE REVELATION OF CHRIST AND PAY THE COST FOR IT?

No. Some of us value our own lives and treasures more than the salvation which God could give us if we surrendered to Christ. If we will not give up our own lives, we cannot receive entrance into the Church for we will not allow ourselves to be joined to Christ alone.

> *... Except a corn of wheat fall into the ground and die, it abideth alone: but if it die, it bringeth forth much fruit. He that loveth his life shall lose it; and he that hateth his life in this world shall keep it unto life eternal. John 12:24,25.*

BIBLE NARRATIVE: The rich young ruler turns away. Luke 18:18–28.

465. HOW DO WE RECEIVE THIS REVELATION THAT CHRIST IS GOD AND THAT IT IS ONLY THROUGH HIM WE CAN BE RECONCILED TO THE FATHER?

The Holy Spirit convinces us until we admit that what He shows us about our relationship to God is true ... we are at war with God through sin and enmity and only Jesus Christ can take away the enmity and make us one with God.

> *Behold, the Lamb of God, which taketh away the sin of the world. John 1:29.*

> *To wit, that God was in Christ, reconciling the world unto himself, not imputing their trespasses unto them; and hath committed unto us the word of reconciliation ... be ye reconciled to God. For he hath made him to be sin for us who knew no sin that we might be made the righteousness of God in him. II Cor. 5:19,20,21.*

466. WHAT DO WE DO WHEN WE RECEIVE THE REVELATION THAT ONLY CHRIST IS THE ANSWER?

We respond with obedience. We repent of our sins; believe that Jesus Christ died in our place; submit to water baptism to be identified with His death, burial and resurrection; and receive the baptism of the Holy Spirit.

> *Therefore let all the house of Israel know assuredly, that God hath made that same Jesus, whom ye have crucified, both Lord and Christ. Now when they heard this, they were pricked in their heart, and said unto Peter and to the rest of the apostles, Men and brethren, what shall we do? Then Peter said unto them, Repent and be baptized every one of you in the name of Jesus Christ for the remission of sins, and ye shall receive the gift of the Holy Ghost. For the promise is unto you, and to your children, and to all*

that are afar off, even as many as the Lord our God shall call. Acts 2:36–39.

67. DOES WATER BAPTISM MAKE US MEMBERS OF CHRIST?

No, not in itself. We only become members of Christ through water baptism when it is combined with repentance, faith toward God, and the revelation of our Lord Jesus Christ.

> *. . . they were pricked in their heart, and said unto Peter and to the rest of the apostles, Men and brethren, what shall we do? Then Peter said unto them, Repent, and be baptized every one of you in the name of Jesus Christ for the remission of sins . . . Acts 2:37,38.*

> *Then they that gladly received his word were baptized: and the same day there were added unto them about three thousand souls. Acts 2:41.*

468. WHAT IS THE REVELATION OF JESUS CHRIST?

It is the same revelation Peter received when the Holy Spirit revealed to him who Jesus is . . . the Christ, the Son of the living God.

> *And Simon Peter answered and said, Thou art the Christ, the Son of the living God. Matt. 16:16.*

469. IS REVELATION WITHOUT WATER BAPTISM, ENOUGH TO MAKE US MEMBERS OF CHRIST?

No. Revelation creates faith and faith is expressed by obedience. If there is no obedience, there has been no revelation.

> *He that believeth and is baptized shall be saved; but he that believeth not shall be damned. Mark 16:16.*

> *. . . I was not disobedient unto the heavenly vision. Acts 26:19*

> *. . . that they should repent and turn to God, and do works meet for repentance. Acts 26:20.*

470. HOW DOES GOD CUT OUR EARTHLY TIES THROUGH WATER BAPTISM?

We experience death and release from all that we were as we are united to Him in His death and burial, and we are given His life as we are united to His resurrection.

> Know ye not, that so many of us as were baptized into Jesus Christ were baptized into his death? Therefore we are buried with him by baptism into death: that like as Christ was raised up from the dead, by the glory of the Father, even so we also should walk in newness of life. For if we have been planted together in the likeness of his death, we shall be also in the likeness of his resurrection. Rom. 6:3-5.

Note: The phrase "planted together in" means "become united with Him by" in the Greek.

> And that he died for all, that they which live should not henceforth live unto themselves, but unto him which died for them, and rose again. Wherefore henceforth know we no man after the flesh: yea, though we have known Christ after the flesh, yet now henceforth know we him no more. Therefore if any man be in Christ, he is a new creature: old things are passed away; behold, all things are become new. And all things are of God, who hath reconciled us to Himself by Jesus Christ, and hath given to us the ministry of reconciliation. II Cor. 5:15-18.

471. HOW DOES GOD JOIN US WITH THE OTHER MEMBERS OF CHRIST THROUGH WATER BAPTISM?

By removing our natural enmity and reconciling us with Himself, we no longer recognize fleshly barriers but are all joined in Christ.

> For he is our peace, who hath made both one, and hath broken down the middle wall of partition between us; Having abolished in his flesh the enmity, even the law of commandments contained in ordinances; for to make in himself of twain one new man, so making peace. And that he might reconcile both unto God in one body by the cross, having slain the enmity thereby. And came and preached peace to you which were afar off, and to them that were

nigh. For through him we both have access by one Spirit unto the Father. Now therefore ye are no more strangers and foreigners, but fellowcitizens with the saints, and of the household of God. Eph. 2:14–19.

472. HOW DOES GOD MAKE OUR UNION TO CHRIST AND HIS MEMBERS STRONGER THAN OUR PREVIOUS NATURAL TIES?

We are brought into God's family and household through the blood of Christ which binds us together as blood-brothers. By taking upon us the circumcision of heart as the seal of the New Covenant and His name, we are further bound together as a covenant nation.

That at that time ye were without Christ, being aliens from the commonwealth of Israel, and strangers from the covenants of promise, having no hope, and without God in the world: But now in Christ Jesus ye who sometimes were far off are made nigh by the blood of Christ. Eph. 2:12,13.

For both he that sanctifieth and they who are sanctified are all of one: for which cause he is not ashamed to call them brethren, Saying, I will declare thy name unto my brethren, in the midst of the church will I sing praise unto thee . . . And again, Behold I and the children which God hath given me. Heb. 2:11–13.

473. WHAT IS OUR NEW NAME AFTER WE HAVE BEEN JOINED TO CHRIST?

We are called Christians. "Christian" means "one who is Christ's."

And the disciples were called Christians first at Antioch. Acts 11:26.

Then Agrippa said unto Paul, Almost thou persuadest me to be a Christian. Acts 26:28.

474. WHAT DO WE BECOME AFTER WE HAVE BEEN JOINED TO CHRIST?

We become new creatures who have been made members of His body.

For we are members of his body, of his flesh, and of his bones. Eph. 5:30.

For in Christ Jesus neither (natural) circumcision availeth any thing, nor uncircumcision, but a new creature. And as many as walk according to this rule, peace be on them, and mercy, and upon the Israel of God. Gal. 6:15,16.

475. HOW DO WE KNOW THAT GOD HAS REMOVED THE ENMITY AND WE ARE INDEED JOINED TO CHRIST?

We love the other members of the Body and are able to recognize them as part of Christ.

We know that we have passed from death unto life, because we love the brethren. He that loveth not his brother abideth in death. I John 3:14.

He that loveth his brother abideth in the light, and there is none occasion of stumbling in him. But he that hateth his brother is in darkness, and walketh in darkness, and knoweth not whither he goeth, because that darkness hath blinded his eyes. I John 2:10,11.

476. HOW CLOSE DOES OUR RELATIONSHIP WITH THE OTHER MEMBERS OF THE BODY BECOME?

Just as we are actually a part of Christ, we become part of one another.

For as the body is one, and hath many members, and all the members of that one body, being many, are one body: so also is Christ. I Cor. 12:12.

. . . for we are members one of another. Eph. 4:25.

477. DO WE ACTUALLY EXPERIENCE THIS CLOSE KINSHIP WITH EACH OTHER IN THE CHURCH?

Yes. We are given real compassion for one another to the extent of feeling each other's joys and sorrows.

That there should be no schism in the body: but that the members should have the same care one for another. And whether one member suffer, all the members suffer with it: or one member be honoured, all the members rejoice with it. I Cor. 12:25,26.

478. DOES THE CHURCH FULFILL THE DESIRE GOD HAS ALWAYS HAD IN HIS HEART?

Yes. God has always wanted a people of His own that He might dwell in their midst. We see pictures of this in ancient Israel but it is only fully realized by the Holy Spirit dwelling in the Church, the members of the body of Christ.

> *And I heard a great voice out of heaven saying, Behold, the tabernacle of God is with men, and he will dwell with them, and they shall be his people, and God himself shall be with them, and be their God. Rev. 21:3.*

Note: The Church is also described as a spiritual building. It is a group of people fitted together by God, not a natural building. Eph. 2:20–22; I Pet. 2:4,5.

STUDY QUESTIONS—Chapter 45

1. What is the meaning of the word "church"?
2. What is the Universal Church?
3. When did this spiritual nation come into being?
4. Who is the spiritual seed of Abraham?
5. How did God create a new nation through Christ?
6. How do we become a part of this new nation?
7. What do we mean by "mystery"?
8. How does God bring us to the place where we surrender our lives and all that is dear to us in order to become a part of Christ?
9. Is everyone willing to receive the revelation of Christ and to pay the cost for it?
10. Does water baptism make us members of Christ?
11. Is revelation without water baptism enough to make us members of Christ?
12. What is the revelation of Jesus Christ?
13. How does God cut our earthly ties through water baptism?
14. How does God join us to the other members of Christ through water baptism?
15. What is our new name after we have been joined to Christ?
16. How close does our relationship with the other members of the body become?
17. Does the Church fulfill the desire God has always had in His heart?

Chapter 46

FELLOWSHIP IN THE LOCAL CHURCH

479. WHAT IS THE LOCAL CHURCH?

The Local Church is any local assembly made up of members of the Universal Church, the Body of Christ, whose common bond is their fellowship with Christ.

> *Unto the church of God which is at Corinth, to them that are sanctified in Christ Jesus, called to be saints, with all that in every place call upon the name of Jesus Christ our Lord, both their's and ours. I Cor. 1:2.*

> *. . . to all the saints in Christ Jesus which are at Philippi, with the bishops and deacons: Phil. 1:1.*

> *. . . unto the church of the Thessalonians which is in God the Father and in the Lord Jesus Christ . . . I Thess. 1:1.*

> *. . . unto the churches of Galatia . . . Gal. 1:2.*

480. WHAT IS THE MISSION OF THE LOCAL CHURCH?

Since the Local Church is the voice of the Universal Church, its mission is to preach and demonstrate the message of the Kingdom of God.

> *And he said unto them, Go ye into all the world, and preach the gospel to every creature. He that believeth and is baptized shall be saved; but he that believeth not shall he damned. Mark 16:15,16.*

481. WHAT IS THE MESSAGE OF THE KINGDOM OF GOD?

The message of the Kingdom is that Jesus Christ, the King, is now offering to all who submit to Him entrance into His Kingdom through repentence, faith toward God, water baptism, and receiving the baptism of the Holy Ghost.

> ... *Repent, and be baptized every one of you in the name of Jesus Christ for the remission of sin, and ye shall receive the gift of the Holy Ghost. Acts 2:38.*

> ... *Except a man be born of water and of the Spirit, he cannot enter into the kingdom of God. John 3:5.*

482. WHAT WARNING MUST THE CHURCH GIVE WITH THE MESSAGE OF THE KINGDOM?

The Church has been commissioned to warn all men that Christ will return to earth again and that all who refuse His offer of grace will be judged.

> *And he commanded us to preach unto the people, and to testify that it is he which was ordained of God to be the Judge of the quick and the dead. To him give all the prophets witness, that through his name whosoever believeth in him shall receive remission of sins. Acts 10:42,43.*

483. WHAT SIGNS OF POWER ACCOMPANY THE MESSAGE OF THE KINGDOM?

The Holy Spirit confirms the message of the Kingdom by granting healing and deliverance as signs of the power of the Kingdom.

> *And they went forth, and preached every where, the Lord working with them, and confirming the word with signs following. Amen. Mark 16:20.*

> *And as ye go, preach, saying, The kingdom of heaven is at hand. Heal the sick, cleanse the lepers, raise the dead, cast out devils: freely ye have received, freely give. Matt. 10:7,8.*

484. HOW LONG IS THE LOCAL CHURCH TO PREACH THE MESSAGE OF THE KINGDOM?

The Local Church is to preach the message of the Kingdom until every man has heard it. Jesus Christ will then return to reign upon the earth.

And this gospel of the kingdom shall be preached in all the world for a witness unto all nations; and then shall the end come. Matt. 24:14.

485. WHAT CONSTITUTES A LOCAL CHURCH?

According to the New Testament, the following factors must be present:

A. Two or more members must be gathered together in the authority and power of the name of the Lord Jesus Christ.

For where two or three are gathered together in my name, there am I in the midst of them. Matt. 18:20.

B. Christ, through His Spirit, is personally present in the congregation.

For He says, I will declare your (the Father's) Name to my brethren; in the midst of the worshipping congregation I will sing hymns of praise to you. Heb. 2:11,12 RV.

C. Two or more members receive direction from the Holy Spirit creating unity in worship, prayer and ministry.

. . . In the mouth of two or three witnesses shall every word be established. II Cor. 13:1.

Now I beseech you, brethren, by the name of our Lord Jesus Christ, that ye all speak the same thing, and that there be no divisions among you; but that ye be perfectly joined together in the same mind and in the same judgment. I Cor. 1:10.

D. All members contribute their share in worship and caring for each other (body ministry).

From (Christ) the whole body fitly joined together and compacted by that which every joint supplieth, according to the effectual working in the measure of every part, maketh increase of the body unto the edifying of itself in love. Eph. 4:16.

That there should be no division in the body, but that the members should have the same care for one another. I Cor. 12:25 NASV.

E. One or more members have been given responsibility and gifts from God to lead and watch over the assembly.

> *For this cause left I thee in Crete, that thou shouldest set in order the things that are wanting, and ordain elders in every city, as I had appointed thee. Titus 1:5.*

> *The elders which are among you I exhort . . . Feed the flock of God which is among you, taking the oversight thereof . . . I Peter 5:1,2.*

Note: See Chapter 53 on "Discipline in the Local Church".

486. WHAT DOES THE LOCAL CHURCH PROVIDE?

The Local Church provides a spiritual family in which we mature under the loving care and protection of pastors and elders.

> *That we henceforth be no more children, tossed to and fro, and, carried about with every wind of doctrine, by the sleight of men, and cunning craftiness, whereby they lie in wait to deceive; But speaking the truth in love may grow up into him in all things, which is the head, even Christ. Eph. 4:14,15.*

487. WHY IS IT NECESSARY FOR US TO BECOME MEMBERS OF THE LOCAL CHURCH?

We can only mature as we accept the responsibilities of growth:

A. Submission to authority.

> *Now I say, that the heir, as long as he is a child, differeth nothing from a servant, though he be lord of all; But is under tutors and governors until the time appointed of the Father. Gal. 4:1,2.*

> *Submitting yourselves one to another in the fear of God. Eph. 5:21.*

> *Obey them that have the rule over you, and submit yourselves . . . Heb. 13:17.*

B. Faithfulness to commitments (obligations, vows, responsibilities, loyalties, etc.).

> *He that is faithful in that which is least is faithful also in much . . . And if we have not been faithful in that which is*

another man's, who shall give you that which is your own?
Luke 16:10,12.

. . . because thou hast been faithful in a very little, have
thou authority . . . Luke 19:17.

C. Involvement with the concerns of others.

Bear one another's burdens, and so fulfill the law of
Christ. Gal. 6:2.

Beloved, if God so loved us, we ought also to love one an-
other . . . If we love one another, God dwelleth in us, and
his love is perfected in us. I John 4:11,12.

488. HOW DO WE BECOME MEMBERS OF THE LOCAL CHURCH?

After we have become members of the Universal Church
through the new birth, we join ourselves to a Local Church by
submitting to those whom God has put in leadership and by following the Local Church's rules for becoming a member.

Obey them that have the rule over you, and submit your-
selves: for they watch for your souls, as they that must give
account, that they may do it with joy, and not with grief
for that is unprofitable for you. Heb. 13:17.

489. FOR WHAT PURPOSE DO WE MEET TOGETHER IN THE LOCAL CHURCH?

God has purposed that we who are joined to the Body of Christ
come together in the local assembly where we may know each
other and share each others joys and burdens.

Not forsaking the assembling of ourselves together, as the
manner of some is; but exhorting one another; and so
much the more, as ye see the day approaching.
Heb. 10:25.

And being let go, they went to their own company, and re-
ported all that the chief priests and elders had said unto
them. And they lifted up their voice to God with one ac-
cord, and said, Lord, thou art God . . . Acts 4:23,24.

490. WHAT IS FELLOWSHIP?

Fellowship is having something in common by participating and sharing in the same spiritual experiences. It is sharing Christ.

> *For we being many are one bread, and one body: For we are all partakers of that one bread. I Cor. 10:17.*

491. HOW DO WE PARTICIPATE IN THE SAME SPIRITUAL EXPERIENCES?

Each of us is joined to Christ and to each other through the new birth. We act out this union by sharing with each other what we have for the benefit of everyone. The best example of this is the Lord's Supper.

> *The cup of blessing (of wine at the Lord's Supper) upon which we ask (God's) blessing, does it not mean (that in drinking it) we participate in and share a fellowship (a communion) in the blood of Christ, the Messiah? The bread which we break, does it not mean (that in eating it) we participate in and share a fellowship (a communion) in the body of Christ? For we (no matter how) numerous we are, are one body, because we all partake of the one Bread (the One Whom the communion bread represents). I Cor. 10:16,17 AMP.*

492. WHY MUST WE SHARE CHRIST WITH EACH OTHER?

None of us has a complete revelation or experience of Christ. God has purposed that what we lack will be supplied to us by others in the Body of Christ.

> *And if they were all one member, where were the body? I Cor. 12:19.*

> *And the eye cannot say unto the hand, I have no need of thee: nor again the head to the feet, I have no need of you ... For our comely parts have no need: but God hath tempered the body together ... I Cor. 12:21,24.*

493. HOW ARE WE ABLE TO SHARE CHRIST WITH EACH OTHER?

The Holy Spirit works in us and through us to communicate to others the portion of Christ which we have received.

... the love of God is shed abroad in our hearts by the Holy Ghost which is given unto us. Rom. 5:5.

If there be therefore any consolation in Christ, if any comfort of love, if any fellowship of the Spirit, if any bowels and mercies, Fulfill ye my joy, that ye be likeminded, having the same love, being of one accord, of one mind. Phil. 2:1,2.

494. WHAT DO WE SHARE WITH EACH OTHER IN FELLOWSHIP?

In fellowship, we share:

A. The ministering of spiritual abilities.

How is it then, brethren? when ye come together, every one of you hath a psalm, hath a doctrine, hath a tongue, hath a revelation, hath an interpretation. Let all things be done unto edifying. I Cor. 14:26.

As every man hath received the gift, even so minister the same one to another, as good stewards of the manifold grace of God. I Peter 4:10.

Note: See Chapter 48 on "Gifts and Ministries".

B. Hospitality.

Use hospitality one to another without grudging. I Peter 4:9.

... given to hospitality. Rom. 12:13.

C. Our money and possessions.

Distributing to the necessity of saints ... Rom. 12:13.

But whoso hath this world's good, and seeth his brother have need, and shutteth up his bowels of compassion from him, how dwelleth the love of God in him? I John 3:17.

D. Our time and strength helping others.

As we have therefore opportunity, let us do good unto all men, especially unto them who are of the household of faith. Gal. 6:10.

Withhold not good from them to whom it is due, when it is in the power of thine hand to do it. Prov. 3:27.

E. Prayer and intercession.

Praying always with all prayer and supplication in the Spirit, and watching thereunto with all perseverance and supplication for all saints. Eph. 6:18.

Ye also helping together by prayer for us ... II Cor. 1:11.

F. Love.

That their hearts might be comforted, being knit together in love ... Col. 2:2.

Let brotherly love continue. Heb. 13:1.

Love the brotherhood. I Peter 2:17.

G. Comfort.

Comfort one another with these words. I Thess. 4:8.

Comfort yourselves together, and edify one another, even as also ye do. I Thess. 5:11.

495. HOW DOES THE LOCAL CHURCH HELP US GROW IN CHRIST?

The Local Church helps us grow:

A. Through feeding and nourishing us.

Take heed therefore unto yourselves, and to all the flock, over which the Holy Ghost hath made you overseers, to feed the church of God, which he hath purchased with his own blood. Acts. 20:28.

B. Through watchful care and protection.

Take heed therefore unto yourselves, and to all the flock, over which the Holy Ghost hath made you overseers ... For I know this, that after my departing shall grievous wolves enter in among you, not sparing the flock. Acts 20:28,29.

C. Through the ministry of the apostles, prophets, evangelists, pastors and teachers.

And he gave some apostles; and some, prophets; and some, evangelists; and some, pastors and teachers; For the perfecting of the saints, for the work of the ministry, for the edifying of the body of Christ: Till we all come in the unity of the faith, and the knowledge of the Son of God, unto a perfect man, unto the measure of the stature of the fulness of Christ. Eph. 4:11–13.

D. Through faithful discipline, warning and exhortation.

These things speak, and exhort and rebuke with all authority . . . Titus 2:15.

Whom we preach, warning every man, and teaching every man in all wisdom; that we may present every man perfect in Christ Jesus. Col. 1:28.

E. Through personal attention according to our need.

Now we exhort you, brethren, warn them that are unruly, comfort the feebleminded, support the weak, be patient toward all men. I Thess. 5:14.

Brethren, if any man be overtaken in a fault, ye which are spiritual, restore such an one in the spirit of meekness; considering thyself, lest thou also be tempted. Gal. 6:1.

496. WHAT ARE WE TO DO SO THAT WE MAY GROW IN CHRIST?

In order to grow in Christ, we must cooperate with the Local Church.

A. We are to desire to be fed by the word of God.

As newborn babes, desire the sincere milk of the word, that ye may grow thereby: If so be ye have tasted that the Lord is gracious. I Peter 2:2–3.

B. We are to receive the word with meekness and faith so that it will profit us.

Wherefore lay apart all filthiness and superfluity of naughtiness, and receive with meekness the engrafted word, which is able to save your souls. James 1:21.

For unto us was the gospel preached, as well as unto them: but the word preached did not profit them, not being mixed with faith in them that heard it. Heb. 4:2.

C. We are to obey them that have the rule over us and submit ourselves to them and to each other that we may grow in God's grace.

Obey them that have the rule over you, and submit yourselves: for they watch for your souls, as they that must give account, that they may do it with joy, and not with grief: for that is unprofitable for you. Heb. 13:17.

Likewise, ye younger, submit yourselves unto the elder. Yea, all of you be subject to one another, and be clothed with humility: for God resisteth the proud, and giveth grace to the humble. I Peter 5:5.

But grow in grace, and in the knowledge of our Lord and Saviour Jesus Christ. To him be glory both now and for ever. Amen. II Peter 3:18.

D. We are to heed the warnings, respond to the exhortations, and be trained by the discipline.

Take heed, brethren, lest there be in any of you an evil heart of unbelief, in departing from the living God. But exhort one another daily, while it is called To day; lest any of you be hardened through the deceitfulness of sin. For we are made partakers of Christ, if we hold the beginning of our confidence stedfast unto the end; Heb. 3:12–14.

Watch ye therefore, and pray always, that ye may be accounted worthy to escape all these things that shall come to pass, and to stand before the Son of man. Luke 21:36.

Now no chastening (discipline) for the present seemeth to be joyous, but grievous: nevertheless afterward it yieldeth the peaceable fruit of righteousness unto them which are exercised thereby. Heb. 12:11.

E. We are to assemble ourselves together that we may receive the help of the Local Church.

*Not forsaking the assembling of ourselves together, as the manner of some is; but exhorting one another: and so much the more, as ye see the day approaching.
Heb. 10:25.*

497. HOW DO WE MATURE AS SONS OF GOD?

We mature as sons by allowing the Holy Spirit to perfect in us the nature of Christ.

But speaking the truth in love, may grow up into him in all things, which is the head, even Christ. Eph. 4:15.

But we all with open face beholding as in a glass the glory of the Lord, are changed into the same image from glory to glory, even as by the Spirit of the Lord. II Cor. 3:18.

498. WHAT HAS CHRIST GIVEN TO THE LOCAL CHURCH TO HELP PERFECT US AS SONS?

Christ has given to the Local Church five ministries to perfect us into the image of Christ.

And he gave some, apostles; and some, prophets; and some, evangelists; and some, pastors and teachers; For the perfecting of the saints, for the work of the ministry, for the edifying of the body of Christ: Till we all come in the unity of the faith, and of the knowledge of the Son of God, unto a perfect man, unto the measure of the stature of the fulness of Christ. Eph. 4:11–13.

499. DO ALL WHO HAVE BEEN BORN OF GOD GROW UP TO BECOME MATURE SONS?

No. All have been given the same life in Christ but all do not submit to the discipline and chastening God requires of those who will mature in Him.

For whom the Lord loveth he chasteneth, and scourgeth every son whom he receiveth. If ye endure chastening, God dealeth with you as with sons, for what son is he whom the father chasteneth not? But if ye be without chastisement, whereof all are partakers, then are ye bastards, and not sons. Heb. 12:6–8.

Note: See Chapter 41 on "Baptism of Fire".

500. WHAT HAPPENS TO THOSE WHO WILL NOT GROW UP?

They remain babes in Christ continually needing milk. They are the carnal (fleshly) Christians who cause divisions in the Local Church by their personal preferences and selfish behavior.

. . . seeing ye are dull of hearing. For when for the time ye ought to be teachers, ye have need that one teach you

again which be the first principles of the oracles of God; and are become such as have need of milk, and not of strong meat. For every one that useth milk is unskilful in the word of righteousness: for he is a babe. Heb. 5:11-13.

And I, brethren, could not speak unto you as unto spiritual, but as unto carnal, even as unto babes in Christ. I have fed you with milk, and not with meat: For hitherto ye were not able to bear it, neither yet now are ye able. For ye are yet carnal: for whereas there is among you envying, and strife, and divisions, are ye not carnal, and walk as men? For while one saith, I am of Paul; and another, I am of Apollos; are ye not carnal? I Cor. 3:1-4.

501. WHAT HAPPENS TO THOSE WHO GO ON TO MATURITY?

They become mature sons whom the Father can trust with authority, knowledge, great responsibility, revelation (meat) in the Word, and intimacy with Himself.

But strong meat belongeth to them that are of full age, even those who by reason of use have their senses exercised to discern both good and evil. Therefore leaving the principles of the doctrine of Christ, let us go on unto perfection; not laying again the foundation ... and this will we do, if God permit. Heb. 5:14; 6:1,3.

Till we all come in the unity of the faith, and of the knowledge of the Son of God, unto a perfect man, unto the measure of the stature of the fulness of Christ: That we henceforth be no more children, tossed to and fro and carried about with every wind of doctrine, by the sleight of men ... But speaking the truth in love, may grow up into him in all things, which is the head, even Christ. Eph. 4:13-15.

502. WHEN CAN WE BEGIN TO MATURE AS SONS?

Only after we have experienced the six foundation stones can we go on to maturity.

Therefore leaving the principles of the doctrine of Christ, let us go on to perfection; not laying again the foundation of repentance from dead works, and of faith toward God, of the doctrine of baptisms, and of laying on of hands, and of resurrection of the dead, and of eternal judgment. And this will we do, if God permit. Heb. 6:1-3.

503.   HOW DO WE LAY THESE FOUNDATION STONES?

As we submit to the teaching of the leaders God has given to us in the Local Church, God will give to us revelation and faith to personally experience these doctrines.

Then they that gladly received his word were baptized, and the same day there were added unto them about three thousand souls. Acts 2:41.

And he gave some, apostles; and some, prophets; and some, evangelists; and some, pastors and teachers; For the perfecting of the saints, for the work of the ministry, for the edifying of the body of Christ: Till we all come in the unity of the faith, and of the knowledge of the Son of God, unto a perfect man, unto the measure of the stature of the fulness of Christ: Eph. 4:11-13.

504.   WHY SHOULD WE DESIRE TO BECOME MATURE SONS?

We should desire maturity that we might be manifested (revealed) as the sons of God to the world. The glory of God can be shown to others through us.

For I reckon that the sufferings of this present time are not worthy to be compared with the glory which shall be revealed in us. For the earnest expectation of the creature waiteth for the manifestation of the sons of God. Rom. 8:18,19.

I press toward the mark for the prize of the high calling of God in Christ Jesus. Phil. 3:14.

STUDY QUESTIONS—Chapter 46.

1. What is the Local Church?
2. What constitutes a Local Church?
3. What is the purpose of the Local Church?
4. Why is it necessary for us to become members of the Local Church?
5. How do we become members of the Local Church?
6. For what purpose do we meet together in the Local Church?
7. What is fellowship?
8. Why must we share Christ with each other?
9. What do we share with each other in fellowship?
10. How does the Local Church help us grow in Christ?
11. What are we to do so that we may grow in Christ?
12. How do we mature as sons of God?
13. What has Christ placed in the Local Church to perfect us as sons?
14. Do all who have been born of God grow up to become mature sons?
15. What happens to those who will grow up?
16. Why should we desire to become mature sons?
17. Write Heb. 10:25; Rom. 8:19; II Cor. 3:18.

Chapter 47

THE PERSON OF THE HOLY GHOST

505. WHO IS THE HOLY GHOST?

The Holy Ghost (Holy Spirit) is the third person of the Holy Trinity, true God with the Father and the Son. He is the out-breathing of God, that is, the life of God going forth to quicken.

Note: Holy Ghost means Holy Breath or Holy Spirit. Other symbols for the Holy Ghost are: wind, power, fire, oil, water, a dove, a voice, rain, dew and a seal.

> *Go ye, therefore, and teach all nations, baptizing them in the name of the Father, and of the Son, and of the Holy Ghost. Matt. 28:19.*

> *The Spirit of God hath made me, and the breath of the Almighty hath given me life. Job. 33:4.*

> *By the word of the Lord were the heavens made; and all the host of them by the breath of His mouth. Ps. 33:6.*

> *And the earth was without form, and void; and darkness was upon the face of the deep. And the Spirit of God moved upon the face of the waters. Gen. 1:2,3.*

> *Thou hidest thy face, they are troubled: thou takest away their breath, they die, and return to their dust. Thou sendest forth thy spirit; they are created; and thou renewest the face of the earth. Ps. 104:29,30.*

506. WHY DO WE BELIEVE THAT THE HOLY SPIRIT IS TRUE GOD?

We believe the Holy Spirit is true God because the Scriptures ascribe to Him:

A. Divine Names—He is called "God" and "Lord".

Peter said, Ananias, why hath Satan filled thine heart to lie to the Holy Ghost? ... Thou hast not lied unto men, but unto God. Acts 5:3,4.

But we all, with open face beholding as in a glass the glory of the Lord, are changed into the same image from glory to glory, even as by the Spirit of the Lord. II Cor. 3:18. See also I Cor. 3:16.

B. Divine Attributes—

Omnipresence—(present everywhere).

Whither shall I go from Thy Spirit, or whither shall I flee from Thy presence? If I ascend up into heaven, thou art there; if I make my bed in hell, behold, thou art there. If I take the wings of the morning, and dwell in the uttermost parts of the sea; even there shall thy hand lead me, and thy right hand shall hold me. Ps. 139:7–10.

Omniscience—(all-knowing).

... The Spirit searcheth all things, yea, the deep things of God. I Cor. 2:10.

Omnipotence—(all-powerful).

But ye shall receive power, after that the Holy Ghost is come upon you: and ye shall be witnesses unto me both in Jerusalem, and in all Judaea, and in Samaria, and unto the uttermost part of the earth. Acts 1:8.

Eternal—

... Christ, who through the eternal Spirit offered himself without spot to God, purge your conscience from dead works to serve the living God. Heb. 9:14.

B. Divine Works—

Creation—

By the word of the Lord were the heavens made; and all the host of them by the breath of his mouth. Ps. 33:6.

Life—

But if the Spirit of him that raised up Jesus from the dead dwell in you, he that raised up Christ from the dead shall also quicken your mortal bodies by his Spirit that dwelleth in you. Rom. 8:11.

It is the spirit that quickeneth; the flesh profiteth nothing: the words that I speak unto you, they are spirit, and they are life. John 6:63.

And the Lord God formed man of the dust of the ground, and breathed into his nostrils the breath of life; and man became a living soul. Gen. 2:7.

Sanctification—

. . . He saved us by the washing of regeneration and renewing of the Holy Ghost. Titus 3:5.

C. Divine Honor and Glory—

. . . The Spirit of glory and of God resteth upon you . . . I Peter 4:14.

507. WHAT ARE THE ACTS OF THE HOLY SPIRIT?

The acts of the Holy Spirit are these:

A. He searches the deep things of God for us.

But God hath revealed them unto us by His Spirit, for the Spirit searcheth all things, yea, the deep things of God. I Cor. 2:10.

B. He speaks to us.

He that hath an ear, let him hear what the Spirit saith unto the churches . . . Rev. 2:7.

C. He makes intercession for us.

Likewise the Spirit also helpeth our infirmities; for we know not what we should pray for as we ought: but the Spirit itself maketh intercession for us with groanings which cannot be uttered. Rom. 8:26.

D. He teaches and comforts us.

But the Comforter, which is the Holy Ghost, whom the Father will send in my name, he shall teach you all things, and bring all things to your remembrance, whatsoever I have said unto you. John 14:26.

E. He leads and guides us.

For as many as are led by the Spirit of God, they are the sons of God. Rom. 8:14.

F. He commissions men for service.

As they ministered to the Lord, and fasted, the Holy Ghost said, Separate me Barnabas and Saul for the work whereunto I have called them. Acts 13:2.

Take heed therefore unto yourselves, and to all the flock over the which the Holy Ghost hath made you overseers, to feed the church of God, which he hath purchased with his own blood. Acts 20:28.

508. **WHAT IS THE WORK OF THE HOLY SPIRIT IN RELATION TO SINNERS?**

The work of the Holy Spirit in relation to sinners is:

A. He strives with them.

And the Lord said, My spirit shall not always strive with man, for that he also is flesh. Gen. 6:3.

B. He witnesses to them.

But when the Comforter is come, whom I will send unto you from the Father, even the Spirit of truth, which proceedeth from the Father, he shall testify of me. John 15:26.

C. He convicts or convinces them.

And when he is come, he will reprove the world of sin, and of righteousness, and of judgment. Of sin, because they believe not on me. Of righteousness, because I go to my Father, and ye see me no more. Of judgment, because the prince of this world is judged. John 16:8–11.

509. **WHAT IS THE WORK OF THE HOLY SPIRIT IN RELATION TO BELIEVERS?**

The work of the Holy Spirit in relation to believers is:

A. He regenerates men, that is, he makes them new creatures.

Jesus answered and said unto him, Verily, verily, I say unto thee, Except a man be born again, he cannot see the kingdom of God. Nicodemus saith unto him, How can a man be born when he is old? Can he enter the second time into his mother's womb, and be born? Jesus answered, Verily, verily, I say unto thee, except a man be born of water and of the Spirit, he cannot enter into the kingdom of God. That which is born of the flesh is flesh; and that which is born of the Spirit is spirit. John 3:3–6.

B. He baptizes them into the Body of Christ.

For by one Spirit are we all baptized into one body, whether we be Jews or Gentiles, whether we be bond or free; and have been all made to drink into one Spirit. I Cor. 12:13.

C. He indwells believers.

Know ye not that ye are the temple of God, and that the Spirit of God dwelleth in you? I Cor. 3:16.

1. He seals us with His Spirit.

In whom ye also trusted, after that ye heard the word of truth, the gospel of your salvation: in whom also after that ye believed, ye were SEALED with that Holy Spirit of promise. Which is the earnest of our inheritance until the redemption of the purchased possession, unto the praise of his glory. Eph. 1:13,14.

2. He gives assurance of salvation.

The Spirit itself beareth witness with our spirit, that we are the children of God. Rom. 8:16.

3. He strengthens our inner man.

That he would grant you, according to the riches of his glory, to be strengthened with might by his Spirit in the inner man. Eph. 3:16.

4. He abides forever.

And I will pray the Father, and he shall give you another Comforter, that he may abide with you for ever. John 14:16.

D. He infills us with His Spirit.

And be not drunk with wine, wherein is excess; but be filled with the Spirit. Eph. 5:18.

E. He liberates us from the power of sin and death.

For the law of the Spirit of life in Christ Jesus hath made me free from the law of sin and death. Rom. 8:2.

F. He directs our steps.

For as many as are led by the Spirit of God, they are the sons of God. Rom. 8:14.

1. He calls to special service.

As they ministered to the Lord, and fasted, the Holy Ghost said, Separate me Barnabas and Saul for the work where-unto I have called them ... So they, being sent forth by the Holy Ghost, departed unto Seleucia; and from thence they sailed to Cyprus. Acts 13:2,4.

2. He guides in service.

And he arose and went: and, behold, a man of Ethiopia, an eunuch of great authority under Candace queen of the Ethiopians, who had the charge of all her treasure, and had come to Jerusalem for to worship, Was returning, and sitting in his chariot read Esaias the prophet. Then the Spirit said unto Philip, Go near, and join thyself to this chariot. Acts 8:27–29.

G. He equips us for service.

1. He illuminates.

Now we have received, not the spirit of the world, but the spirit which is of God; that we might know the things that are freely given to us of God ... But the natural man re-ceiveth not the things of the Spirit of God: for they are foolishness unto him; neither can he know them, because they are spiritually discerned. I Cor. 2:12,14.

2. He instructs.

Howbeit when he, the Spirit of truth is come, he shall guide you into all truth: for he shall not speak of himself; but whatsoever he shall hear, that shall he speak; and he will shew you things to come. John 16:13.

3. He empowers.

For our gospel came not unto you in word only, but also in power, and in the Holy Ghost, and in much assurance; as ye know what manner of men we were among you for your sake. I Thess. 1:5.

H. He produces the fruit of Christlike graces.

But the fruit of the Spirit is love, joy, peace, longsuffering, gentleness, goodness, faith. Meekness, temperance: against such there is no law. Gal. 5:22,23.

I. He makes possible all forms of communion with God.

1. Prayer.

But ye, beloved, building up yourself on your most holy faith, praying in the Holy Ghost. Jude 20.

2. Worship and praise.

For we are the circumcision, who worship by the Spirit of God and glory in Christ Jesus, and have no confidence in the flesh. Phil. 3:3 RSV.

3. Thanksgiving.

And be not drunken with wine, wherein is riot, but be filled with the Spirit, speaking one to another in psalms and hymns and spiritual songs, singing and making melody with your heart to the Lord; Giving thanks always for all things in the name of our Lord Jesus Christ to God even the Father. Eph. 5:18–20 RSV.

J. He shall quicken the believer's body.

But if the Spirit of him that raised up Jesus from the dead dwell in you, he that raised up Christ from the dead shall also quicken your mortal bodies by his Spirit that dwelleth in you ... And not only they, but ourselves also, which have the first-fruits of the Spirit, even we ourselves groan within ourselves, waiting for the adoption, to wit, the re-demption of our body. Rom. 8:11,23.

510. WHAT IS THE WORK OF THE HOLY SPIRIT IN RELA-TION TO JESUS CHRIST?

A. Jesus Christ was conceived by the Holy Ghost.

And the angel answered and said unto her, The Holy

Ghost shall come upon thee, and the power of the Highest shall overshadow thee: therefore also that holy thing which shall be born of thee shall be called the Son of God. Luke 1:35.

B. Jesus was anointed with the Holy Spirit.

How God anointed Jesus of Nazareth with the Holy Spirit and with power: who went about doing good, and healing all that were oppressed of the devil; for God was with him. Acts 10:38.

C. Jesus was led by the Spirit.

Then was Jesus led up of the spirit into the wilderness to be tempted of the devil. Matt. 4:1.

D. Jesus was filled with the Holy Spirit.

And Jesus being full of the Holy Ghost returned from Jordan, and was led by the Spirit into the wilderness. Luke 4:1.

E. Jesus accomplished His ministry in the power of the Spirit.

The Spirit of the Lord is upon me, because he hath anointed me to preach the gospel to the poor; he hath sent me to heal the brokenhearted, to preach deliverance to the captives, and recovering of sight to the blind, to set at liberty them that are bruised, To preach the acceptable year of the Lord. Luke 4:18,19.

F. Jesus sacrificially offered Himself through the Spirit.

How much more shall the blood of Christ, who through the eternal Spirit offered himself without spot to God, purge your conscience from dead works to serve the living God. Heb. 9:14.

G. Jesus was resurrected by the power of the Spirit.

But if the Spirit of him that raised up Jesus from the dead dwell in you, he that raised up Christ from the dead shall also quicken your mortal bodies by his Spirit that dwelleth in you. Rom. 8:11.

H. Jesus' commandment to the Apostles after His resurrection was given through the Holy Spirit.

The former treatise have I made, O Theophilus, of all that

Jesus began both to do and teach, Until the day in which he was taken up, after that he through the Holy Ghost had given commandments, unto the apostles whom he had chosen. Acts 1:1,2.

I. Jesus was the bestower of the Holy Spirit.

. . . he shall baptize you with the Holy Ghost and with fire: Luke 3:16b.

Note: Jesus Christ lived His life in absolute dependence upon and in subjection to the Holy Spirit.

511. WHAT IS THE WORK OF THE HOLY SPIRIT IN RELATION TO THE SCRIPTURES?

The work of the Holy Spirit in relation to the Scriptures is:

A. He is the Author of all Scripture.

Knowing this first, that no prophecy of the Scripture is of any private interpretation. For the prophecy came not in old time by the will of man: but holy men of God spake as they were moved by the Holy Ghost. II Peter 1:20,21.

B. He is the Interpreter of all Scripture.

That the God of our Lord Jesus Christ, the Father of glory, may give unto you the spirit of wisdom and revelation in the knowledge of him. Eph. 1:17.

512. WHAT TREATMENT HAS THE HOLY SPIRIT RECEIVED BY MEN?

The Holy Spirit has been:

A. Rebelled against and grieved.

But they rebelled and grieved His Holy Spirit; therefore he was turned to be their enemy and himself fought against them. Isa. 63:10 RSV.

B. He has been intentionally deceived.

But Peter said, Ananias, why hath Satan filled thine heart to lie to the Holy Ghost, and to keep back part of the price of the land? Acts 5:3.

C. He is blasphemed.

Wherefore I say unto you, All manner of sin and blasphemy shall be forgiven unto men: but the blasphemy against the Holy Ghost shall not be forgiven unto men. Matt. 12:31.

513. WHAT IS THE UNPARDONABLE SIN?

When a knowledgeable person willfully attributes to the devil those works which could only be wrought by the Spirit of God, this is blasphemy against the Holy Spirit, i.e., the unpardonable sin.

Verily I say unto you, All sins shall be forgiven unto the sons of men, and blasphemies wherewith soever they shall blaspheme: But he that shall blaspheme against the Holy Ghost hath never forgiveness, but is in danger of eternal damnation: Because they said, he hath an unclean spirit. Mark 3:28–30.

Wherefore I say unto you, All manner of sin and blasphemy shall be forgiven unto men: but the blasphemy against the Holy Ghost shall not be forgiven unto men. And whosoever speaketh a word against the Son of man, it shall be forgiven him: but whosoever speaketh against the Holy Ghost, it shall not be forgiven him, neither in this world, neither in the world to come. Matt. 12:31,32.

Who (Paul) was before a blasphemer, *and a persecutor, and injurious: but I obtained mercy, because I did it ignorantly in unbelief. I Tim. 1:13.*

For if we sin willfully *after that we have received the* knowledge *of the truth, there remaineth no more sacrifice for sins. Heb. 10:26.*

514. WHAT PUNISHMENT IS METED TO THOSE WHO GRIEVE THE HOLY SPIRIT?

The punishment that is meted to those who mistreat or grieve the Holy Spirit is very severe:

A. Those who rebel against Him and grieve Him are in danger of having Him fight against them.

But they rebelled, and vexed (grieved) his holy Spirit:

therefore he was turned to be their enemy, and he fought against them. Isa. 63:10.

B. Those who lie to the Holy Spirit are in danger of death.

But Peter said, Ananias, why hath Satan filled thine heart to lie to the Holy Ghost, and to keep back part of the price of the land? Whiles it remained, was it not thine own? and after it was sold, was it not in thine own power? why hast thou conceived this thing in thine heart? thou hast not lied unto men, but unto God. And Ananias hearing these words fell down, and gave up the ghost: and great fear came on all them that heard these things. And the young men arose, wound him up, and carried him out, and buried him. Acts 5:3–6.

C. Those who are knowledgeable and blaspheme the Holy Spirit willfully can never have this sin forgiven in this life or in the life to come.

Wherefore I say unto you, All manner of sin and blasphemy shall be forgiven unto men: but the blasphemy against the Holy Ghost shall not be forgiven unto men. And whosoever speaketh a word against the Son of man, it shall be forgiven him: but whosoever speaketh against the Holy Ghost, it shall not be forgiven him, neither in this world, neither in the world to come. Matt. 12:31,32.

515. WHY IS BLASPHEMY AGAINST THE HOLY SPIRIT AN UNFORGIVEABLE SIN?

Blasphemy against the Holy Spirit is unforgiveable because the Holy Spirit departs from the man who blasphemes His name. Without the presence of the Holy Spirit, it is impossible for man to approach the throne of grace or find repentance for sin.

516. WHAT SHOULD BE OUR ATTITUDE TOWARD THE HOLY SPIRIT?

We should regard Him as a real person, indeed, as Jesus Christ. We should hold Him in high esteem, as loving, wise and strong and worthy of our confidence, love and surrender. He has been sent to us to be to us what Jesus Christ was to His disciples during the days of His personal companionship with them. We should strive to know the communion and fellowship of the Holy Spirit.

And grieve not the holy Spirit of God, whereby ye are sealed unto the day of redemption. Eph. 4:30.

Quench not the Spirit. I Thess. 5:19.

STUDY QUESTIONS—Chapter 47

1. Who is the Holy Ghost?
2. What are the acts of the Holy Ghost?
3. What is the work of the Holy Spirit in relation to believers?
4. Who is the author of all Scripture?
5. What does it mean to blaspheme the Holy Ghost?
6. What is the unforgiveable sin?
7. How should we regard the person of the Holy Ghost?
8. What punishment is meted to those who grieve the Holy Ghost?
9. Write John 14:26; John 15:26; Matt. 12:31,32.

Chapter 48

THE GIFTS AND CALLINGS
OF THE HOLY SPIRIT

517.   **WHAT ARE THE GIFTS OF THE HOLY SPIRIT?**

The gifts of the Holy Spirit are the special abilities given to believers to extend the work of Christ on earth.

> *But ye shall receive power, after that the Holy Ghost is come upon you: and you shall be witnesses unto me both in Jerusalem, and in all Judea, and in Samaria, and unto the uttermost parts of the earth. Acts 1:8.*

518.   **WHAT IS THE DIFFERENCE BETWEEN THE GIFT AND THE GIFTS OF THE HOLY SPIRIT?**

The gift of the Holy Spirit is the baptism into the Holy Spirit. After experiencing this infilling, the Spirit begins to bestow special abilities that are manifestations of the presence of the Holy Spirit within the believer.

> *Then Peter said unto them, Repent, and be baptized every one of you in the name of Jesus Christ for the remission of sins, and you shall receive the gift of the Holy Ghost. Acts 2:38.*

> *But all these worketh that one and the selfsame Spirit, dividing to every man severally as he will. I Cor. 12:11.*

519.   **HOW MANY GIFTS ARE THERE?**

There are nine gifts (special abilities).

520.   **WHAT ARE THEY?**

There are three gifts of power: faith, miracles and healing; three gifts of utterance: prophecy, tongues and the interpretation of tongues; three gifts of revelation: word of wisdom, word of knowledge and discerning of spirits.

> *For to one is given by the Spirit, the word of wisdom, to another the word of knowledge by the same Spirit; To another faith by the same Spirit; to another gifts of healing by the same Spirit; to another the working of miracles; to another prophecy; to another discerning of spirits; to another divers kinds of tongues; to another the interpretation of tongues. I Cor. 12:8–12.*

Note: The same word "gifts" (abilities, endowments of grace) is used in Romans 12:4—6 to include ministry (preaching, teaching, exhorting, giving (sharing), ruling (leading), and showing mercy; and in I Cor. 12:28—31 to include helps and governments.

521. WHAT IS THE GIFT OF FAITH?

Faith is the ability to believe God's Word and to respond to it as it is divinely inspired to us.

> *So then faith cometh by hearing, and hearing by the word of God. Rom. 10:17.*

> *And the apostles said unto the Lord, Increase our faith. Luke 17:5.*

522. WHAT IS THE GIFT OF MIRACLES?

The gift of miracles is a God-given ability to interfere with and change the course of nature, events or circumstances.

> *God also bearing them witness, both with signs and wonders, and with divers miracles, and gifts of the Holy Ghost, according to his own will. Heb. 2:4.*

523. WHAT ARE THE GIFTS OF HEALING?

The gifts of healing are the divine abilities to heal the sick apart from the aid of natural means or human skills.

> *And these signs shall follow them that believe ... they shall lay hands on the sick, and they shall recover. Mark 16:17,18.*

524. WHAT IS THE GIFT OF PROPHECY?

Prophecy is the voice of the Holy Spirit speaking through a believer to men for edification, exhortation and comfort.

> *But he that prophesieth speaketh unto men to edification, and exhortation, and comfort. I Cor. 14:3.*
>
> *. . . the Lord God hath spoken, who can but prophesy? Amos 3:8.*

525. WHAT IS EDIFICATION?

Edification is the outflowing of the Holy Spirit through prophecy that strengthens, encourages and builds up the faith of believers.

> *He that speaketh in an unknown tongue edifieth himself; but he that prophesieth edifieth the church. I would that ye all speak with tongues, but rather that ye prophesied; for greater is he that prophesieth than he that speaketh with tongues, except he interpret, that the church may receive edifying. I Cor. 14:4,5.*

526. WHAT IS EXHORTATION?

Exhortation is an earnest flow of words expressed through a believer under the direction of the Holy Spirit imploring or warning sinner or believer to seek repentence or guidance, or giving direction to the Church.

> *And we beseech you, brethren, to know them which labour among you, and are over you in the Lord and admonish you; And to esteem them very highly in love for their work's sake. And be at peace among yourselves. Now we exhort you, brethren, warn them that are unruly, comfort the feebleminded, support the weak, be patient toward all men. I Thess. 5:12–14.*
>
> *Confirming the souls of the disciples and exhorting them to continue in the faith, and that we must through much tribulation enter into the kingdom of God. Acts. 14:22.*

527. WHAT IS COMFORT?

Comfort is the impartation of courage and strength by the Holy Spirit to the believer in times of grief and/or anxiety. The promises and assurances of God are also included in this realm.

Blessed be God, even the Father of our Lord Jesus Christ, the Father of mercies, and the God of all comfort; Who comforteth us in all our tribulation that we may be able to comfort them which are in any trouble by the comfort wherewith we ourselves are comforted of God. II Cor. 1:3,4.

528. WHAT IS THE GIFT OF TONGUES?

It is an ability given to a believer by the Holy Spirit to utter divinely inspired words. The speaker is given words to speak that are unknown to him but which can be understood by the person to whom the message is sent. Such a message is a sign to those who do not believe to turn them to God.

Wherefore tongues are for a sign, not to them that believe, but to them that believe not . . . I Cor. 14:22.

529. WHAT IS INTERPRETATION OF TONGUES?

Interpretation of tongues is the ability to fully explain the meaning of divinely inspired words spoken in an unknown tongue. The interpreter has no knowledge of the language spoken by the messenger who gave the message in tongues.

If any man speak in an unknown tongue, let it be by two, or at the most by three, and that by course; and let one interpret. But if there be no interpreter, let him keep silent in the church; and let him speak to himself, and to God. I Cor. 14:27,28.

530. WHAT IS THE WORD OF WISDOM?

The word of wisdom is a God-given ability to understand the mysteries of God and to speak the mind of the Lord. In answering questions, solving problems and giving instructions, the wisdom of the words is so complete that they leave no room for further discussion.

Howbeit we speak wisdom among them that are perfect: yet not the wisdom of this world, nor of the princes of this world that come to nought: But we speak the wisdom of God in a mystery, even the hidden wisdom, which God ordained before the world unto our glory. I Cor. 2:6,7.

Settle it, therefore in your hearts, not to meditate before what ye shall answer: For I will give you a mouth and wisdom, which all your adversaries shall not be able to gainsay nor resist. Luke 21:14,15.

531.   WHAT IS THE WORD OF KNOWLEDGE?

The word of knowledge is the God-given ability to know certain facts about a situation without having any previous knowledge concerning the situation or the individual involved.

But if all prophesy, and there come in one that believeth not, or one unlearned, he is convinced of all, he is judged of all: And thus are the secrets of his heart made manifest; and so falling down on his face he will worship God, and report that God is in you of a truth. I Cor. 14:24,25.

But Peter said, Ananias, why hath Satan filled thine heart to lie to the Holy Ghost, and to keep back part of the price of the land? Whiles it remained, was it not thine own? And after it was sold, was it not in thine own power? Why hast thou conceived this thing in thine heart? Thou hast not lied unto men, but unto God, And Ananias hearing these words fell down, and gave up the ghost; and great fear came on all them that heard these things. Acts 5:3-5.

532.   WHAT IS DISCERNING OF SPIRITS?

The discerning of spirits is the God-given ability to reveal the identity of the spirit that is holding a person captive or is causing distress, or to reveal that a person is acting by the direction of the Holy Spirit.

For I perceive that thou art in the gall of bitterness, and in the bond of iniquity. Acts 8:23.

533.   WHY ARE SPIRITUAL GIFTS GIVEN TO US?

They are given as a sign of the divine life and power of the Holy Spirit working within us and to enable us to minister according to God's will.

. . . Jesus of Nazareth, a man approved of God among you by miracles and wonders and signs, which God did by him in the midst of you, as ye yourselves also know. Acts 2:22.

534. IS IT NECESSARY FOR EVERY BELIEVER TO HAVE SPIRITUAL GIFTS?

Yes. Every member of the Body of Christ must have a function, a place to fill, a duty to perform within the Church.

> *For as we have many members in one body, and all members have not the same office: So we being many, are one body in Christ, and every one members one of another. Having then gifts differing according to the grace that is given to us, whether prophecy, let us prophesy according to the proportion of faith. Rom. 12:4–6.*

535. WHAT ARE SPIRITUAL CALLINGS?

Spiritual callings are divine appointments to a vocation or service in the church of Jesus Christ. There are five vocations: apostle, prophet, evangelist, pastor and teacher. There are four classifications of service: elders, deacons, helps and governments.

> *And he gave some, apostles; and some prophets; and some evangelists; and some, pastors and teachers; For the perfecting of the saints, for the work of the ministry, for the edifying of the body of Christ. Eph. 4:11,12.*

> *And God hath set some in the church, first apostles, secondarily prophets, thirdly teachers, after that miracles, then gifts of healings, helps, governments, diversities of tongues. I Cor. 12:28.*

536. WHAT IS THE DIFFERENCE BETWEEN A CALLING AND A MINISTRY?

A calling is a divine appointment for service that includes the special abilities needed for a particular ministry. When these abilities are developed by consistent exercise, they become a ministry.

> *Having then gifts differing according to the grace that is given to us, whether prophecy, let us prophesy according to the proportion of faith; Or ministry, let us wait on our ministering: or he that teacheth, on teaching; or he that exhorteth, on exhortation: he that giveth, let him do it with simplicity; he that ruleth, with diligence; he that sheweth mercy, with cheerfulness. Rom. 12:6–8.*

537. ARE WE ALL CALLED TO THE SAME MINISTRIES IN THE BODY OF CHRIST?

No. God has chosen each one to fulfill a particular purpose and to fill a place in the Body of Christ that no one else can fill.

> *For the body is not one member, but many. If the foot shall say, Because I am not the hand, I am not of the body; it is therefore not of the body ... if the whole body were an eye, where were the hearing? If the whole were hearing, where were the smelling? But now hath God set the members everyone of them in the body, as it hath pleased him. And if they were all one member, where were the body? I Cor. 12:14–15,17–19.*

538. WHY HAS GOD GIVEN US DIFFERENT CALLINGS WITHIN THE ONE BODY?

It increases unity and love to know that we truly need one another. We are not self-sufficient in the ministry of the Spirit but are perfected and completed by every other member of the Body.

> *And the eye cannot say unto the hand, I have no need of thee: nor again the head to the feet, I have no need of you. Nay, much more those members of the body, which seem to be more feeble, are necessary ... For our comely parts have no need: but God hath tempered the body together, having given more abundant honour to that part which lacked: that there should be no scism (division) in the body; but that the members should have the same care one for another. I Cor. 12:21–25.*

> *Now ye are the body of Christ, and members in particular. I Cor. 12:27.*

> *For as we have many members in one body, and all members have not the same office: So we, being many, are one body in Christ, and every one members one of another. Rom. 12:4,5.*

539. HOW CAN WE DEVELOP OUR SPECIAL ABILITIES IN ORDER TO BECOME EFFECTIVE IN MINISTRY?

By spending time alone with God in prayer and in the Scriptures, by learning to serve other people, by exercising our gifts in the Local Church where spiritual leaders can guide and correct us, and by fully dedicating ourselves to the perfecting of our personal lives and ministry, we can develop our special abilities.

> *Neglect not the gift that is in thee, which was given thee by prophecy, with the laying on of the hands of the presbytery. Meditate upon these things; give thyself wholly to them; that thy profiting may appear to all. Take heed unto thyself, and unto the doctrine; Continue in them: for in doing this thou shalt both save thyself, and them that hear thee. I Tim. 4:14–16.*

> *Study to shew thyself approved unto God, a workman that needeth not to be ashamed, rightly dividing the word of truth. II Tim. 2:15.*

> *The husbandman that laboureth must be first partaker of the fruits. II Tim. 2:6.*

540. HOW ARE SPIRITUAL GIFTS AND CALLINGS GIVEN?

Spiritual gifts and callings are given in different ways:

A. A manifestation of the Spirit or an appointment to a vocation or service may become evident following the baptism of the Holy Spirit.

> *And when Paul had laid his hands upon them, the Holy Ghost came on them, and they spake with tongues and prophesied. Acts 19:6.*

B. Spiritual gifts and ministries are imparted by the laying on of the hands of the presbytery (ministers) and accompanied by prophecy.

> *Neglect not the gift that is in thee, which was given thee by prophecy, with the laying on of the hands of the presbytery. I Tim. 4:14.*

> *For I long to see you, (said Paul) that I may impart unto you some spiritual gift, to the end you may be established. Rom. 1:11.*

> *This charge I commit unto thee, son Timothy, according to the prophecies which went before on thee, that thou by them mightest war a good warfare. I Tim. 1:18.*

C. Spiritual gifts are given in answer to fervent prayer arising out of an evident spiritual need.

And when they heard that, they lifted up their voice to God with one accord, and said, Lord, thou art God, which hast made heaven, and earth, and the sea, and all that in them is . . . And now, Lord, behold their threatenings: and grant unto thy servants, that with all boldness they may speak thy word, By stretching forth thine hand to heal; and that signs and wonders may be done by the name of thy holy child Jesus. And when they had prayed, the place was shaken where they were assembled together; and they were all filled with the Holy Ghost, and they spake the word of God with boldness. Acts 4:24,29–31.

541. DOES GOD GIVE SPIRITUAL GIFTS AND CALLINGS TO EVERY BELIEVER?

The gifts and callings of God are given to every dedicated and consecrated believer according to the plan and purpose of God.

If ye then, being evil, know how to give good gifts unto your children, how much more shall your Father, which is in heaven, give good things to them that ask him? Matt. 7:11.

But covet earnestly the best gifts . . . I Cor. 12:31.

But now hath God set the members every one of them, in the body, as it hath pleased him. I Cor. 12:18.

Thou hast ascended on high, thou hast led captivity captive: thou hast received gifts for men; yea, for the rebellious also, that the Lord God may dwell among them. Ps. 68:18.

542. DO SPIRITUAL GIFTS AND CALLINGS THAT COME TO US SOVEREIGNLY OR IN ANSWER TO PRAYER DIFFER FROM THOSE GIVEN TO US BY THE LAYING ON OF HANDS?

There is no difference in God's gifts or callings. The prophecy that comes from the presbytery confirms what has been given to us in times of prayer and meditation. The blessing we receive by the laying on of hands and prophecy is the confirmation that strengthens and establishes us.

For I long to see you, (said Paul) that I may impart unto you some spiritual gift, to the end ye may be established. Rom. 1:11.

. . . In the mouth of two or three witnesses shall every word be established. II Cor. 13:1.

STUDY QUESTIONS—Chapter 48

1. What are the gifts of the Holy Spirit?
2. What are the nine gifts?
3. Briefly define each of the nine gifts.
4. Why are spiritual gifts given to us?
5. What are spiritual callings?
6. What is the difference between a calling and a ministry?
7. Why has God given us different callings within the one body?
8. How can we develop our special abilities in order to become effective in ministry?
9. How are spiritual gifts and callings given?
10. Write: I Cor. 12:8–12.

Chapter 49

THE MINISTRIES OF THE HOLY SPIRIT

543. WHAT ARE THE MINISTRIES OF THE HOLY SPIRIT?

The ministries of the Holy Spirit are the five direct gifts Christ gave to His Church after His ascension.

Now there are diversities of gifts, but the same Spirit . . . But the manifestation of the Spirit is given to every man to profit withal. I Cor. 12:4,7.

544. WHAT ARE THE FIVE MINISTRIES?

Christ gave to the Church the ministries of apostles, prophets, evangelists, pastors and teachers.

. . . When he ascended up on high, he led captivity captive, and gave gifts unto men . . . And he gave some, apostles; and some, prophets; and some, evangelists; and some, pastors and teachers; For the perfecting of the saints, for the work of the ministry, for the edifying of the body of Christ. Eph. 4:8,11,12.

545. FOR WHAT PURPOSE DID CHRIST GIVE THESE MINISTRIES TO THE CHURCH?

Christ gave these basic ascension gift ministries to the Church for the perfection, edification and strengthening of the saints.

For the perfecting of the saints, for the work of the ministry, for the edifying of the body of Christ: Till we all come in the unity of the faith, and of the knowledge of the Son of God, unto a perfect man, unto the measure of the stature of the fulness of Christ: That we henceforth be no more children, tossed to and fro, and carried about with every wind of doctrine, by the sleight of men, and cunning craftiness, whereby they lie in wait to deceive; But speaking the truth in love, may grow up into him in all things, which is the head, even Christ. Eph. 4:12–15.

546. WHAT IS AN APOSTLE?

An apostle is a specially-sent messenger and leader whose ministries are:

1. To preach the Gospel.

   By whom we have received grace and apostleship, for obedience to the faith among all nations, for his name: Among whom are ye also the called of Jesus Christ. Rom. 1:5,6.

2. To plant and establish churches.

   Confirming the souls of the disciples, and exhorting them to continue in the faith, and that we must through much tribulation enter into the kingdom of God. Acts 14:22.

3. To bring forth and develop those called to the ministry by giving them guidance and instruction until they can be confirmed in their calling.

   And when they had ordained them elders in every church, and had prayed with fasting, they commended them to the Lord, on whom they believed. Acts 14:23.

4. To carry responsibility in prayer and counsel for the churches and elders who have been confirmed.

   For though ye have ten thousand instructors in Christ, yet have ye not many fathers: for in Christ Jesus I have begotten you through the gospel. For this cause have I sent unto you Timotheus, who is my beloved son, and faithful in the Lord, who shall bring you into remembrance of my ways which be in Christ, as I teach every where in every church. I Cor. 4:15,17.

   My little children, of whom I travail in birth again until Christ be formed in you. Gal. 4:19.

5. To be trail-blazers of first-hand revelation until it is received as doctrine by the church.

   But I certify you, brethren, that the gospel which was

preached of me is not after man. For I neither received it of man, neither was I taught it, but by the revelation of Jesus Christ. But when it pleased God, who separated me from my mother's womb, and called me by his grace, To reveal his Son in me, that I might preach him among the heathen; immediately I conferred not with flesh and blood. Gal. 1:11,12,15,16.

6. To establish believers in foundation truths.

According to the grace of God which is given unto me, as a wise master-builder, I have laid the foundation, and another buildeth thereon. But let every man take heed how he buildeth thereupon. I Cor. 3:10.

7. To take the Gospel in word and demonstration to unreached people.

Yea, so have I strived to preach the gospel, not where Christ was named, lest I should build upon another man's foundation. Rom. 15:20.

8. To correct errors in doctrine or conduct, directly or through giving authority to local churches.

. . . And the rest will I set in order when I come. I Cor. 11:34b.

For I verily, as absent in body, but present in spirit, have judged already, as though I were present, concerning him that hath so done this deed, In the name of our Lord Jesus Christ, when ye are gathered together, and my spirit, with the power of our Lord Jesus Christ, To deliver such an one unto Satan for the destruction of the flesh, that the spirit may be saved in the day of the Lord Jesus. I Cor. 5:3–5.

Now we exhort you, brethren, warn them that are unruly, comfort the feebleminded, support the weak, be patient toward all men. I Thess. 5:14.

547. DID THE MINISTRY OF AN APOSTLE END WITH THE ORIGINAL TWELVE APOSTLES?

No. In the New Testament, many persons were given this title.

Note: Paul became the apostle to the Gentiles.

> *For I speak to you Gentiles, inasmuch as I am the apostle of the Gentiles, I magnify mine office: Rom. 11:13.*

Paul made reference to the "other apostles, and the brothers of the Lord, Cephas . . . and Barnabas."

> *Have we not power to lead about a sister, a wife, as well as other apostles, and as the brethren of the Lord, and Cephas? I Cor. 9:5.*

> *Salute Andronicus and Junia, my kinsmen, and my fellow-prisoners, who are of note among the apostles, who also were in Christ before me. Rom. 16:7.*

548.   WHAT IS A PROPHET?

A prophet is an appointed spokesman for God with the special ministry of:

1. Speaking the word of God.

> *Let the prophets speak two or three, and let the others judge. I Cor. 14:29.*

2. Bringing forth revelation and increased spiritual understanding of the Scriptures.

> *If any thing be revealed to another that sitteth by, let the first hold his peace. I Cor. 14:30.*

3. Predicting and warning of future events.

> *And in these days came prophets from Jerusalem unto Antioch. And there stood up one of them named Agabus, and signified by the spirit that there should be great dearth throughout all the world: which came to pass in the days of Claudius Caesar. Acts 11:27,28.*

4. Providing direction in ministry, doctrine and worship.

> *Now there were in the church that was at Antioch certain prophets and teachers . . . As they ministered to the Lord, and fasted, the Holy Ghost said, Separate me Barnabas and Saul for the work whereunto I have called them. Acts 13:12.*

5. Keeping the flow of God's Word fresh and alive in the Local Church.

But he that prophesieth speaketh unto men to edification, and exhortation, and comfort. I Cor. 14:3.

6. Revealing the secrets of men's hearts as a sign to unbelievers.

But if all prophesy, and there come in one that believeth not, or one unlearned, he is convinced of all, he is judged of all: And thus are the secrets of his heart made manifest; and so falling down on his face he will worship God, and report that God is in you of a truth. I Cor. 14:24,25.

7. Acting as members of the presbytery, they confirm and impart spiritual blessings and gifts.

And Judas and Silas, being prophets themselves, exhorted the brethren with many words, and confirmed them. Acts 15:32.

549.   WHAT IS AN EVANGELIST?

An evangelist is one who proclaims the Gospel with the special ministries of:

1. Extending the message of the kingdom to unreached areas.

Therefore they that were scattered abroad went every where preaching the word. Acts 8:4.

And this gospel of the kingdom shall be preached in all the world for a witness unto all nations ... Matt. 24:14.

2. Demonstrating the Gospel of the Kingdom by works of faith and power.

And they went forth and preached every where, the Lord working with them, and confirming the word with signs following ... Mark 16:20.

And the hand of the Lord was with them: and a great number believed, and turned to the Lord. Acts 11:21.

3. Exhorting men to repent, believe and obey the Gospel.

Preach the word; be instant in season, out of season; reprove, rebuke, exhort with all longsuffering and doctrine. But watch thou in all things, endure afflictions, do the work of an evangelist, make full proof of thy ministry. II Tim. 4:2,5.

. . . it pleased God by the foolishness of preaching to save them that believe. I Cor. 1:21.

These things speak, and exhort, and rebuke with all authority, Let no man despise thee. Titus 2:15.

4. Maintaining communication among the churches and ministers.

I . . . sent Timotheus, our brother, and minister of God, and our fellow-labourer in the gospel of Christ, to establish you, and comfort you concerning your faith. But now when Timotheus came from you unto us, and brought us good tidings of your faith and charity, and that ye have good remembrance of us always, desiring greatly to see us, as we also to see you. I Thess. 3:2,6.

5. Ordaining elders and establishing or restoring order in various churches.

For this cause left I thee in Crete, that thou shouldest set in order the things that are wanting, and ordain elders in every city, as I had appointed thee. Titus 1:5.

550. WHAT IS A PASTOR?

A pastor is an undershepherd appointed by the Great Shepherd, Jesus Christ, to tend a local fold. His special ministries are:

1. Feeding and nourishing the people God puts under his care.

Feed the flock of God which is among you, taking the oversight thereof, not by constraint, but willingly; not for filthy lucre, but of a ready mind. Neither as being lords over God's heritage, but being ensamples to the flock. And when the chief Shepherd shall appear, ye shall receive a crown of glory that fadeth not away. I Peter 5:2–4.

. . . Feed my sheep. John 21:16.

2. Taking the responsibility of protecting the door of the fold from false teachers.

Take heed therefore unto yourselves and to all the flock over which the Holy Ghost hath made you overseers, to feed the church of God which he hath purchased with his own blood. For I know this, that after my departing shall grievous wolves enter in among you, not sparing the flock. Also of your own selves shall men arise, speaking perverse things, to draw away disciples after them. Therefore watch . . . Acts 20:28–31.

. . . He that entereth not by the door into the sheepfold, but climbeth up some other way, the same is a thief and a robber. John 10:1.

3. Disciplining the local congregation as a whole or dealing in love with any individual who needs reproof or correction.

And we beseech you, brethren, to know them which labour among you, and are over you in the Lord, and admonish you. Now we exhort you, brethren, warn them that are unruly, comfort the feebleminded, support the weak, be patient toward all men. I Thess. 5:12,14.

4. Governing and guiding the congregation.

Obey them that have the rule over you, and submit yourselves: for they watch for your souls, as they that must give account, that they may do it with joy, and not with grief: for that is unprofitable for you. Heb. 13:17.

Let the elders that rule well be counted worthy of double honor, especially they who labor in the word and doctrine. I Tim. 5:17.

For if a man know not how to rule his own house, how shall he take care of the church of God? I Tim. 3:5.

551. WHAT IS A TEACHER?

A teacher brings the knowledge of truth to others by careful instructions, illustrations and example. His special ministries include:

1. Clarifying the application of truth in our lives to enable us to obey the word.

But be ye doers of the word, and not hearers only, deceiving your own selves. James 1:22.

2. Organizing truth into topical studies and practical disciplines.

. . . If ye continue in my word, then are ye my disciples indeed; And ye shall know the truth, and the truth shall make you free. John 8:31,32.

3. Providing motivation for further study in the Scriptures by making truth interesting and rewarding.

> *These (Bereans) were more noble than those in Thessalonica, in that they received the word with all readiness of mind, and searched the scriptures daily, whether these things were so. Acts 17:11.*

4. Carefully examining the truth they have already experienced and communicating revealed truth to bring unity of the faith through understanding.

> *Now I beseech you, brethren, by the name of our Lord Jesus Christ, that ye all speak the same thing, and that there be no divisions among you; but that ye be perfectly joined together in the same mind and in the same judgment. I Cor. 1:10.*

552. WHAT ARE GOVERNMENTS IN THE CHURCH?

Governments are those who guide, steer or pilot the church. This ministry includes:

1. Taking oversight of the local congregation.

> *The elders which are among you I exhort ... feed the flock of God which is among you, taking the oversight thereof, not by constraint, but willingly; not for filthy lucre, but of a ready mind; Neither as being lords over God's heritage, but being ensamples to the flock. I Peter 5:1–3.*

2. Presiding in council meetings to initiate action and finalize decisions.

> *And after they had held their peace, James answered, saying, Men and brethren, hearken unto me: ... wherefore my sentence is that we trouble not them, which from among the Gentiles are turned to God: But that we write unto them ... Acts 15:13,19,20.*

3. Administrative duties, managing business and being stewards of money and property of the local church.

Note: Governments are not only for the pastor but rather may be exercised by any of the five ministry gifts or by the elders, deacons and deaconesses who make up the presbytery of the

Church and who work with the pastor. This is a spiritual ministry.

553. WHAT IS AN ELDER?

An elder is one whose ministry is consistent with his age, experience and dignity. He shares with the presbytery the responsibility of governing the Church, exercises authority in spiritual matters of the congregation and is set apart for anointing the sick with oil, serving the Lord's Supper and teaching.

> Let the elders that rule well be counted worthy of double honour, especially they who labour in the word and doctrine. I Tim. 5:17.

Note: An elder, a presbyter or bishop all refer to an overseer—one who watches over the Local Church. One of these elders comes to be recognized by the other elders as the one to whom God gives the leadership.

> For this cause left I thee in Crete, that thou shouldest set in order the things that are wanting, and ordain elders in every city, as I had appointed thee: If any be blameless, the husband of one wife, having faithful children not accused of riot or unholy. For a bishop (elder) must be blameless, as a steward of God; not selfwilled, not soon angry, not given to wine, no striker, not given to filthy lucre; But a lover of hospitality, a lover of good men, sober, just, holy, temperate; Holding fast the faithful word as he hath been taught, that he may be able by sound doctrine both to exhort and to convince the gainsayers. Titus 1:5–9.

554. WHAT IS A DEACON?

A deacon is a Christian teacher who is called to serve and minister to the needs of the poor and to the needs of the Local Church. His duties include the serving of the Lord's Supper, prayer for the sick, exhortation of the Scriptures.

> And in those days, when the number of the disciples was multiplied, there arose a murmuring of the Grecians against the Hebrews, because their widows were neglected in the daily ministration. Then the twelve called the multitude of the disciples unto them, and said, It is not reason

> *that we should leave the word of God, and serve tables.
> Wherefore, brethren, look ye out among you seven men of
> honest report, full of the Holy Ghost and wisdom, whom
> we may appoint over this business. But we will give our-
> selves continually to prayer, and to the ministry of the
> word. And the saying pleased the whole multitude: and
> they chose Stephen, a man full of faith and of the Holy
> Ghost, and Philip, and Prochorus, and Nicanor, and
> Timon, and Parmenas, and Nicolas a proselyte of An-
> tioch: Whom they set before the apostles: and when they
> had prayed, they laid their hands on them. Acts 6:1–6.*

555. WHAT IS A DEACONESS?

A deaconess is a Christian teacher who is called to minister to
the Local Church. Her responsibilities include instructing other
women in the care of the sick, tending to the needs of the poor,
preparing the Lord's Supper, praying and interceding for the
saints, exhorting the Word.

> *The aged women likewise, that they be in behavior as be-
> cometh holiness, not false accusers, not given to much
> wine, teachers of good things; That they may teach the
> young women to be sober, to love their husbands, to love
> their children, To be discreet, chaste, keepers at home,
> good, obedient to their husbands, that the word of God be
> not blasphemed. Titus 2:3–5.*

556. DOES A WOMAN HAVE A MINISTRY IN THE CHURCH?

Yes. In Christ (the body of Christ—the Church), there is neither
male nor female. Christ, who is the Head, anoints whom He will
to minister in His Church.

> *There is neither Jew nor Greek, there is neither bond nor
> free, there is neither male nor female: for ye are all one in
> Christ Jesus. Gal. 3:28.*

557. WHAT ARE HELPS IN THE CHURCH?

The ministry of helps in the church is a Spirit-led ministry that
addicts itself to bearing the natural and spiritual burdens of the
saints.

> *And God hath set some in the church, first apostles, sec-*

ondarily prophets, thirdly teachers, after that miracles, then gifts of healings, helps, governments, diversities of tongues. I Cor. 12:28.

I commend unto you Phebe, our sister, who is a servant of the church which is at Cenchrea, That ye receive her in the Lord, as becometh saints, and that ye assist her in whatever business she hath need of you; for she hath been a (helper) of many, and of myself also. Greet Priscilla and Aquila, my helpers in Christ Jesus, Greet Mary, who bestowed much labor on us. Greet Urbanus, our helper in Christ, and Stachys, my beloved. Greet Tryphena and Tryphosa, who labored much in the Lord. Rom. 16:1,2,3,6,9,12. New Scofield Reference Bible.

I beseech you, brethren (ye know the house of Stephanas, that it is the first fruits of Achaia, and that they have (devoted) themselves to the ministry of the saints). I Cor. 16:15. New Scofield Reference Bible.

STUDY QUESTIONS—Chapter 49

1. What are the ministries of the Holy Spirit? Name them.
2. For what purpose did God give these ministries to the church?
3. Briefly define each of the five ministries.
4. What is a deacon?
5. What is a deaconess?
6. What is the ministry of helps?
7. Write: Eph. 4:11,12 and Rom. 12:4–6.

Chapter 50

THE MINISTRY OF WORSHIP, PRAISE AND THANKSGIVING

558. **WHAT IS WORSHIP, PRAISE AND THANKSGIVING?**

It is a ministry of giving to God spiritual offerings and sacrifices.

> *Ye also, as lively stones are built up a spiritual house, an holy priesthood, to offer up spiritual sacrifices, acceptable to God by Jesus Christ. I Peter 2:5.*

559. **WHAT ARE SPIRITUAL OFFERINGS?**

Spiritual offerings are the praise and thanksgiving we willingly present to God.

> *I will praise the name of God with a song, and will magnify him with thanksgiving. This also shall please the Lord better than an ox or bullock, that has horns and hoofs. Ps. 69:30,31.*

560. **WHAT IS A SACRIFICE?**

A sacrifice is anything that is consecrated (set aside) and offered to God that costs us something. It always involves the denying of self or surrender of the will.

> *. . . Nay, but I will surely buy it of thee at a price: neither will I offer burnt-offerings unto the Lord my God of that which doth cost me nothing . . . II Sam. 24:24.*

> *. . . Nay; but I will verily buy it for the full price: for I will not take that which is thine for the Lord, nor offer burnt-offerings without cost. I Chron. 21:24.*

561. WHAT SPIRITUAL SACRIFICES DOES GOD DESIRE OF US?

There are three spiritual sacrifices God desires from us as worshippers:

A. Our bodies.

> *I beseech you therefore, brethren, by the mercies of God, that ye present your bodies a living sacrifice, holy, acceptable unto God, which is your reasonable service. Rom. 12:1.*

B. Our lips.

> *By him therefore let us offer the sacrifice of praise to God continually, that is, the fruit of our lips giving thanks to his name. Heb. 13:15.*

> *I will bless the Lord at all times: his praise shall continually be in my mouth. Ps. 34:1.*

C. Our service and hospitality.

> *And do not neglect doing good and sharing for with such sacrifices God is pleased. Heb. 13:16 NASV.*

562. WHAT IS WORSHIP?

Worship is the purest form of adoration we can offer to God. It is initiated in us through God who reveals Himself to us through the Holy Spirit causing us to completely trust and submit ourselves to the Lord. It is giving glory to God with the aid of the Holy Spirit for circumstances or situations that are hard to understand or accept.

> *But the hour cometh, and now is, when the true worshippers shall worship the Father in spirit and in truth: for the Father seeketh such to worship him. God is a Spirit: and they that worship him must worship him in spirit and in truth. John 4:23,24.*

> *And behold, there came a great wind from the wilderness, and smote the four corners of the house, and it fell upon the young men and they are dead; and I only am escaped alone to tell thee. Then Job arose, and rent his mantle, and shaved his head, and fell down upon the ground, and*

*worshipped. And said, Naked came I out of my mother's
womb, and naked shall I return thither: The Lord gave,
and the Lord hath taken away; blessed be the name of the
Lord. Job 1:19–21.*

563. CAN WE WORSHIP GOD WITHOUT SUBMITTING TO HIS WILL?

No. Worship demands the yielding of our will to the will of God.
Worship is saying "yes" to everything God sends or requires of
us.

*And we know that all things work together for good to
them that love God, to them who are the called according
to his purpose. Rom. 8:28.*

*Then Job arose, and rent his mantle, and shaved his head,
and fell down upon the ground, and worshipped. And said,
Naked came I out of my mother's womb, and naked shall
I return thither: the Lord gave, and the Lord hath taken
away; blessed be the name of the Lord. Job 1:20,21.*

BIBLE NARRATIVE: Daniel worshipped God against the
command of the king and was cast into the lion's den. Dan. 6.

564. HOW DOES NEW COVENANT WORSHIP DIFFER FROM OLD COVENANT WORSHIP?

Under the Old Covenant, God's people worshipped Him in temples. To them, he was a God who was outside of them. In the
New Covenant, we become the temples of God and God dwells
in us by the Holy Spirit. Some basic differences between the two
covenants are:

A. Under the Old Covenant, a few men were chosen as priests
   (Levites) and one as a high priest. In the New Covenant, we
   are all priests and our worship is made acceptable to God by
   our high priest, Jesus Christ.

   *Unto him that loved us, and washed us from our sins in his
   own blood, and hath made us kings and priests unto God
   and his Father; to him be glory and dominion for ever and
   ever. Amen. Rev. 1:5,6.*

B. Under the Old Covenant, only the high priest could enter
   God's actual presence and then only once a year. Under the

New Covenant, we all have access into His presence and God comes to live within us.

Having therefore, brethren, boldness to enter into the holiest by the blood of Jesus, By a new and living way, which he hath consecrated for us, through the veil, that is to say, his flesh. Heb. 10:19,20.

C. Under the Old Covenant, the blood of bulls and goats covered sins for a time but this sacrifice had to be repeated again and again. In the New Covenant, the blood of Jesus Christ takes away sin forever and frees our conscience from the remembrance of sin.

But in those sacrifices there is a remembrance again made of sins every year. For it is not possible that the blood of bulls and goats should take away sins. Heb. 10:3,4.

How much more shall the blood of Christ, who through the eternal Spirit offered himself without spot to God, purge your conscience from dead works to serve the living God? Heb. 9:14.

D. Under the Old Covenant, God required sacrifices of animals and birds for sin. In the New Covenant, there is no sacrifice for sin since Jesus Christ offered Himself as a sacrifice for us. In turn, we offer ourselves as living sacrifices in joyful service to God.

By him therefore let us offer the sacrifices of praise to God continually, that is, the fruit of our lips giving thanks to his name. But to do good and to communicate forget not; for with such sacrifices God is well pleased. Heb. 13:15,16.

E. Under the Old Covenant, the will of God was written on tablets of stone and imposed from without. In the New Covenant, God puts the desire to please Him within us.

I delight to do thy will, O my God: yea, thy law is within my heart. Ps. 40:8.

F. Under the Old Covenant, worship was restricted to one special place. In the New Covenant, worship is in the Spirit and is not limited to sacred places or times.

And there I will meet with thee, and I will commune with thee from above the mercy seat, from between the two

> *cherubim which are upon the ark of the testimony* . . .
> *Exod. 25:22.*

565. HOW DID THE EARLY CHRISTIANS WORSHIP?

They came together and allowed the Holy Spirit to direct their worship ministry to each other.

> *For we are the true circumcision, who worship in the Spirit of God and glory in Christ Jesus and put no confidence in the flesh. Phil. 3:3 NASV.*

> *How is it then, brethren? When ye come together, every one of you hath a psalm, hath a doctrine, hath a tongue, hath a revelation, hath an interpretation. Let all things be done unto edifying. I Cor. 14:26.*

566. HOW DO WE WORSHIP TODAY?

God is restoring spiritual worship to His Church by sending visitation of his Spirit upon his people everywhere.

> *And it shall come to pass afterward, that I will pour out of my spirit upon all flesh; and your sons and your daughters shall prophesy, your old men shall dream dreams, your young men shall see visions: And also upon the servants and upon the handmaids in those days will I pour out my spirit. Joel 2:28,29.*

> *Repent ye therefore, and be converted, that your sins may be blotted out, when the times of refreshing shall come from the presence of the Lord. Acts 3:19.*

567. WHAT IS A SPIRITUAL VISITATION?

It is a season of refreshing caused by the unusual presence of God. It is like rain falling upon dry ground.

> *Be glad then, ye children of Zion, and rejoice in the Lord your God: for he hath given you the former rain moderately, and he will cause to come down for you the rain, the former rain, and the latter rain in the first month. Joel 2:23.*

568.   WHAT BLESSINGS COME WITH SPIRITUAL VISITATION?

As God sends the rain of His Presence upon us, we drink until the well within us overflows and becomes a river to others. The blessings which we can experience at times of visitation include:

A. Fresh revelation from the Scriptures.

> *My doctrine shall drop as the rain, my speech shall distil as the dew, as the small rain upon the tender herb, and as the showers upon the grass. Deut. 32:2.*

B. Birth of spiritual songs and choruses.

> *. . . be filled with the Spirit; Speaking to yourselves in psalms and hymns and spiritual songs, singing and making melody in your heart to the Lord. Eph. 5:18,19.*

> *Let the word of Christ dwell in you richly in all wisdom; teaching and admonishing one another in psalms and hymns and spiritual songs, singing with grace in your hearts to the Lord. Col. 3:16.*

C. Restoration of life and truth.

> *Be glad then, ye children of Zion, and rejoice in the LORD your God: for he hath given you the former rain moderately, and he will cause to come down for you the rain, the former rain, and the latter rain in the first month . . . And I will restore to you the years that the locust hath eaten, the cankerworm, and the caterpillar, and the palmerworm, my great army which I sent among you. And ye shall eat in plenty, and be satisfied, and praise the name of the LORD your God, that hath dealt wondrously with you: and my people shall never be ashamed. And ye shall know that I am in the midst of Israel, and that I am the LORD your God, and none else: and my people shall never be ashamed. Joel 2:23,25–27.*

D. Miracles of deliverance.

> *And it shall come to pass, that whosoever shall call on the name of the LORD shall be delivered: for in mount Zion and in Jerusalem shall be deliverance, as the LORD hath said, and in the remnant whom the LORD shall call. Joel 2:32.*

Then the eyes of the blind shall be opened, and the ears of the deaf shall be unstopped. Then shall the lame man leap as an hart, and the tongue of the dumb sing: for in the wilderness shall waters break out, and streams in the desert. Isa. 35:5,6.

E. Calling out of God's true people to gather around the Lord.

. . . and unto him shall the gathering of the people be. Gen. 49:10.

And the ransomed of the Lord shall return, and come to Zion with songs and everlasting joy upon their heads: they shall obtain joy and gladness, and sorrow and sighing shall flee away. Isa. 35:10.

Gather my saints together unto me; those that have made a covenant with me by sacrifice. Ps. 50:5.

F. Unity of the Spirit.

Thy watchmen shall lift up the voice; with the voice together shall they sing: for they shall see eye to eye, when the Lord shall bring again Zion. Break forth into joy, sing together, ye waste places of Jerusalem: for the Lord hath comforted his people, he hath redeemed Jerusalem. Isa. 52:8,9.

569. WHAT DID JESUS TEACH US ABOUT WORSHIPPING GOD?

Jesus came to teach us a new way of worshipping God . . . worshipping Him in spirit and in truth.

God is a Spirit: and they that worship him must worship him in spirit and in truth. John 4:24.

570. HOW CAN WE WORSHIP "IN SPIRIT AND IN TRUTH"?

When we give ourselves to God in faith with the sincere desire to bless Him, the Holy Spirit makes His Presence real to us and gives us the ability to express our love for God.

Bless the Lord, O my soul: and all that is within me, bless his holy name. Ps. 103:1.

I will praise thee, O Lord, with my whole heart; I will

shew forth all thy marvellous works. I will be glad and rejoice in thee: I will sing praise to thy name, O thou most High. Ps. 9:1,2.

571. WHY DOES GOD WANT ONLY SPIRITUAL WORSHIP?

Natural man cannot please God. He has given us the gift of His Spirit to give us a spiritual language and an entrance into His Presence.

For to be carnally minded is death; but to be spiritually minded is life and peace. Because the carnal mind is enmity against God: for it is not subject to the law of God, neither indeed can be. So then they that are in the flesh cannot please God. Rom. 8:6–8.

But the natural man receiveth not the things of the Spirit of God: for they are foolishness unto him: neither can he know them, because they are spiritually discerned. I Cor. 2:14.

572. HOW DO WE ENTER INTO GOD'S PRESENCE?

We follow the order He has given us giving Him thanksgiving for what He has done and praise for what He means to us.

Enter into his gates with thanksgiving (a thank offering) and into his courts with praise: be thankful unto him, and bless his name. Ps. 100:4.

573. WHAT IS THANKSGIVING?

In thanksgiving, we express our gratitude to God for His divine goodness and mercies and His gifts to us.

Praise ye the Lord. O give thanks unto the Lord; for he is good: for his mercy endureth for ever. Who can utter the mighty acts of the Lord? who can shew forth all his praise? Ps. 106:1,2.

Great is the Lord, and greatly to be praised; and his greatness is unsearchable. Ps. 145:3.

574. WHAT IS PRAISE?

In praise, we express honor and love for the person of God rather than His gifts.

I will give thee thanks in the great congregation: I will praise thee among much people. Ps. 35:18.

Whoso offereth praise glorifieth me: and to him that ordereth his conversation aright will I shew the salvation of God. Ps. 50:23.

Note: Praise and thanksgiving both give glory to God and are frequently combined as one ministry.

575.   WHY DOES GOD WANT US TO PRAISE HIM?

Praise creates a dwelling place for the presence of God in and with His people.

But thou art holy, O thou that inhabitest the praises of Israel. Ps. 22:3.

Saying, I will declare thy name unto my brethren, in the midst of the church will I sing praise unto thee. Heb. 2:12.

576.   HOW DO WE EXPRESS OUR PRAISE?

By presenting our bodies to God, we co-operate with the Holy Spirit in any of the following ways:

I urge you therefore, brethren, by the mercies of God, to present your bodies a living and holy sacrifice, acceptable to God, which is your spiritual service of worship. Rom. 12:1 NASV.

A. Lifting up our hands.

Because thy lovingkindness is better than life, my lips shall praise thee. Thus will I bless thee while I live: I will lift up my hands in thy name. Ps. 63:3–4.

B. Clapping our hands.

O clap your hands, all ye people; shout unto God with the voice of triumph. Ps. 47:1.

C. Singing.

Sing unto God, sing praises to his name: extol him that rideth upon the heavens by his name JAH, and rejoice before him. Ps. 68:4.

D. Playing musical instruments.

Praise him with the sound of the trumpet; praise him with psaltery and harp. Praise him with the timbrel and dance: praise him with stringed instruments and organs. Ps. 150:4,5.

E. Rejoicing and laughing.

Rejoice in the Lord alway: and again I say rejoice. Phil. 4:4.

Then was our mouth filled with laughter, and our tongue with singing: then said they among the heathen, The Lord hath done great things for them. Ps. 126:2.

F. Shouting and cries of victory.

Cry out and shout, thou inhabitant of Zion: for great is the Holy One of Israel in the midst of thee. Isa. 12:6.

G. Extravagant giving.

BIBLE NARRATIVES: Mary of Bethany broke the alabaster box, Matt. 26:6–13; The widow gave all, Luke 21:1–4.

577. WHY IS WORSHIP AND PRAISE IMPORTANT IN THE LOCAL CHURCH?

Through worship and praise we minister to God creating a spiritual dwelling place for Him where He can come and minister to us.

In whom all the building fitly framed together groweth into an holy temple in the Lord: In whom ye also are builded together for an habitation of God through the Spirit. Eph. 2:21,22.

578. HOW DO WE MINISTER TO GOD?

We minister to God through psalms, hymns, and spiritual songs.

579. WHAT ARE HYMNS?

Hymns are Christian songs of praise.

580. WHY DO WE SING HYMNS?

Hymns are a reminder to us that the Lord has been good to us and shall continue to visit us with His goodness and mercy.

*I call to remembrance my song in the night: I commune
with mine own heart: and my spirit made diligent search.
Ps. 77:6.*

581. WHEN SHOULD WE SING HYMNS?

We should sing hymns in times of testing and when we bless the
Lord in the Local Church services.

*Speaking to yourselves in psalms and hymns and spiritual
songs, singing and making melody in your heart to the
Lord; Giving thanks always for all things unto God and
the Father in the name of our Lord Jesus Christ.
Eph. 5:19,20.*

582. SHOULD WE MEMORIZE THE HYMNS?

Yes. If we learn the hymns of the Church, and can sing them
when we are in trouble, the Lord will relieve us of the tension,
anxiety and fear we have during times of hardship and testing.

*Why art thou cast down, O my soul? and why art thou dis-
quieted within me? hope in God: for I shall yet praise him,
who is the health of my countenance, and my God.
Ps. 43:5.*

583. WHAT ARE SPIRITUAL SONGS?

Spiritual songs are songs or choruses of experience or meditation
filled with spiritual truth containing exhortations, prophecies
and praise.

*O come, let us sing unto the Lord: let us make a joyful
noise to the rock of our salvation. Let us come before his
presence with thanksgiving, and make a joyful noise unto
him with psalms. Ps. 95:1,2.*

584. WHEN DO WE SING SPIRITUAL SONGS?

We sing spiritual songs when the Holy Spirit begins to fill the
mind and heart with melody.

*O sing unto the Lord a new song; for he hath done mar-
vellous things: his right hand, and his holy arm, hath got-
ten him the victory. Ps. 98:1.*

585.   WHEN DOES THIS HAPPEN?

In times of prayer, meditation or when we bless the Lord in ou
services.

*Serve the Lord with gladness: come before his presence
with singing. Ps. 100:2.*

586.   HOW IS THIS DONE?

When the Holy Spirit gives us a song, we do not need to search
for words, for words come to mind and flow out of us as a river.
We begin to sing the spiritual songs we feel in our heart . . . our
words . . . our feelings . . . our song.

*I will sing of the mercies of the Lord forever: with my
mouth will I make known thy faithfulness to all generations. Ps. 89:1.*

587.   HOW DO WE LEARN TO PRAISE GOD?

We learn to praise the Lord as we join others in blending our
voices in a great chorus of praise to God.

*Let the word of Christ dwell in you richly in all wisdom;
teaching and admonishing one another in psalms and
hymns and spiritual songs, singing with grace in your
hearts to the Lord. Col. 3:16.*

STUDY QUESTIONS—Chapter 50

1. What three sacrifices does God desire from us?
2. Can we worship God without submitting to His will?
3. How does New Covenant worship differ from Old Covenant worship?
4. How did the early Christians worship?
5. What blessings come with spiritual visitation?
6. Why does God want only spiritual worship?
7. What is praise?
8. How do we express our praise?
9. Why do we sing hymns?
10. What are spiritual songs?
11. Write Ps. 100:4; Col. 3:16; Ps. 69:30,31.

Chapter 51

PRAYER AND FASTING

588. WHAT IS PRAYER?

Prayer is communicating with God.

589. HOW DO WE COMMUNICATE WITH GOD?

We communicate with God by talking directly to Him.

> *O thou that hearest prayer, unto thee shall all flesh come. Ps. 65:2.*

590. HOW DO WE TALK TO GOD?

We talk to God orally or mentally, in a formal or informal fashion.

> *I will therefore that men pray everywhere, lifting up holy hands, without wrath and doubting. I Tim. 2:8.*

591. IS PRAYER A FORM OF WORSHIP?

Yes. It is acknowledging the sovereignty and power of God with thanksgiving.

> *Be careful for nothing; but in every thing by prayer and supplication with thanksgiving let your requests be made known unto God. Phil. 4:6.*

592. WHAT METHOD OF PRAYER IS MOST ACCEPTABLE TO GOD?

All methods of prayer are acceptable to God when they are:

1. Sincere.

> *He forgetteth not the prayer of the humble. Ps. 9:12.*

2. Offered with reverence and godly fear.

Seek the Lord and his strength, seek his face continually. Say ye, Save us, O God of our salvation, and gather us together, and deliver us from the heathen, that we may give thanks to thy holy name, and glory in thy praise. I Chron. 16:11,35.

3. Accompanied with faith ... believing God will hear, answer and fulfill His Word.

I will call upon the Lord, who is worthy to be praised: so shall I be saved from mine enemies. Ps. 18:3.

593.   HOW MANY KINDS OF PRAYER ARE THERE?

There are five kinds of prayer:

1. Personal prayer (private prayers).

But thou, when thou prayest, enter into thy closet, and when thou hast shut thy door, pray to thy Father which is in secret; and thy Father which seeth in secret shall reward thee openly. Matt. 6:6.

2. Community prayer (family prayers or group worship not held in the church).

Help us, O Lord our God; for we rest on thee, and in thy name we go against this multitude. O Lord, thou art our God; let not man prevail against thee. II Chron. 14:11.

3. Congregational prayers (held in the service of the sanctuary).

Peter therefore was kept in prison: but prayer was made without ceasing of the church unto God for him. Acts 12:5.

4. Intercessory prayer.

And he saw that there was no man, and wondered that there was no intercessor ... Isa. 59:16.

5. Travailing prayer.

My little children, of whom I travail in birth again until Christ be formed in you. Gal. 4:19.

594.   WHAT IS PERSONAL PRAYER?

Personal prayer is the private prayer we pray to God in secret for the sake of fellowship with Him or to tell Him our personal, private needs.

> *But thou, when thou prayest, enter into thy closet, and when thou hast shut thy door, pray to thy Father which is in secret; and thy Father which seeth in secret shall reward thee openly. Matt. 6:6.*

595. WHAT IS OUR ROLE IN PERSONAL PRAYER?

Our role in personal prayer is:

A. To come into God's presence with praise and thanksgiving inviting Him to meet with us for fellowship or to hear our personal petitions.

> *Enter into his gates with thanksgiving, and into his courts with praise: be thankful unto him, and bless his name. Ps. 100:4.*

B. To yield ourselves to the Holy Spirit in worship and as our spirit responds to Him, we begin speaking mysteries to God in an unknown tongue.

> *Likewise the Spirit also helpeth our infirmities: for we know not what we should pray for as we ought: but the Spirit itself maketh intercession for us with groanings which cannot be uttered. And he that searcheth the hearts knoweth what is the mind of the Spirit, because he maketh intercession for the saints according to the will of God. Rom. 8:26,27.*

C. To meditate reverently in God's presence——listening, learning and rejoicing. During this time, the Holy Spirit may inspire a word of Scripture, or a word of comfort or instruction.

> *Let the words of my mouth, and the meditations of my heart, be acceptable in thy sight, O Lord, my strength, and my redeemer. Ps. 19:14.*

> *I will stand upon my watch, and set me upon the tower, and will watch to see what he will say unto me, and what I shall answer when I am reproved. And the Lord answered me, and said, Write the vision, and make it plain upon tables, that he may run that readeth it. Hab. 2:1,2.*

Now we have received, not the spirit of the world, but the spirit which is of God; that we might know the things that are freely given to us of God. Which things also we speak, not in the words which man's wisdom teacheth; but which the Holy Ghost teacheth; comparing spiritual things with spiritual. I Cor. 2:12,13.

D. To read the Scriptures the Holy Spirit has inspired to us and search out related Scriptures.

These were more noble than those in Thessalonica, in that they received the word with all readiness of mind, and searched the scriptures daily, whether those things were so. Acts 17:11.

E. To leave the place of personal prayer renewed in spirit and in mind.

And be not conformed to this world, but be ye transformed by the renewing of your mind, that ye may prove what is that good and acceptable, and perfect, will of God. Rom. 12:2.

596. WHAT BENEFITS DO WE RECEIVE FROM PERSONAL PRAYER?

We receive the joy of having fellowship with the Lord, understanding of the Scriptures, comfort, guidance and power to overcome temptations.

And he said unto them, why sleep ye? rise and pray, lest ye enter into temptation. Luke 22:46.

But ye, beloved, building up yourselves on your most holy faith, praying in the Holy Ghost, Keep yourselves in the love of God . . . Jude 20, 21a.

So shall they fear the name of the Lord from the west, and his glory from the rising of the sun. When the enemy shall come in like a flood, the Spirit of the Lord shall lift up a standard against him. Isa. 59:19.

597. WHAT IS COMMUNITY PRAYER?

Community prayer is prayer offered up to God by a group of believers who pray for each other and intercede on behalf of others.

BIBLE NARRATIVES: Church prays for boldness in preaching, Acts. 4:23–31; Church prays for Peter's release from prison, Acts 12:5–17.

Note: It is important that proper leadership be present at all community prayer meetings.

598. DOES GOD HELP US TO PRAY?

Yes. He has given us the Holy Spirit to pray for us if we turn ourselves over to Him and has given us a language of the Spirit (tongues) that He may use our lips to pray through us according to God's will.

> *Likewise the Spirit also helpeth our infirmities: for we know not what we should pray for as we ought: but the Spirit itself maketh intercession for us with groanings which cannot be uttered. And he that searcheth the hearts knoweth what is the mind of the Spirit, because he maketh intercession for the saints according to the will of God. Rom. 8:26,27.*

599. WHY IS PRAYING IN TONGUES NECESSARY?

Since we do not know how to pray, the Holy Spirit comes to our aid and pleads with God in our behalf.

> *. . . for we do not know how to pray as we should, but the Spirit Himself intercedes for us with groanings too deep for words. Rom. 8:26 NASV.*

600. WHAT DOES PRAYING IN TONGUES DO FOR US?

It is the means God has given to us to pray in the Spirit and be built up in faith.

> *But ye, beloved, building up yourselves on your most holy faith, praying in the Holy Ghost. Jude 20.*

> *He that speaketh in an unknown tongue edifieth himself . . . I Cor. 14:4.*

> *For he that speaketh in an unknown tongue speaketh not unto men, but unto God: for no man understandeth him; howbeit in the spirit he speaketh mysteries. I Cor. 14:2.*

601.   IS IT BETTER TO PRAY IN TONGUES OR WITH UNDER-STANDING?

Both are necessary. We pray in a way that fits the occasion. If we are praying aloud with others, we pray with the understanding. In personal prayer, it is better to pray in tongues.

> *What is it then? I will pray with the spirit, and I will pray with the understanding also. I will sing with the spirit, and I will sing with the understanding also. Else when thou shalt bless with the spirit, how shall he that occupieth the room of the unlearned say Amen at thy giving of thanks, seeing he understandeth not what thou sayest? For thou verily givest thanks well, but the other is not edified. I Cor. 14:15–17.*

602.   HOW LONG DOES IT TAKE THE SPIRIT TO PRAY THROUGH US?

The time varies ... it can take a few minutes or continue for many days or months.

BIBLE NARRATIVE: Daniel prayed for twenty-one days. Dan. 10.

603.   HOW DO WE KNOW WHEN OUR PETITION HAS BEEN HEARD BY GOD?

The burden of prayer lifts from us and we have great inner peace.

> *And this is the confidence that we have in him, that, if we ask anything according to his will, he heareth us: And if we know that he hear us, whatsoever we ask, we know that we have the petitions that we desired of him. I John 5:14,15.*

604.   WHAT IS CONGREGATIONAL PRAYER?

Congregational prayer is prayer offered to God by the members of a Local Church for the Body of Christ, the government and all mankind.

> *I exhort therefore, that, first of all, supplications, prayers, intercessions, and giving of thanks, be made for all men; For kings, and for all that are in authority; that we may*

lead a quiet and peaceable life in all godliness and honesty. I Tim. 2:1,2.

605. WHAT SHOULD WE PRAY FOR IN COMMUNITY OR CONGREGATIONAL PRAYER MEETINGS?

As the Holy Spirit directs, we should intercede for the needs of the church and of the world praying for:

A. Government authorities.

I exhort therefore, that first of all, supplications, prayers, intercessions, and giving of thanks, be made for all men; For kings, and for all that are in authority; that we may lead a quiet and peaceable life in all godliness and honesty. I Tim. 2:1,2.

B. God's servants and their ministries.
And now, Lord, behold their threatenings: and grant unto thy servants that with all boldness they may speak thy word. Acts 4:29.

C. Deliverance of those in distress and need.

Peter therefore was kept in prison: but prayer was made without ceasing of the church unto God for him ... he came to ... where many were gathered together praying. Acts 12:5,12.

D. God to thrust out laborers to harvest.

Then He said to His disciples, The harvest is indeed plentiful, but the laborers are few. So pray the Lord of the harvest to force out and thrust laborers into his harvest. Matt. 9:37,38. Amp.

E. All members of the body of Christ.

Praying always with all prayer and supplication in the Spirit, and watching thereunto with all perseverance and supplication for all saints. Eph. 6:18.

606. WHAT IS THE PURPOSE OF PRAYING TOGETHER?

Praying together was one of the most important activities of the early Church. Only as we pray together does God bring us into one accord by the Spirit uniting our hearts and giving us power with God.

And they continued steadfastly in the apostle's doctrine and fellowship, and in breaking of bread, and in prayers. Acts 2:42.

Behold, how good and how pleasant it is for brethren to dwell together in unity! Ps. 133:1.

And when they heard that, they lifted up their voice to God with one accord, and said, Lord, thou art God, which hast made heaven, and earth, and the sea, and all that in them is ... And when they had prayed, the place was shaken where they were assembled together; and they were all filled with the Holy Ghost, and they spake the word of God with boldness. Acts 4:24,31.

BIBLE NARRATIVES: Prayer meeting after persecution. Acts 4:23–31; Prayer for Peter's release from prison. Acts 12:5–17.

607.   WHAT IS INTERCESSORY PRAYER?

Intercessory Prayer is prayer that is prayed in behalf of another.

Praying always with all prayer and supplication in the Spirit. Eph. 6:18.

As for me, God forbid that I should sin against the Lord in ceasing to pray for you. I Sam. 12:23.

608.   WHO MAY PRAY AS AN INTERCESSOR?

Every believer is called to be a priest before the Lord to intercede and bear the burdens of others through prayer.

... the effectual fervent prayer of a righteous man availeth much. James 5:16.

And hath made us kings and priests unto God and his Father; to him be glory and dominion for ever and ever. Amen. Rev. 1:6.

609.   WHO DIRECTS THE PRAYERS OF AN INTERCESSOR?

The Holy Spirit directs the intercessor's prayer enabling him to pray accurately and effectively according to the wisdom of God.

Likewise the Spirit also helpeth our infirmities: for we know not what we should pray for as we ought: but the

Spirit itself maketh intercession for us with groanings which cannot be uttered. Rom. 8:26.

610. WHAT IS THE ROLE OF AN INTERCESSOR?

The intercessor carries the burden to God in prayer by:

1. Praising God with psalms, hymns and spiritual songs until the Holy Spirit enables him to enter into the holy presence of God.

   Enter into his gates with thanksgiving, and into his courts with praise: be thankful unto him, and bless his name. Ps. 100:4.

2. Praying in the Holy Ghost who initiates the prayer and intercedes through the believer in an unknown tongue ... the intercessor not understanding the petition.

   And he that searcheth the hearts knoweth what is the mind of the Spirit, because he maketh intercession for the saints according to the will of God. Rom. 8:27.

3. Calling on the name of Jesus Christ, the Lord Himself endorses the prayer that is prayed in His name and takes the petition into the presence of the Father.

   ... Verily, verily, I say unto you, Whatsoever ye shall ask the Father in my name, he will give it you. John 16:23.

   Wherefore he is able also to save them to the uttermost that come unto God by him, seeing he (Jesus) ever liveth to make intercession for them. Heb. 7:25.

4. Thanking Christ for the assurance that the prayers have been heard and will be answered.

   And this is the confidence that we have in him, that, if we ask any thing according to his will, he heareth us: And if we know that he hear us, whatsoever we ask, we know that we have the petitions that we desired of him. I John 5:14,15.

611. WHAT IS TRAVAILING PRAYER?

Travailing prayer is Holy Spirit inspired prayer in which we agonize and labor for our own need or for the need of someone near and dear to us.

I have seen the travail, which God hath given to the sons of men to be exercised in it. Eccl. 3:10.

Who in the days of his flesh, when he had offered up prayers and supplications with strong crying and tears unto him that was able to save him from death, and was heard in that he feared. Heb. 5:7.

My little children, of whom I travail in birth again until Christ be formed in you. Gal. 4:19.

612.   WHAT IS THE PURPOSE OF TRAVAILING PRAYER?

Travailing prayer is for the purpose of causing change in an individual or a situation through divine intervention.

My little children, of whom I travail in birth again until Christ be formed in you. Gal. 4:19.

Behold, the Lord God will come with strong hand, and his arm shall rule for him: behold, his reward is with him, and his work before him. Isa. 40:10.

. . . The effectual fervent prayer of a righteous man availeth much. Elias was a man subject to like passions as we are, and he prayed earnestly that it might not rain: and it rained not on the earth by the space of three years and six months. And he prayed again, and the heaven gave rain, and the earth brought forth her fruit. James 5:16–18.

613.   WHAT IS THE ROLE OF THE TRAVAILER?

The role of the travailer is to carry on spiritual warfare against the opposing forces.

For though we walk in the flesh, we do not war after the flesh: (For the weapons of our warfare are not carnal, but mighty through God to the pulling down of strong holds;) Casting down imaginations, and every high thing that exalteth itself against the knowledge of God, and bringing into captivity every thought to the obedience of Christ. II Cor. 10:3–5.

Blessed be the Lord my strength, which teacheth my hands to war, and my fingers to fight: My goodness, and my fortress; my high tower, and my deliverer; my shield, and he

*in whom I trust; who subdueth my people under me.
Ps. 144:1,2.*

614. WHAT IS SPIRITUAL WARFARE?

Spiritual warfare is a battle in which the Holy Spirit equips
the believer with spiritual armor to fight against the forces of
wickedness.

> *Finally, my brethren, be strong in the Lord, and in the
> power of his might. Put on the whole armour of God, that
> ye may be able to stand against the wiles of the devil. Eph.
> 6:10,11.*

615. WHAT IS THE SPIRITUAL ARMOR THE HOLY SPIRIT GIVES US?

The Holy Spirit gives us the following armor:

1. **Truth for the loins.** Through previous encounters in prayer,
   we are strengthened in the knowledge that we can come
   against the lies of the devil.
2. **Righteousness as a breastplate.** According to the Scriptures,
   God hears the prayers of a righteous man . . . one who has the
   freedom to approach God because his conscience is pure and
   he feels no guilt for sin.
3. **Peace for the feet.** Our motive in seeking the Lord must be the
   desire to bring reconciliation between God and man . . . not
   revenge.
4. **Faith as a shield.** Through experience, we believe God gives us
   power not only to overcome the attacks of the devil but to defeat him as well.
5. **Salvation for a helmet.** Having assurance of our salvation
   through the blood of Jesus Christ, we have confidence knowing that we belong to Him and He will help us to fight the
   battle.
6. **The Word for a sword.** The Word that is born in us as a result
   of travailing prayer becomes the sword that destroys the
   enemy.

> *Put on the whole armour of God, that ye may be able to
> stand against the wiles of the devil. Stand therefore, hav-
> ing your loins girt about with truth, and having on the*

breastplate of righteousness; And your feet shod with the preparation of the gospel of peace; Above all, taking the shield of faith, wherewith ye shall be able to quench all the fiery darts of the wicked. And take the helmet of salvation, and the sword of the Spirit, which is the word of God. Eph. 6:11,14–17.

616.   HOW DO WE ENGAGE IN SPIRITUAL WARFARE?

We engage in spiritual warfare in the following ways:

1. After entering into the presence of God through praise and thanksgiving and receiving the armor of God, we confront the enemy with travailing prayer.

   Enter into his gates with thanksgiving, and into his courts with praise: be thankful unto him, and bless his name. Ps. 100:4.

2. The Holy Spirit gives us power and direction through the name of Jesus to fight the forces of evil that have encompassed the mind ... wild imaginings, thoughts infested with unbelief or deceitful or unreal avenues of escape.

   (For the weapons of our warfare are not carnal, but mighty through God to the pulling down of strong holds;) Casting down imaginations, and every high thing that exalteth itself against the knowledge of God, and bringing into captivity every thought to the obedience of Christ. II Cor. 10:4,5.

   Blessed be the Lord my strength, which teacheth my hands to war, and my fingers to fight. Ps. 144:1.

3. The battle is verbal. As we continue to pray in the Spirit in an unknown tongue, we rebuke the lies of the tempter and false accuser.

   Likewise the Spirit also helpeth our infirmities: for we know not what we should pray for as we ought: but the Spirit itself maketh intercession for us with groanings which cannot be uttered. Rom. 8:26.

   And they came to him, and awoke him, saying, Master, master, we perish. Then he arose, and rebuked the wind and the raging of the water: and they ceased, and there was a calm. Luke 8:24.

4. The travailing prayer brings to birth the sword of the Spirit which is the word of God ... that inspired Word that creates faith and hope.

> *Who hath heard such a thing? who hath seen such things? Shall the earth be made to bring forth in one day? or shall a nation be born at once? for as soon as Zion travailed, she brought forth her children. Shall I bring to the birth, and not cause to bring forth? saith the Lord: shall I cause to bring forth, and shut the womb? saith thy God. Isa. 66:8,9.*

> *Neither did we eat any man's bread for nought: but wrought with labour and travail night and day, that we might not be chargeable to any of you: Not because we have not power, but to make ourselves an ensample unto you to follow us. II Thess. 3:8,9.*

5. The song of victory breaks forth. We have overcome by the blood of Jesus and the Word of the Lord!

> *... and this is the victory that overcometh the world, even our faith. Who is he that overcometh the world, but he that believeth that Jesus is the Son of God? I John 5:4,5.*

> *... greater is he that is in you, than he that is in the world. I John 4:4.*

617. HOW OFTEN DO WE PRAY THE INTERCESSORY OR TRAVAILING PRAYER?

We pray the intercessory or travailing prayer again and again until victory is ours.

> *My little children, of whom I travail in birth again until Christ be formed in you. Gal. 4:19.*

> *Praying always with all prayer and supplication in the Spirit, and watching thereunto with all perseverance and supplication for all saints. Eph. 6:18.*

618. CAN WE INDUCE SPIRIT PRAYER WITHIN OURSELVES?

No. The Spirit's aid for intercessory or travailing prayer can only be induced by the Spirit of God within us.

Draw me, we will run after thee . . .
Song of Solomon. I:4.

Draw nigh to God, and he will draw nigh to you . . .
James 4:8.

619. DID JESUS GIVE US A PATTERN FOR PRAYER?

Yes. In the Lord's prayer, Jesus gave us the basic pattern for prayer which is praying for the following things: to honor God's name; to see the Fatherhood of God and accept his will; to ask for our daily needs; to forgive so we may be forgiven; to ask for power to overcome evil forces; to ask to see the demonstration of the power of God on earth.

> *After this manner therefore pray ye: Our Father which art in heaven, Hallowed be thy name. Thy kingdom come. Thy will be done in earth, as it is in heaven. Give us this day our daily bread. And forgive us our debts, as we forgive our debtors. And lead us not into temptation, but deliver us from evil: For thine is the kingdom, and the power, and the glory forever. Amen. Matt. 6:9–13.*

620. WHAT SHOULD BE AVOIDED IN PRAYER?

We should avoid:

1. Vain repetitions. (Saying the same prayers over and over again.)

   > *But when ye pray, use not vain repetitions, as the heathen do: for they think that they shall be heard for their much speaking. Matt. 6:7.*

2. Imposing our will above the will of God.

   > *Ye lust, and have not: ye kill, and desire to have, and cannot obtain: ye fight and war, yet ye have not, because ye ask not. Ye ask, and receive not, because ye ask amiss, that ye may consume it upon your lusts. Jas. 4:2,3.*

3. Bargaining with God.

   > *. . . It is said, Thou shalt not tempt the Lord thy God. Luke 4:12.*

4. Seeking revenge.

But I say unto you, Love your enemies, bless them that curse you, do good to them that hate you, and pray for them which despitefully use you, and persecute you; That ye may be the children of your Father which is in heaven: for he maketh his sun to rise on the evil and on the good, and sendeth rain on the just and on the unjust. For if ye love them which love you, what reward have ye? do not even the publicans the same? Matt. 5:44–46.

621. ACCORDING TO SCRIPTURE, WHAT POSITIONS ARE ASSUMED BY US IN PRAYER?

Four positions are recorded in the Scriptures. They are: standing, kneeling, bowing or falling prostrate; spreading out the hands.

And he kneeled down, and cried with a loud voice, Lord, lay not this sin to their charge . . . Acts 7:60.

And he went a little farther, and fell on his face (Jesus), and prayed, saying, O my Father, if it be possible, let this cup pass from me: nevertheless not as I will, but as thou wilt. Matt. 26:39.

I will therefore that men pray everywhere, lifting up holy hands, without wrath and doubting. I Tim. 2:8.

And when ye stand praying, forgive, if ye have ought against any: that your Father also which is in heaven may forgive you your trespasses. Mark 11:25.

622. WHEN DO WE COMBINE FASTING WITH PRAYER?

Fasting is combined with prayer when:

1. Intercessory or travailing prayer seems to elude us.

   So we fasted and besought our God for this: and he was intreated of us. Ezra 8:23.

   Then shalt thou call, and the LORD shall answer; thou shalt cry, and he shall say, Here I am . . . Isa. 58:9.

2. A serious situation demands it.

   Is not this the fast that I have chosen? to loose the bands of wickedness, to undo the heavy burdens, and to let the oppressed go free, and that ye break every yoke? Isa. 58:6.

3. We need to receive an answer from God for a particular need.

And I set my face unto the Lord God, to seek by prayer and supplications, with fastings, and sackcloth, and ashes: And I prayed unto the LORD my God . . . Dan. 9:3,4.

623. WHAT IS FASTING?

Fasting is voluntarily refraining from food and drink at a time and for a time to give us the opportunity to give our full attention to a particular matter. It must be accompanied with sincere prayer to be effective in securing an answer from God.

624. HOW MANY KINDS OF FASTS ARE THERE?

There are three kinds of fasts . . . regular, partial and complete.

625. WHAT IS A REGULAR FAST?

During a regular fast we refrain from all food and drink except water.

And when he had fasted forty days and forty nights, he was afterward an hungred. Matt. 4:2.

Note: The Bible does not say He was thirsty.

626. WHAT IS A PARTIAL FAST?

In a partial fast, we omit a certain meal each day and strictly restrict the quantity of food and drink we consume.

I ate no delicacies, no meat or wine entered my mouth. Dan. 10:3.

627. WHAT IS A COMPLETE FAST?

In a complete fast, we do not eat or drink liquid of any kind. This kind of fast is not to exceed three days.

And he was three days without sight, and neither did eat nor drink. Acts 9:9.

Go, gather together all the Jews . . . and fast ye for me, and neither eat nor drink three days, night or day: I also and my maidens will fast likewise . . . Esth. 4:16.

628. WHAT IS A LIQUID FAST?

A liquid fast is a partial fast that allows liquids of all kinds to be taken for any period of time (juice, broth or beverages).

Note: A liquid fast is recommended for an extended fast.

629. WHAT SHOULD BE OUR MOTIVE FOR FASTING?

When fasting, our main objective should be to minister to the Lord through worship and by giving ourselves wholly to Him.

> *When ye fasted . . . did ye at all fast unto me, even to me? Zech. 7:5 RV.*

> *As they ministered unto the Lord, and fasted, the Holy Ghost, said Separate me Barnabas and Saul for the work whereunto I have called them. Acts 13:2.*

630. HOW CAN WE MINISTER TO THE LORD?

Through worship and prayer.

> *They ministered to the Lord, and fasted. Acts 13:2 RV.*

631. WHAT ARE THE BENEFITS OF FASTING?

The benefits of fasting are:

1. It brings deliverance.

> *Is not this the fast that I have chosen? to loose the bands of wickedness, to undo the heavy burdens, and to let the oppressed go free, and that ye break every yoke? Isa. 58:6.*

2. It disciplines the body.

> *But I keep under my body, and bring it into subjection: lest that by any means, when I have preached to others, I myself should be a castaway. I Cor. 9:27.*

3. It releases our faith for healing.

> *Beloved, I pray that . . . you may be in health. III John 2.*

> *Your healing shall spring up speedily. Isa. 58:8.*

4. It gives force to our prayers.

> *So we fasted and besought our God for this: and he was intreated of us. Ezra 8:23.*

5. It purges our spirit.

But as for me, when they were sick, my clothing was sackcloth: I humbled my soul with fasting. Ps. 35:13.

632.   DOES GOD ANSWER EVERY PRAYER?

God answers every prayer He hears. Sometimes He says "No" to our requests because He has a plan for our lives that would be hindered if our petition was granted.

After they were come to Mysia, they assayed to go into Bithynia: but the Spirit suffered them not. Acts 16:7.

633.   ARE THERE TIMES WHEN GOD DOES NOT HEAR OUR PRAYERS?

Yes. God does not hear our prayers if we are concealing sin in our lives or have an unforgiving spirit.

If I regard iniquity in my heart, the Lord will not hear me. Ps. 66:18.

Now we know that God heareth not sinners: but if any man be a worshipper of God, and doeth his will, him he heareth. John 9:31.

STUDY QUESTIONS—Chapter 51

1. What is prayer?
2. How do we communicate with God?
3. Why is prayer a form of worship?
4. What method of prayer is most acceptable to God?
5. How does God help us to pray?
6. Why is praying in tongues necessary?
7. What does prayer in tongues do for us?
8. Is it better to pray in tongues or with the understanding?
9. What should we pray for in community or congregational prayer meetings?
10. What is the purpose of praying together?
11. What is intercessory prayer?
12. What is travailing prayer?
13. What is spiritual warfare?
14. What spiritual armor does the Holy Spirit give to us?
15. What should be avoided in prayer?
16. When do we combine fasting with prayer?
17. What is fasting?
18. What is a regular fast?
19. What should be our motive for fasting?
20. What are the benefits of fasting?

Chapter 52

THE MINISTRY OF GIVING

634. **WHAT IS THE MINISTRY OF GIVING?**

The ministry of giving is an act of worship. It is the giving first of ourselves and then of all we possess to God.

> *Praying us with much intreaty that we would receive the gift, and take upon us the fellowship of the ministering to the saints. And this they did, not as we hoped, but first gave their own selves to the Lord, and unto us by the will of God. II Cor. 8:4,5.*

635. **HOW DO WE MINISTER TO THE LORD IN GIVING?**

We present our bodies as living sacrifices and our possessions not only to praise Him but to serve others in love.

> *I beseech you therefore, brethren, by the mercies of God, that ye present your bodies a living sacrifice, holy, acceptable unto God, which is your reasonable service. Rom. 12:1.*

> *For brethren, ye have been called unto liberty; only use not liberty for an occasion to the flesh, but by love serve one another. Gal. 5:13.*

636. **WHY IS MINISTRY TO OTHERS IN THE CHURCH A MINISTRY TO GOD?**

Ministry to others in the church is a ministry to God because those who are in Christ are a part of Christ.

> *... Inasmuch as ye have done it unto one of the least of these my brethren, ye have done it unto me. Matt. 25:40.*

637. WHAT ARE WE TO GIVE TO OTHERS IN THE CHURCH?

We are to give of our substance, our time and energy, and our hospitality.

> *And do not negelct doing good and sharing; for with such sacrifices God is pleased. Heb. 13:15 NASV.*

638. HOW MUCH ARE WE TO GIVE TO OTHERS IN THE CHURCH?

The Holy Spirit directs our giving once we have given ourselves to Him. We give according to what we have, what is needed, and what is our fair share of responsibility.

> *Contributing to the needs of the saints, practicing hospitality. Rom. 12:13 NASV.*

> *For if there be first a willing mind, it is accepted according to that a man hath, and not according to that he hath not. For I mean not that other men be eased, and ye burdened: But by an equality, that now at this time your abundance may be a supply for their want, that their abundance also may be a supply for your want; that there may be equality. II Cor. 8:12–14.*

639. ARE THERE ANY SCRIPTURAL GUIDELINES AS TO WHAT PERCENTAGE OF OUR ASSETS IS A FAIR SHARE?

Yes. God instructed Israel to give in detailed ways as a picture of how each one in the New Covenant Church is responsible to give.

> *Now all these things happened unto them for ensample: And they are written for our admonition, upon whom the ends of the world are come. I Cor. 10:11.*

640. WHAT LESSONS DO WE LEARN ABOUT GIVING FROM THE INSTRUCTIONS GIVEN TO ISRAEL?

Specifically we learn:

A. God expects us to give a basic percentage of all we possess and to help others who are in need.

> *Give, and it shall be given unto you; good measure,*

pressed down, and shaken together, and running over, shall men give unto your bosom. For with the same measure that ye mete withal it shall be measured to you again. Luke 6:38.

Bring ye all the tithes into the storehouse, that there may be meat in mine house, and prove me now herewith, saith the LORD of hosts, if I will not open you the windows of heaven, and pour you out a blessing, that there shall not be room enough to receive it. Mal. 3:10.

B. Giving is a systematic, regular support of the ministers God has placed over us.

And (they) brought in the offerings and the tithes and the dedicated things faithfully: over which Cononiah the Levite was ruler, and Shimei his brother was the next. II Chron. 31:12.

And the priest the son of Aaron shall be with the Levites, when the Levites take tithes: and the Levites shall bring up the tithe of the tithes unto the house of our God, to the chambers, into the treasure house. Neh. 10:38.

C. We are to give the first and the best of what we have to God.

Honour the Lord with thy substance, and with the firstfruits of all thine increase. Prov. 3:9.

D. God expects us to be merciful to the poor.
But the seventh year thou shalt let it (the land) rest and lie still; that the poor of thy people may eat . . . Exod. 23:11.
For the poor shall never cease out of the land: therefore I command thee, saying, Thou shalt open thine hand wide unto thy brother, to thy poor, and to thy needy in thy land. Deut. 15:11.

E. We are to give to God's house and allow His ministers to be directed in determining how our gifts are to be used.

Bring ye all the tithes into the storehouse, that there may be meat in mine house . . . Mal. 3:10.

And of the Levites, Ahijah was over the treasures of the house of God, and over the treasures of the dedicated things. I Chron. 26:20.

641. WHAT IS A TITHE?

A tithe is a tenth. It is the portion that belongs to God.

> *And all the tithe of the land, whether of the seed of the land, or of the fruit of the tree, is the Lord's: it is holy unto the Lord. Lev. 27:30.*

642. DID THE GIVING OF TITHES BEGIN WITH THE LAW OF MOSES?

No. Abraham gave a tenth of the spoils of victory to Melchizedek, a priest of God. Jacob devoted a tenth of all he owned to God after his vision at Luz.

> *And Melchizedek king of Salem brought forth bread and wine: and he was the priest of the most high God. And he blessed him ... And (Abraham) gave him tithes of all. Gen. 14:18–20.*

Bible Narrative: Jacob's vow, Gen. 28:11–22.

643. WHY DID ABRAHAM GIVE TITHES TO GOD?

Abraham had seen that God owned everything and had blessed him with abundance. Through his giving, Abraham told God that he was trusting Him alone to provide for him.

> *And (Melchizedek) blessed him, and said, Blessed be Abram of the most high God, possessor of heaven and earth: and blessed be the most high God, which hath delivered thine enemies into thy hand. And (Abraham) gave him tithes of all. Gen. 14:19,20.*

BIBLE NARRATIVE: Abraham's tithing vow protected him from coveting anything from the King of Sodom. Gen. 14:21–24.

644. WHAT BLESSINGS DID GOD PROMISE TO THOSE WHO TITHED?

God promised every kind of prosperity to those who were obedient in their giving.

> *Bring ye all the tithes into the storehouse, that there may be meat in mine house, and prove me now herewith, saith the Lord of hosts, if I will not open you the windows of heaven, and pour you out a blessing, that there shall not be*

room enough to receive it. And I will rebuke the devourer for your sake, and he shall not destroy the fruits of your ground; neither shall your vine cast her fruit before the time in the field, saith the Lord of hosts. Mal. 3:10,11.

645.   WHAT DOES THE SCRIPTURE MEAN BY "THE STORE-HOUSE"?

It is the place where we regularly receive our spiritual food. In Israel, the Tabernacle or the Temple were the central places of worship. Under the New Covenant, the Local Church is the place of regular worship.

Now concerning the collection for the saints, as I have given order to the churches of Galatia even so do ye. Upon the first day of the week let every one of you lay by him in store, as God hath prospered him, that there be no gatherings when I come. I Cor. 16:1,2.

646.   WHAT IS AN OFFERING?

An offering is a gift to the work of God that is beyond the tithe. It is a free will contribution to support a special need or person or to express thanks.

647.   WHAT ARE ALMS?

Alms are works of mercy or charitable gifts to relieve the poor.

. . . hath given his bread to the hungry, and hath covered the naked with a garment. Ezek. 18:7.

He that hath a bountiful eye shall be blessed; for he giveth of his bread to the poor. Prov. 22:9.

648.   WHAT DID JESUS TEACH US ABOUT GIVING?

Jesus taught that the most important part of giving is the attitude of our heart. He taught:

A. That clinging to earthly wealth can make us lose out in eternal wealth.

Sell that ye have, and give alms; provide yourselves bags which wax not old, a treasure in the heavens that faileth not, where no thief approacheth, neither moth corrupteth.

For where your treasure is, there will your heart be also. Luke 12:33,34.

B. We should not give expecting to be rewarded by men.

Take heed that ye do not your alms before men, to be seen of them: otherwise ye have no reward of your Father which is in heaven. Matt. 6:1.

C. We are not to keep more than we need but are to share what we have.

He answereth and saith unto them, He that hath two coats, let him impart to him that hath none; and he that hath meat, let him do likewise. Luke 3:11.

D. Giving in genuine sacrifice pleases God more than much wealth given without meaning.

... Verily, I say unto you, that this poor widow hath cast more in, than all they which have cast into the treasury: For all they did cast in of their abundance; but she of her want did cast in all that she had, even all her living. Mark 12:43,44.

E. Giving is as much a part of serving God as prayer and fasting.

But when thou doest alms ... And when thou prayest ... moreover when ye fast ... Matt. 6:3,5,16.

F. Our giving is the measure of what we can receive.

Give and it shall be given unto you; good measure, pressed down, and shaken together, and running over, shall men give unto your bosom. For with the same measure that ye mete withal it shall be measured to you again. Luke 6:38.

649. HOW DID THE EARLY CHURCH MINISTER IN GIVING?

Giving was an important part of the outreach of the church which was giving to others as well as caring for its own members.

A. The first deacons were appointed to provide for the widows.

And in those days, when the number of disciples was multiplied there arose a murmuring of the Grecians against the Hebrews, because their widows were neglected in the daily ministration. Then the twelve called the multitude of the disciples unto them, and said, It is not reason that we should leave the word of God, and serve tables. Wherefore, brethren, look ye out among you seven men of honest report, full of the Holy Ghost and wisdom, whom we may appoint over this business. Acts 6:1–3.

B. In the Jerusalem church, no man considered his goods as his own.

And all that believed were together, and had all things common; And sold their possessions and goods, and parted them to all men, as every man had need. Acts 2:44,45.

C. Prospering local churches supported poorer churches in other places.

Moreover, brethren, we do you to wit of the grace of God bestowed on the churches of Macedonia; How that in a great trial of affliction the abundance of their joy and their deep poverty abounded unto the riches of their liberality. For to their power, I bear record, yea, and beyond their power they were willing of themselves; Praying us with much intreaty that we would receive the gift, and take upon us the fellowship of the ministering to the saints. And this they did, not as we hoped, but first gave their own selves to the Lord, and unto us by the will of God. II Cor. 8:1–5.

D. The Philippian Church helped to support traveling ministers.

Notwithstanding ye have well done, that ye did communicate with my affliction. Now ye Phillippians know also, that in the beginning of the gospel, when I departed from Macedonia, no church communicated with me as concerning giving and receiving, but ye only. Phil. 4:14,15.

650.   HOW DOES GOD WANT US TO MINISTER BY GIVING TODAY?

God wants us to give in ways which glorify Him and which prepare us to receive more blessing from Him. Therefore, we should give:

A. Willingly.

For if there be first a willing mind, it is accepted according to that a man hath, and not according to that he hath not. II Cor. 8:12.

B. Generously.

But this I say, He which soweth sparingly shall reap also sparingly; and he which soweth bountifully shall reap also bountifully. II Cor. 9:6.

C. Gladly.

Every man as he purposeth in his heart, so let him give; not grudgingly, or of necessity; for God loveth a cheerful giver. II Cor. 9:7.

D. Simply.

. . . he that giveth, let him do it with simplicity. Rom. 12:8.

651.   HOW IS GIVING RELATED TO BROTHERLY LOVE?

The only way the love within us is shown to others is by what we do. Compassion is shown by taking care of our brother's needs.

But whoso hath this world's good, and seeth his brother have need, and shutteth up his bowels of compassion from him, how dwelleth the love of God in him? My little children, let us not love in word, neither in tongue; but in deed and in truth. I John 3:17,18.

652.   HOW SHOULD WE LOVE THE BRETHREN?

We should love the brethren with complete self-giving just as Christ loved us.

Hereby perceive we the love of God, because he laid down his life for us: and we ought to lay down our lives for the brethren. I John 3:16.

653.   CAN WE LOVE GOD WITHOUT SHOWING LOVE TO OTHERS?

No. The Bible tells us very forcefully that we cannot love God and hate our brother at the same time.

If a man say, I love God, and hateth his brother, he is a liar: for he that loveth not his brother whom he hath seen, how can he love God whom he hath not seen? And this commandment have we from him, That he who loveth God love his brother also. I John 4:20,21.

654. WHAT IS HOSPITALITY?

Hospitality is showing kindness and care to others by inviting them to your own home. It is a very personal way of giving to others.

Use hospitality one to another without grudging. I Peter 4:9.

Distributing to the necessity of saints; given to hospitality. Rom. 12:13.

655. TO WHOM SHOULD WE GIVE HOSPITALITY?

We should give hospitality to those in the Church, to strangers and to those in special need.

Let brotherly love continue. Be not forgetful to entertain strangers: for thereby some have entertained angels unawares. Remember them that are in bonds, as bound with them; and them which suffer adversity, as being yourselves also in the body. Heb. 13:1–3.

656. WHAT IS TO BE OUR REAL REASON FOR GIVING?

Giving is our response to God's love that is so freely given to us.

. . . freely ye have received, freely give. Matt. 10:8.

657. WHAT ARE OUR RESPONSIBILITIES FOR GIVING TODAY?

Our first responsibility is to support the ministry and work of the Local Church. Then we are to give to our brother and to the needy.

Bring ye all the tithes into the storehouse, that there may be meat in mine house . . . Mal. 3:10.

Now concerning the collection for the saints, as I have given order to the churches of Galatia, even so do ye. Upon the first day of the week let everyone of you lay by him in store, as God hath prospered him, that there be no gatherings when I come. I Cor. 16:2,3.

As we have therefore opportunity, let us do good unto all men, especially unto them who are of the household of faith. Gal. 6:10.

658.   DOES GOD REQUIRE US TO SUPPORT OUR MINISTERS FINANCIALLY?

Yes. God frees His servants to give all their time and energy to providing for our spiritual needs. We are to care for their material needs.

... For if the Gentiles have been made partakers of their spiritual things, their duty is also to minister unto them in carnal things. Rom. 15:27.

Or I only and Barnabas, have not we power to forbear working? Who goeth a warfare anytime at his own charges? who planteth a vineyard, and eateth not of the fruit thereof? or who feedeth a flock, and eateth not of the milk of the flock? Say I these things as a man? or saith not the law the same also? For it is written in the law of Moses, Thou shalt not muzzle the mouth of the ox that treadeth out the corn. Doth God take care for oxen? Or saith·he it altogether for our sakes? For our sakes, no doubt, this is written: that he that ploweth should plow in hope; and that he that thresheth in hope should be partaker of his hope. If we have sown unto you spiritual things, is it a great thing if we shall reap your carnal things? . . . Even so hath the Lord ordained that they which preach the gospel should live of the gospel. I Cor. 9:6–11,14.

... for the labourer is worthy of his hire ... Luke 10:7.

659.   WHO DOES GOD USE TO SUPPLY THE NEEDS OF HIS SERVANTS?

God has purposed that we who benefit from the ministry should share our material goods with those who minister to us.

And let the one who is taught the word share all good things with him who teaches. Gal. 6:6 NASV.

660.   WHY DOES GOD USE US TO SUPPLY THE NEEDS OF THE MINISTRY?

Our giving keeps us free to continue to receive and it makes us fruitful people.

> *Not because I desire a gift: but I desire fruit that may abound to your account. Phil. 4:17.*

> *Give, and it shall be given unto you; good measure, pressed down, and shaken together, and running over, shall men give unto your bosom. For with the same measure that ye mete withal it shall be measured to you again. Luke 6:38.*

661.   WHAT LESSON ARE WE TO LEARN THROUGH GIVING?

We are to learn that God is the source of supply of all that we need and enjoy.

> *But my God shall supply all your need according to his riches in glory by Christ Jesus. Phil. 4:19.*

> *Charge them that are rich in this world, that they be not highminded, nor trust in uncertain riches, but in the living God, who giveth us richly all things to enjoy; That they do good, that they be rich in good works, ready to distribute, willing to communicate (share). I Tim 6:17,18.*

662.   WHAT BLESSINGS ARE PROMISED TO THE GENEROUS GIVER?

As we allow God to create a generosity in our spirits, He promises us the following blessings:

A. Increase.

> *There is that scattereth, and yet increaseth; and there is that withholdeth more than is meet, but it tendeth to poverty. The liberal soul shall be made fat: and he that watereth shall be watered also himself. Prov. 11:24,25.*

B. Health.

> *Beloved, I wish above all things that thou mayest prosper and be in health, even as thy soul prospereth. III John 2.*

C. A spiritual foundation for the future.

Laying up in store for themselves a good foundation against the time to come, that they may lay hold on eternal life. I Tim. 6:19.

D. Fruits of Righteousness.

Now he that ministereth seed to the sower both minister bread for your food, and multiply your seed sown, and increase the fruits of your righteousness. II Cor. 9:10.

663. WHEN WE TAKE OUR TITHES AND OFFERINGS TO GOD'S HOUSE, HOW DO WE KNOW THEY WILL BE USED FOR THE ADVANCEMENT OF THE KINGDOM?

Our responsibility is to give, not to concern ourselves with what has been done with what we have given. After we have brought our tithes and offerings to His house as He commanded, our duty has been fulfilled. The stewards in charge of God's money after it comes into God's house now become responsible for it.

Moreover it is required in stewards, that a man be found faithful. I Cor. 4:2.

. . . what is that to thee? Follow thou me. John 21:22.

664. WHAT IS A STEWARD?

A steward is one who is in charge of the goods or property belonging to another. God has made us stewards over everything He has given us of worldly goods. We own nothing. Rather, we are stewards of God's possessions. We must be faithful to take good care of what has been put in our charge.

For every beast of the forest is mine, and the cattle upon a thousand hills. I know all the fowls of the mountains: and the wild beasts of the field are mine. If I were hungry, I would not tell thee: for the world is mine, and the fulness thereof. Ps. 50:10–12.

The silver is mine, and the gold is mine, saith the LORD of hosts. Hag. 2:8.

BIBLE NARRATIVES: The parable of the pounds. Luke 19:11–27; The rich fool. Luke 12:16–20.

665.   WHY DOES GOD USE US AS STEWARDS OF HIS POSSESSIONS?

He uses us to develop our character in preparation for inheriting the Kingdom. We are heirs of God and shall rule with Him if we are faithful. Faithfulness determines our reward. (See Chapter 44 "Eternal Judgment")

> *And if children, then heirs; heirs of God, and joint-heirs with Christ ... Rom. 8:17.*

> *To an inheritance, incorruptible, and undefiled, and that fadeth not away, reserved in heaven for you. I Peter 1:4.*

> *And he said unto him, Well, thou good servant: because thou hast been faithful in a very little, have thou authority over ten cities. Luke 19:17.*

STUDY QUESTIONS—Chapter 52

1. What is the ministry of giving?
2. How do we minister to the Lord in giving?
3. What are we to give to others in the church?
4. Are there any Scriptural guidelines as to what percentage of our assets is a fair share?
5. What lessons do we learn about giving from the instructions given to Israel?
6. What is a tithe?
7. Did the giving of tithes begin with the law of Moses?
8. What does the Scripture mean by "the storehouse"?
9. What is an offering?
10. What did Jesus teach us about giving?
11. How does God want us to minister by giving today?
12. How is giving related to brotherly love?
13. How should we love the brethren?
14. What are our responsibilities for giving today?
15. What lesson are we to learn through giving?
16. What is a steward?
17. Write Mal. 3:10; Luke 6:38; Prov. 11:24,25.

Chapter 53

DISCIPLINE IN THE LOCAL CHURCH

666. **WHAT IS "DISCIPLINE"?**

Discipline is the training we receive from those in authority over us in the Local Church. It is designed to train character through instruction, control, correction and strengthening.

> *Give instruction to a wise man, and he will be yet wiser: teach a just man, and he will increase in learning. Prov. 9:9.*

> *Stern discipline (correction) is for him who forsakes the way; He who hates reproof will die. Prov. 15:10 NASV.*

> *All scripture is given by inspiration of God, and is profitable for doctrine, for reproof, for correction, for instruction in righteousness. That the man of God may be perfect, throughly furnished unto all good works. II Tim. 3:16,17.*

667. **WHAT IS THE PURPOSE OF DISCIPLINE?**

Discipline teaches us obedience through submitting our will to the will of God.

> *Obey them that have the rule over you and submit yourselves: for they watch for your souls, as they that must give account, that they may do it with joy, and not with grief: for that is unprofitable for you. Heb. 13:17.*

668. **WHY MUST WE LEARN OBEDIENCE?**

We must learn obedience because God demands it of His children. He not only requires us to be obedient in keeping the Ten Commandments but we are to practice obedience in all areas of life.

> *Train up a child in the way he should go: and when he is old, he will not depart from it. Prov. 22:6.*

> *For whom the Lord loveth he chasteneth, and scourgeth every son whom he receiveth. Heb. 12:6.*

669. DOES GOD REQUIRE OBEDIENCE OF EVERYONE?

Yes, everyone is required to learn obedience. God presents to us the example of His own Son, Jesus Christ, who was obedient in all things. The Bible gives us examples of His obedience:

1. To His parents.

> *And he went down with them, and came to Nazareth, and was subject unto them: but his mother kept all these sayings in her heart. Luke 2:51.*

2. To those in authority.

> *And Jesus answering said unto them, Render to Caesar the things that are Caesar's, and to God the things that are God's. And they marvelled at him. Mark 12:17.*

3. In His suffering.

> *Though he were a Son, yet learned he obedience by the things which he suffered. And being made perfect, he became the author of eternal salvation unto all them that obey him. Heb. 5:8,9.*

4. In His death.

> *And being found in fashion as a man, he humbled himself, and became obedient unto death, even the death of the cross. Phil. 2:8.*

5. To God, the Father.

> *For I came down from heaven, not to do mine own will, but the will of him that sent me. John 6:38.*

670. WHY IS DISCIPLINE AND OBEDIENCE NEEDED IN THE LOCAL CHURCH?

It is needed in the Local Church for the development of our spiritual growth, to train us in God's ways and to correct us when we are wrong or disobedient.

> *Son of man, I have made thee a watchman unto the house of Israel: Therefore hear the word at my mouth, and give them warning from me. When I say unto the wicked, Thou shalt surely die; and thou givest him not warning, nor speakest to warn the wicked from his wicked way, to save his life; the same wicked man shall die in his iniquity; but his blood will I require at thine hand. Nevertheless if thou warn the righteous man, that the righteous sin not, and he doth not sin, he shall surely live, because he is warned; also thou has delivered thy soul. Ezek. 3:17,18,21.*

671. WHO HAS THE AUTHORITY TO DISCIPLINE US IN THE LOCAL CHURCH?

The Church Council.

> *When therefore Paul and Barnabas had no small dissension and disputation with them, they determined that Paul and Barnabas, and certain other of them, should go up to Jerusalem unto the apostles and elders about this question. And when they were come to Jerusalem, they were received of the church, and of the apostles and elders, and they declared all things that God had done with them. Acts 15:2,4.*

672. WHAT IS THE CHURCH COUNCIL?

The pastor and elders and those to whom God has given the responsibility of oversight and the ministry of governments have the authority to discipline us. This would also include department supervisors, teachers, ushers, etc.

> *And we beseech you, brethren, to know them which labour among you, and are over you in the Lord, and admonish you. I Thess. 5:12.*

> *I beseech you, brethren, (ye know the house of Stephanas, that it is the first fruits of Achaia, and that they have addicted themselves to the ministry of the saints,) that ye submit yourselves unto such, and to every one that helpeth with us, and laboureth. I Cor. 16:15,16.*

673.   WHO GIVES THE AUTHORITY TO THE PASTOR AND ELDERS, ETC.?

All authority comes from God and those who are placed over us receive it only when we submit ourselves to it.

> *Submit yourselves to every ordinance of man for the Lord's sake: whether it be to the king, as supreme; Or unto governors, as unto them that are sent by him for the punishment of evildoers, and for the praise of them that do well. I Peter 2:13,14.*

674.   WHEN IS DISCIPLINE NEEDED IN THE LOCAL CHURCH?

Discipline is needed in the Local Church at all times. Correction is needed when the members become unruly or it is needed to maintain fellowship with Christ and with each another.

> *. . . Know ye not that a little leaven leaveneth the whole lump? Purge out therefore the old leaven, that ye may be a new lump, as ye are unleavened. For even Christ our passover is sacrificed for us. Therefore let us keep the feast, not with old leaven, neither with the leaven of malice and wickedness; but with the unleavened bread of sincerity and truth. I Cor. 5:6–8.*

> *Ye did run well; who did hinder you that ye should not obey the truth? This persuasion cometh not of him that calleth you. A little leaven leaveneth the whole lump. I have confidence in you through the Lord, that ye will be none otherwise minded: but he that troubleth you shall bear his judgment, whosoever he be. Gal. 5:7–10.*

> *Looking diligently lest any man fail of the grace of God; lest any root of bitterness springing up trouble you, and thereby many be defiled. Lest there be any fornicator, or profane person, as Esau . . . Heb. 12:15,16.*

675.   WHAT SHOULD BE DONE WHEN A DIFFERENCE EXISTS BETWEEN TWO MEMBERS OF THE LOCAL CHURCH?

The one who has been wronged is to go to the one at fault and attempt to make reconciliation.

Moreover if thy brother shall trespass against thee, go and tell him his fault between thee and him alone: if he shall hear thee, thou hast gained thy brother. Matt. 18:15.

Take heed to yourselves: If thy brother trespass against thee, rebuke him; and if he repent, forgive him. And if he trespass against thee seven times in a day, and seven times in a day turn again to thee, saying, I repent; thou shalt forgive him. Luke 17:3,4.

676. HOW MANY ATTEMPTS SHOULD BE MADE?

According to the Scriptures, two attempts should be made—the first one is to be made privately; the second, in the presence of two or three witnesses.

But if he will not hear thee, then take with thee one or two more, that in the mouth of two or three witnesses every word may be established. Matt. 18:16.

677. WHAT ACTION SHOULD BE TAKEN IF THE TWO ATTEMPTS FAIL?

The matter should be brought before the Church (leaders).

And if he shall neglect to hear them, tell it unto the church . . . Matt. 18:17.

Dare any of you, having a matter against another, go to law before the unjust, and not before the saints? Do ye not know that the saints shall judge the world? And if the world shall be judged by you, are ye unworthy to judge the smallest matters? I Cor. 6:1,2.

678. IF THE ONE AT FAULT REFUSES TO HEAR THE CHURCH (LEADERS), WHAT IS THE NEXT STEP?

He is to be excluded from the Local Church.

. . . but if he neglect to hear the church, let him be unto thee as an heathen man and a publican. Matt. 18:17.

Now we command you, brethren, in the name of our Lord Jesus Christ, that ye withdraw yourselves from every brother that walketh disorderly, and not after the tradition which he received of us. II Thess. 3:6.

679. ARE WE TO HAVE FELLOWSHIP WITH ONE WHO HAS BEEN EXCLUDED FROM THE LOCAL CHURCH?

Having fellowship with an individual who has been excluded from the Church indicates we condone what he has done. It also shows that we do not support those in authority over us whose responsibility is to keep the fellowship between Christ and His body, the Church, flowing freely.

> *Now I beseech you, brethren, mark them which cause divisions and offenses contrary to the doctrine which ye have learned, and avoid them. Rom. 16:17.*

680. FOR WHAT REASONS WERE PEOPLE EXCLUDED FROM THE EARLY CHURCH?

The early Church excluded those who would not receive correction or those who would not repent of sins of fornication, covetousness, extortion, idolatry, railing, habitual drunkenness, gossiping, homosexuality and other sexual perversions.

> *Or do you not know that the unrighteous shall not inherit the Kingdom of God. Do not be deceived; neither fornicators, nor idolaters, nor adulterers, nor effeminate (by perversion), nor homosexuals, nor thieves, nor covetous, nor drunkards, nor revilers, nor swindlers, shall inherit the Kingdom of God. I Cor. 6:9–11 NASV.*

> *I wrote unto you in an epistle not to company with fornicators. Yet not altogether with the fornicators of this world, or with the covetous, or extortioners, or with idolaters; for then must ye needs go out of the world. But now I have written unto you not to keep company, if any man that is called a brother be a fornicator, or covetous, or an idolater, or a railer, or a drunkard, or an extortioner; with such an one, no, not to eat. I Cor. 5:9–11.*

> *Now we command you, brethren, in the name of our Lord Jesus Christ, that ye withdraw yourselves from every brother that walketh disorderly, and not after the tradition which he received of us ... For we hear that there are some which walk among you disorderly, working not at all, but are busybodies. II Thess. 3:6,11.*

681. FOR WHAT OTHER REASON DOES THE CHURCH EXCLUDE MEMBERS?

For heresy. The Church is commanded to exclude heretics after they have been warned twice.

> *A man that is an heretick after the first and second admonition reject: Knowing that he that is such is subverted, and sinneth, being condemned of himself. Titus 3:10,11.*

682. WHAT IS A HERETIC?

A heretic is one who deliberately refuses to believe truth and stubbornly clings to error. If heretics are allowed to remain in the Church, they will lead others into error.

> *But there were false prophets also among the people, even as there shall be false teachers among you, who privily shall bring in damnable heresies, even denying the Lord that bought them and bring upon themselves swift destruction. And many shall follow their pernicious ways; by reason of whom the way of truth shall be evil spoken of. II Peter 2:1,2.*

> *Whosoever transgresseth, and abideth not in the doctrine of Christ, hath not God. He that abideth in the doctrine of Christ, he hath both the Father and the Son. If there come any unto you, and bring not this doctrine, receive him not into your house, neither bid him God speed: For he that biddeth him God speed is partaker of his evil deeds. II John 9–11.*

683. IF A CHURCH MEMBER TEACHES FALSE DOCTRINE, HOW SHOULD THE CHURCH DEAL WITH HIM?

In the application of discipline for false teaching, two things must be considered.

A. Consider if the one concerned is wrong due to the fact that he is not fully instructed or misunderstands the meaning of the Scriptures. Heresy is a deliberate choice against truth.

B. Consider if it is doctrine that is heretical, satanic in origin and accompanied by practices and doctrine that sever our fellowship with the Lord.

If any man teach otherwise, and consent not to wholesome words, even the words of our Lord Jesus Christ, and to the doctrine which is according to godliness, He is proud, knowing nothing but doting about questions and strifes of words, whereof cometh envy, strife, railings, evil surmisings, perverse disputings of men of corrupt minds, and destitute of the truth, supposing that gain is godliness: from such withdraw thyself. I Tim. 6:3–5.

Now I beseech you, brethren, mark them which cause divisions and offences contrary to the doctrine which ye have learned; and avoid them. Rom. 16:17.

. . . that they may learn not to blaspheme. I Tim. 1:20b.

684. WHAT DISCIPLINE MAY BE IMPOSED UPON MEMBERS WHO PERSIST IN SIN?

The elders have authority from God to turn a sinning member over to Satan who will inflict great distress or sickness upon the individual so that he will learn not to blaspheme and sin against God. This is only done in extreme cases and in the will of God when the individual persists in his sin and all other Scriptural attempts fail.

In the name of our Lord Jesus Christ, when ye are gathered together, and my spirit, with the power of our Lord Jesus Christ, To deliver such an one unto Satan for the destruction of the flesh, that the spirit may be saved in the day of the Lord Jesus. I Cor. 5:4,5.

. . . for he that hath suffered in the flesh hath ceased from sin; That he no longer should live the rest of his time in the flesh to the lusts of men, but to the will of God. I Peter 4:1,2.

Of whom is Hymenaeus and Alexander; whom I have delivered unto Satan, that they may learn not to blaspheme. I Tim. 1:20.

685. HOW SHOULD CORRECTION BE GIVEN?

Correction should be given in a spirit of meekness knowing that we are all open to the same temptations.

Brethren, if a man be overtaken in a fault, ye which are

spiritual restore such an one in the spirit of meekness, considering thyself, lest thou also be tempted. Gal. 6:1.

And why beholdest thou the mote that is in thy brother's eye, but perceivest not the beam that is in thine own eye? Luke 6:41.

686. IS DISCIPLINE NECESSARY FOR THE CONTROL OF SPIRITUAL GIFTS?

God wants all to be done in order and in peace. He has given us leaders to direct our use of spiritual gifts that harmony and peace may prevail in His Church.

For God is not the author of confusion, but of peace, as in all churches of the saints. I Cor. 14:33.

Let all things be done decently and in order. I Cor. 14:40.

For though I be absent in the flesh, yet am I with you in the spirit, joying and beholding your order, and the steadfastness of your faith in Christ. Col. 2:5.

687. WHAT WAS THE PURPOSE OF PAUL'S CORRECTION IN THE CORINTHIAN CHURCH CONCERNING SPEAKING IN TONGUES AND PROPHECY?

Paul's aim was to show the Corinthians how to edify (build up) the church by the use of these gifts. He encouraged the use of self-control to make things understandable for the profit of all.

Even so ye, forasmuch as ye are zealous of spiritual gifts, seek that ye may excel to the edifying of the church. Wherefore let him that speaketh in an unknown tongue pray that he may interpret. I Cor. 14:12,13.

See Chapter 48 on Gifts and Ministries.

688. HOW ARE THOSE IN AUTHORITY TO DISCIPLINE THEMSELVES?

Those in authority must judge themselves constantly, submitting themselves one to another and walking in such a way that the ministry will not be disgraced or dishonored.

For a bishop (elder) must be blameless, as the steward of God; not self-willed, not soon angry, not given to wine, no striker, not given to filthy lucre; But a lover of good men, sober, just, holy, temperate; Titus 1:7,8.

BIBLE NARRATIVE: Eli and sons: I Sam. 2:12–36.

689. WHAT ACTION SHOULD BE TAKEN IN THE CASE OF A SINNING ELDER?

An accusation against an elder must not be made except before two or three witnesses. He is then rebuked before the Church that others might not fall into sin.

Against an elder receive not an accusation, but before two or three witnesses. Them that sin rebuke before all, that others also may fear. I Tim. 5:19,20.

One witness shall not rise up against a man for any iniquity, or for any sin, in any sin that he sinneth; at the mouth of two witnesses or at the mouth of three witnesses shall the matter be established. Deut. 19:15.

690. HOW CAN WE HELP OURSELVES TO LEARN OBEDIENCE?

We can help ourselves to learn obedience by practicing self-discipline and obeying the laws of the Local Church.

... Behold, to obey is better than sacrifice, and to hearken than the fat of rams. I Sam. 15:22.

691. WHAT IS SELF-DISCIPLINE?

Self-discipline is practicing temperance (self-control) in our own lives.

And in exercising knowledge develop self-control; and in exercising self-control develop steadfastness (patience, endurance), and in exercising steadfastness develop godliness (piety). II Peter 1:6 AMP.

For if we would judge ourselves, we should not be judged. I Cor. 11:31.

But he that is spiritual judgeth all things, yet he himself is judged of no man. I Cor. 2:15.

692. WHAT ARE CHURCH LAWS?

Church laws are man-made laws that are set up by the Local Church for the purpose of avoiding the vices that bring men into bondage.

> *But let all things be done properly and in an orderly manner. I Cor. 14:40 NASV.*

> *For God is not the author of confusion, but of peace, as in all churches of the saints. I Cor. 14:33.*

693. ARE CHURCH LAWS THE SAME AS GOD'S LAWS?

No. Church laws are the rules made by the leaders of a Local Church. God's laws are the Ten Commandments.

694. IS IT A SIN TO DISOBEY A CHURCH LAW?

Yes. To disobey a church law means to dishonor those in authority over us. We are commanded in the Fifth Commandment to obey all those God has placed in authority over us.

> *Obey them that have the rule over you, and submit yourselves: for they watch for your souls, as they that must give account, that they may do it with joy, and not with grief: for that is unprofitable for you. Heb. 13:17.*

695. DID THE CHURCHES IN THE NEW TESTAMENT HAVE CHURCH LAWS?

Yes. The Jerusalem Church Council set down the rules for Gentile believers.

> *Wherefore my sentence is, that we trouble not them which from among the Gentiles are turned to God: But that we write unto them, that they abstain from pollutions of idols, and from fornication, and from things strangled, and from blood. Acts 15:19,20.*

696. WHAT CHURCH LAWS DO LOCAL CHURCHES OBSERVE TODAY?

Local Churches command us not to participate in anything that can enslave us.

> *All things are lawful for me, but all things are not expe-*

dient: All things are lawful for me, but all things edify not. I Cor. 10:23.

While they promise them liberty, they themselves are the servants of corruption: for of whom a man is overcome, of the same is he brought in bondage. For if after they have escaped the pollutions of the world through the knowledge of the Lord and Saviour Jesus Christ, they are again entangled therein, and overcome, the latter end is worse with them than the beginning. II Peter 2:19,20.

697. ACCORDING TO CHURCH LAWS, WHAT PRACTICES ARE WE COMMANDED TO AVOID?

We are commanded to avoid all forms of intemperance:

A. Drinking and gluttony.

Be not among winebibbers; among riotous eaters of flesh: For the drunkard and the glutton shall come to poverty: And drowsiness shall clothe a man with rags. Prov. 23:20,21.

B. Smoking and drugs.

Know ye not that ye are the temple of God, and that the Spirit of God dwelleth in you? If any man defile the temple of God, him shall God destroy, for the temple of God is holy, which temple ye are. Let no man deceive himself. If any man among you seemeth to be wise in this world, let him become a fool, that he may be wise. For the wisdom of this world is foolishness with God. For it is written, He taketh the wise in their own craftiness. And again, the Lord knoweth the thoughts of the wise, that they are vain. I Cor. 3:16–20.

C. Gambling.

And he said unto them, Take heed, and beware of covetousness: for a man's life consisteth not in the abundance of the things which he possesseth. Luke 12:15.

For the love of money is the root of all evil: which while some coveted after, they have erred from the faith, and pierced themselves through with many sorrows. I Tim. 6:10.

D. Questionable movies, books, and entertainment; pornography; indecent dress and immodesty, indecent dancing, "petting", necking and passionate kissing.

Let no man say when he is tempted, I am tempted of God: for God cannot be tempted with evil, neither tempteth he any man: But every man is tempted, when he is drawn away of his own lust, and enticed. Then when lust hath conceived, it bringeth forth sin; and sin when it is finished, bringeth forth death. James 1:13–15.

And have no fellowship with the unfruitful works of darkness, but rather reprove them. For it is a shame even to speak of those things which are done of them in secret. Eph. 5:11,12.

abstain from fleshly lusts, which war against the soul. I Peter 2:11.

In like manner also, that women adorn themselves in modest apparel ... I Tim. 2:9.

E. Occult literature, meetings, and practices.

There shall not be found among you any one that maketh his son or his daughter to pass through the fire, or that useth divination, or an observer of times, or an enchanter, or a witch, Or a charmer, or a consulter with familiar spirits, or a wizard, or a necromancer. For all that do these things are an abomination unto the Lord. Deut. 18:10–12.

Note: Occult practices bring spiritual death to us when we participate in them for any reason. These include: clairvoyance, ESP, sorcery, witchcraft, necromancy (communing with the dead), hypnotism, automatic writing, ouija boards, fortune telling, astrology and horoscopes, magic charms.

698. WHY MUST WE NOT PARTAKE OF THINGS THAT WILL ENSLAVE US?

If we yield ourselves to these things, they will become our masters.

Know ye not, that to whom ye yield yourselves servants to obey, his servants ye are to whom ye obey; whether of sin unto death, or of obedience unto righteousness? Rom. 6:16.

699.   HOW ARE CHURCH LAWS ENFORCED?

The elders deal with offenders and if they do not change their habits, fellowship with the Local Church is severed.

> *Obey them that have the rule over you, and submit yourselves: for they watch for your souls, as they that must give account, that they may do it with joy, and not with grief: for that is unprofitable for you. Heb. 13:17.*

STUDY QUESTIONS—Chapter 53

1. What is discipline?
2. How was Jesus obedient?
3. Who has the authority to discipline us in the Local Church?
4. When is discipline needed in the Local Church?
5. What action should be taken when a difference between two members exists?
6. For what reasons were people excluded from the early church?
7. What is a heretic?
8. What should our attitude be if we are corrected?
9. How should correction be given?
10. Why is discipline necessary for the control of spiritual gifts?
11. How are those in authority to discipline themselves?
12. What action is taken in the case of a sinning elder?
13. What are church laws?
14. Why must we not partake of things that will enslave us?
15. Write Heb. 13:17; Matt. 18:15–17; Rom. 16:17.

COVENANTS AND SACRAMENTS

Chapter 54

THE COVENANTS AND SACRAMENTS OF THE CHURCH

700. WHAT IS A COVENANT?

A covenant is a solemn agreement between two parties. The Hebrew word "berith" means "to cut or divide, to make a binding agreement."

701. HOW ARE COVENANTS MADE?

Covenants are made when both parties commit themselves by oath to the agreement between them.

> *For men verily swear by the greater: and an oath for confirmation is to them an end of all strife. Heb. 6:16.*

702. WHAT WAYS OF COMMITTING OURSELVES BY OATH DO WE FIND IN SCRIPTURE?

Along with swearing in word, some visible act shows commitment to the oath. This visible act means that we pledge ourselves, our very lives, to keep the oath. Bible examples include cutting animals in half and passing between the two halves, lifting up hands, joining hands, eating sacrificial meals together, using salt, placing the hand under the thigh of the person to whom the oath is made.

> *And Abram said to the king of Sodom, I have lift up mine*

> *hand unto the Lord, the most high God, the possessor of heaven and earth, That I will not take from a thread even to a shoelatchet, and that I will not take any thing that is thine, lest thou shouldest say, I have made Abram rich: Gen. 14:22,23.*

> *The God of Abraham, and the God of Nahor, the God of their father, judge betwixt us. And Jacob sware by the fear of his father Isaac. Then Jacob offered sacrifice upon the mount, and called his brethren to eat bread: and they did eat bread. Gen. 31:53,54.*

BIBLE NARRATIVES: King Zedekiah's people made a covenant by passing between parts of a calf, Jer. 34:8–20; Pharaoh gave his hand in oath, Ezek. 17:18,19; David's kingdom was secured by salt, II Chron. 13:5; Abraham's servant placed his hand under his thigh. Gen. 24:1–9.

703.   HOW DO WE SWEAR AN OATH?

We call on the name of someone greater than ourselves to place us under penalty if we do not keep our word.

> *For men swear by one greater than themselves, and with them an oath given as confirmation is an end of every dispute. Heb. 6:16 NASV.*

BIBLE NARRATIVES: Phrases used in swearing oaths, Gen. 31:53; Ruth 1:17; 3:13; I Sam. 3:17; II Cor. 1:23; Gal. 1:20; I Thess. 2:5.

704.   HOW DOES GOD TAKE AN OATH WHEN HE MAKES COVENANT WITH MAN?

God swears by Himself, since there is no one greater than He.

> *Wherein God, willing more abundantly to show unto the heirs of promise the immutability (unchangeableness) of his counsel, confirmed it by an oath. Heb. 6:17.*

> *For when God made promise to Abraham, because he could swear by no greater, he sware by himself. Heb. 6:13.*

705.   WHAT COVENANT DO WE ENTER INTO WITH GOD?

We enter into the New Covenant through the blood of Jesus Christ.

For this is the blood of the new testament (covenant), which is shed for many for the remission of sins. Matt. 26:28.

Likewise also the cup after supper, saying, This cup is the new testament (covenant) in my blood, which is shed for you. Luke 22:20.

Note: The Greek word translated "testament" is the word for "covenant". See also Mark 14:24 and I Cor. 11:25.

706. WHY IS THE NEW COVENANT SEALED BY BLOOD?

It is the blood of Jesus Christ that joins us to God.

That at that time ye were without Christ, being aliens from the commonwealth of Israel, and strangers from the covenants of promise, having no hope; and without God in the world. But now in Christ Jesus ye who sometimes were far off are made nigh by the blood of Christ. Eph. 2:12,13.

And having made peace through the blood of his cross, by him to reconcile all things unto himself; by him, I say, whether they be things in earth, or things in heaven. Col. 1:20.

707. WHY DOES GOD USE CEREMONIES IN MAKING COVENANT WITH MAN?

Only by acting out the meanings of entering into covenant with God do we realize the power of the agreement to bring us life or death. Words alone cannot make spiritual truth real to the heart. Actions, visible symbols, emotions, and experience shared with others make a lasting impression upon us which we will then call to mind each time we hear the words of the covenant oath. God wants to single out the occasion, time and place where we make a covenant by giving us an experience we will not forget. This experience should be so dramatic and meaningful that we pass it on to our children.

Only take heed to thyself, and keep thy soul diligently, lest thou forget the things which thine eyes have seen, and lest they depart from thy heart all the days of thy life: but teach them thy sons, and thy sons' sons, Specially the day that thou stoodest before the Lord thy God in Horeb, when

*the Lord said unto me, Gather me the people together, and
I will make them hear my words, that they may learn to
fear me all the days that they shall live upon the earth, and
that they may teach their children. Deut. 4:9,10.*

BIBLE NARRATIVES: The blood covenant ceremony at Mt.
Sinai, Deut. 5–7; Mountains of blessing and cursing remind Israel to keep the covenant, Deut. 27:9–26,28.

708. HOW DO WE RELATE TO GOD'S COVENANT TODAY?

Through participating in the sacraments, we relate personally to
God's covenant and God, in turn, blesses us and manifests His
Presence.

*Also the sons of the stranger, that join themselves to the
Lord, to serve him, and to love the name of the Lord, to be
his servants, every one that keepeth the sabbath from pol-
luting it, and taketh hold of my covenant; Even them
will I bring to my holy mountain, and make them joyful in
my house of prayer: their burnt offerings and their
sacrifices shall be accepted upon mine altar; Isa. 56:6,7.*

709. WHAT IS A SACRAMENT?

The word "sacrament" comes from the Latin, and means "an
oath of allegiance, consecration, or solemn obligation". The
church uses the word to describe "something sacred in character
or significance: a spiritual sign, seal or bond (or a covenant held
to exist between God and man)". (Webster's Third New International Dictionary of the English Language, 1966).

710. HOW DO WE RELATE TO THE COVENANT THROUGH PARTICIPATING IN THE SACRAMENTS?

We believe that God has given Himself to us through these
means and give ourselves to Him in obedience. We meet God by
coming to Him in the ways He has given to the Church.

*Draw nigh to God, and he will draw nigh to you.
James 4:8.*

711. HOW MANY SACRAMENTS ARE THERE?

There are seven sacraments. They are: Water Baptism, Lord's

Supper, Foot Washing, Confirmation, Anointing with Oil, Matrimony and Dedication of Children.

712. WHO MAY PARTAKE OF THE SACRAMENTS?

Believers may partake of the sacraments of the church.

713. IS THERE A DIFFERENCE BETWEEN A SACRAMENT AND A RELIGIOUS RITE?

Yes. The difference between a sacrament and a religious rite is:

1. A religious rite has but one part ... the outward visible sign or ceremony which is usually based upon traditional practices.

   > *Howbeit in vain do they worship me, teaching for doctrines the commandments of men. For laying aside the commandments of God, ye hold the traditions of men ... Full well ye reject the commandment of God, that ye may keep your own tradition. Mark 7:7–9.*

   > *... why do ye also transgress the commandment of God by your tradition? ... thus have ye made the commandment of God of none effect by your tradition. Matt. 15:3,6.*

   > *Beware lest any man spoil you through philosophy and vain deceit, after the tradition of men, after the rudiments of the world, and not after Christ. Col. 2:8.*

2. A sacrament has two parts: (1) the outward visible sign, act or ceremony that is observed exactly as it is taught in the Scriptures and (2) the inward spiritual work of the Holy Spirit that imparts life and change.

714. HOW CAN A SACRAMENT IMPART LIFE AND CHANGE?

The believer who prepares his heart and obeys in faith receives spiritual life and change through revelation and experience.

715. HOW DO WE PREPARE OURSELVES FOR RECEIVING A SACRAMENT?

A. By repentance (recognition and acknowledgment of our need).

   > *... repent, and be baptized every one of you ... Acts 2:38.*

But let a man examine himself, and so let him eat of that bread, and drink of that cup. I Cor. 11:28.

B. By allowing the Holy Spirit to give us understanding of the Word. (Instruction may be the means God uses to give understanding.)

So then faith cometh by hearing, and hearing by the word of God. Rom. 10:17.

Teaching them to observe all things whatsoever I have commanded you: and, lo, I am with you alway, even unto the end of the world. Matt. 28:20.

And they continued steadfastly in the apostles' doctrine and fellowship, and in breaking of bread, and in prayers. Acts. 2:42.

C. By asking God in faith to give us what He has ordained for us in this act of obedience.

Buried with him in baptism, wherein also ye are risen with him through the faith of the operation of God, who hath raised him from the dead. Col. 2:12.

But without faith it is impossible to please him: for he that cometh to God must believe that he is, and that he is a rewarder of them that diligently seek him. Heb. 11:6.

D. By willingly submitting ourselves to obey all that is commanded in the sacrament. This means that we will do it exactly the way it is taught in the Scriptures, not substituting man-made revisions.

Howbeit in vain do they worship me, teaching for doctrines the commandments of men. For laying aside the commandments of God, ye hold the tradition of men ... Full well ye reject the commandment of God, that ye may keep your own tradition. Mark 7:7–9.

... why do ye also transgress the commandment of God by your tradition. .... Thus have ye made the commandment of God of none effect by your tradition. Matt. 15:3,6.

Beware lest any man spoil you through philosophy and vain deceit, after the tradition of men, after the rudiments of the world, and not after Christ. Col. 2:8.

. . . See . . . that thou make all things according to the pattern shewed to thee in the mount. Heb. 8:5.

STUDY QUESTIONS—Chapter 54

1. What is a covenant?
2. How are covenants made?
3. What visible acts were used in taking oaths in Scripture?
4. How do we swear an oath?
5. How does God take an oath when He makes covenant with man?
6. What covenant do we enter into with God?
7. Why does God use ceremonies in making covenant with man?
8. How do we relate to God's covenant today?
9. What is a sacrament?
10. How many sacraments are there?
11. What is the difference between a sacrament and a religious rite?
12. How can a sacrament impart life and change?
13. How do we prepare ourselves for receiving a sacrament?
14. Write Isa. 56:6,7; Matt. 28:20; Col. 2:8.

Chapter 55

THE SACRAMENT OF BAPTISM

716. WHAT IS WATER BAPTISM?

Water Baptism is a sacrament instituted by Jesus Christ by which we are baptized into Christ and into His death.

> *Know ye not, that so many of us as were baptized into Jesus Christ were baptized into his death? Therefore we are buried with him by baptism into death: that like as Christ was raised up from the dead by the glory of the Father, even so we also should walk in newness of life. Rom. 6:3,4.*

717. WHY IS BAPTISM NECESSARY?

Baptism is necessary because we cannot enter into the kingdom of God unless:

1. We have been identified with the death, burial and resurrection of Jesus Christ which He experienced in our place.
2. The enmity (hostility) that is in us because of original sin is removed.

> *For if we have been planted together in the likeness of his death, we shall be also in the likeness of his resurrection. Rom. 6:5.*

> *Verily, verily, I say unto thee, Except a man be born of water and of the Spirit, he cannot enter into the kingdom of God. John 3:5.*

> *He that believeth and is baptized shall be saved; but he that believeth not shall be damned. Mark 16:16.*

718.   WHAT IS ORIGINAL SIN?

Original sin (inherited sin) is the total corruption of our whole human nature. Man, by nature, is without true fear, love and trust in God. He is without righteousness, is inclined only to evil, and is spiritually blind, dead and an enemy of God.

> *. . . The imagination of man's heart is evil from his youth. Gen. 8:21.*

> *. . . (We) were by nature the children of wrath, even as others. Eph. 2:3.*

> *The carnal mind is enmity against God. Rom. 8:7.*

719.   WHAT HAPPENS TO ORIGINAL SIN IN BAPTISM?

Original sin and all other sins that have been committed are cancelled (remitted) along with the punishment due for them.

> *Therefore we are buried with him by baptism into death: that like as Christ was raised up from the dead by the glory of the Father, even so we also should walk in newness of life. For if we have been planted together in the likeness of his death, we shall be also in the likeness of his resurrection: Knowing this, that our old man is crucified with him, that the body of sin might be destroyed, that henceforth we should not serve sin. Rom. 6:4–6.*

> *Blotting out the handwriting of ordinances that was against us, which was contrary to us, and took it out of the way, nailing it to his cross. Col. 2:14.*

720.   DO WE HAVE ANY WORDS IN THE NEW TESTAMENT FOR ORIGINAL SIN?

The New Testament refers to it as "the old man" or "the body of sin"

> *That ye put off concerning the former conversation the old man, which is corrupt according to the deceitful lusts. Eph. 4:22.*

> *Knowing this, that our old man is crucified with him, that the body of sin might be destroyed, that henceforth we should not serve sin. Rom. 6:6.*

721. HOW DID WE ACQUIRE ORIGINAL SIN?

We acquired original sin through the sin of Adam.

> *Wherefore, as by one man sin entered into the world, and death by sin; and so death passed upon all men, for that all have sinned. Rom. 5:12.*

722. WHAT WAS THE SIN OF ADAM?

The sin of Adam was deliberate disobedience.

> *And unto Adam he said, Because thou hast hearkened unto the voice of thy wife, and hast eaten of the tree, of which I commanded thee, saying, Thou shalt not eat of it: cursed is the ground for thy sake . . . Gen. 3:17.*

723. WHY DID ADAM DISOBEY GOD?

Adam disobeyed God because Satan led him to believe that by eating of the Tree of Knowledge of Good and Evil, the knowledge he would gain would make him self-sufficient and, therefore, independent of God.

> *And the serpent said unto the woman, Ye shall not surely die; For God doth know that in the day ye eat thereof, then your eyes shall be opened, and ye shall be as gods, knowing good and evil. And when the woman saw that the tree was good for food, and that it was pleasant to the eyes, and a tree to be desired to make one wise, she took of the fruit thereof and did eat, and gave also unto her husband with her; and he did eat. Gen. 3:4–6.*

724. WHAT EFFECT DOES ADAM'S SIN HAVE ON US?

We are spiritually dead. Adam's rebellion against Divine Authority is passed on to us. In this day and age, we tend to rebel not only against the authority of God but against parental and civil authority as well. Original sin causes us to commit all manner of actual sins. We have enmity (hostility) against God. The conscience is stained with guilt.

> *This know also, that in the last days perilous times shall come. For men shall be lovers of their own selves, covetous, boasters, proud, blasphemers, disobedient to parents, unthankful, unholy, Without natural affection, truce-*

breakers, false accusers, incontinent, fierce, despisers of those that are good, Traitors, heady, highminded, lovers of pleasures more than lovers of God; Having a form of godliness, but denying the power thereof: from such turn away. For of this sort are they which creep into houses, and lead captive silly women laden with sins, led away with divers lusts. Ever learning, and never able to come to the knowledge of the truth. II Tim. 3:1–7.

. . . A corrupt tree bringeth forth evil fruit. Matt. 7:17.

Note: See Chapter 38—Faith toward God (questions 327, 328).

725. WHAT IS THE PENALTY FOR ORIGINAL SIN?

The penalty for original sin is spiritual and physical death.

And the Lord God commanded the man, saying, Of every tree of the garden thou mayest freely eat: But of the tree of the knowledge of good and evil, thou shalt not eat of it: for in the day that thou eatest thereof thou shalt surely die. Gen. 2:16–17.

Note: Spiritual death is separation of man from God; physical death is separation of man's body from his soul and spirit.

726. HOW CAN WE HAVE THE SENTENCE OF SIN REVOKED?

We must become partakers of Christ's death so that the penalty for sin is paid for us through the shedding of His blood.

. . . Without shedding of blood is no remission. Heb. 9:22.

For this is my blood of the new testament, which is shed for many for the remission of sins. Matt. 26:28.

Jesus said unto her, I am the resurrection, and the life: he that believeth in me, though he were dead, yet shall he live . . . John 11:25.

I am the living bread which came down from heaven: if any man eat of this bread, he shall live for ever: and the bread that I will give is my flesh, which I will give for the life of the world. John 6:51.

727. HOW DO WE BECOME PARTAKERS OF CHRIST'S DEATH?

We become partakers of Christ's death by repentance, faith and being buried with Him in water baptism.

> *Know ye not that so many of us as were baptized into Jesus Christ were baptized into his death. Therefore we are buried with him by baptism into death: that like as Christ was raised up from the dead by the glory of the Father, even so we also should walk in newness of life. Rom. 6:3,4.*

> *For if, when we were enemies, we were reconciled to God by the death of his Son, much more, being reconciled, we shall be saved by his life. Rom. 5:10.*

728. WHEN WE ARE BAPTIZED, WHAT HAPPENS TO THE ENMITY THAT IS IN US?

The enmity is cut away, and the feud between God and man is brought to an end.

> *For if, when we were enemies, we were reconciled to God by the death of his Son, much more, being reconciled, we shall be saved by his life. Rom. 5:10.*

729. HOW IS THE ENMITY CUT AWAY?

The Holy Spirit performs a spiritual operation on the heart that is called circumcision of the heart. He cuts away our old, corrupt nature with its passions and lusts.

> *In Him also you were circumcised with a circumcision not made with hands, but in a (spiritual) circumcision (performed by) Christ by stripping off the body of the flesh (the whole corrupt, carnal nature with its passions and lusts).*

> *(Thus you were circumcised when) you were buried with him in (your) baptism, in which you were also raised with (Him to a new life) through (your) faith in the working of God (as displayed when He) raised Him up from the dead. Col. 2:11,12 AMP.*

730. WHY MUST THE HEART BE CIRCUMCISED?

The heart must be circumcised before a believer can enter into covenant relationship with God. The rite of circumcision was instituted by God as a seal of His covenant (agreement) with Abraham and his seed. The Israelites circumcised every male child to keep the covenant but they abandoned the worship of God and broke His commandments. Because of the hardness of their hearts, they broke their covenant with God. By his death on the cross, Jesus Christ made a new covenant between God and man. The sign of the new covenant is circumcision of the heart by the Holy Spirit.

> For he is not a Jew, which is one outwardly; neither is that circumcision, which is outward in the flesh: But he is a Jew, which is one inwardly: and circumcision is that of the heart, in the spirit, and not in the letter: whose praise is not of men, but of God. Rom. 2:28,29.

> But now hath he obtained a more excellent ministry, by how much also he is the mediator of a better covenant, which was established upon better promises. For if that first covenant had been faultless, then should no place have been sought for the second. For finding fault with them, he saith, Behold, the days come, saith the Lord, when I will make a new covenant with the house of Israel and with the house of Judah: Not according to the covenant that I made with their fathers in the day when I took them by the hand to lead them out of the land of Egypt; because they continued not in my covenant, and I regarded them not, saith the Lord. For this is the covenant that I will make with the house of Israel after those days, saith the Lord; I will put my laws into their minds and write them in their hearts: and I will be to them a God, and they shall be to me a people: And they shall not teach every man his neighbor, and every man his brother, saying, Know the Lord: for all shall know me, from the least to the greatest. For I will be merciful to their unrighteousness, and their sins and their iniquities will I remember no more. In that he saith, A new covenant, he hath made the first old. Now that which decayeth and waxeth old is ready to vanish away. Heb. 8:6–13. (See Chapter 39—Doctrine of Baptisms.)

731. WHAT DOES CIRCUMCISION OF HEART DO FOR US?

1. When the heart is circumcised, God places His seal of righteousness upon us making us heirs to the promises made to Abraham.

And he received the sign of circumcision, a seal of the righteousness of the faith which he had yet being uncircumcised: that he might be the father of all them that believe, though they be not circumcised; that righteousness might be imputed unto them also. Rom. 4:11.

2. When the enmity (hostility) is cut away, true love for God begins to develop in the heart.

And the Lord thy God will circumcise thine heart, and the heart of thy seed, to love the Lord thy God with all thine heart, and with all thy soul, that thou mayest live. Deut. 30:6.

3. When the conscience is cleansed, we approach God in confidence because we no longer feel guilty in His presence.

The like figure whereunto even baptism doth also now save us (not the putting away of the filth of the flesh, but the answer of a good conscience toward God,) by the resurrection of Jesus Christ. I Peter 3:21.

732. CAN WE LOVE GOD BEFORE EXPERIENCING CIRCUMCISION OF HEART?

We cannot love God as we should until the enmity in us against God is destroyed.

And the Lord thy God will circumcise thine heart, and the heart of thy seed, to love the Lord thy God with all thine heart, and with all thy soul, that thou mayest live. Deut. 30:6.

And I will give them one heart, and I will put a new spirit within you; and I will take the stony heart out of their flesh, and will give them an heart of flesh: That they may walk in my statutes, and keep mine ordinances, and do them: and they shall be my people, and I will be their God. Ezek. 11:19–20.

733. HOW DOES CIRCUMCISION OF HEART CHANGE US?

Circumcision of heart changes us by breaking down barriers that have separated Christians because of social status, race, nationality or sex. We find fellowship with other Christians who are sincerely following Christ even though their beliefs are different from ours.

For as many of you as have been baptized into Christ have put on Christ. There is neither Jew nor Greek, there is neither bond nor free, there is neither male nor female: for ye are all one in Christ Jesus. Gal. 3:27,28.

734. IS THE CIRCUMCISION OF HEART AN ESSENTIAL PART OF THE NEW BIRTH?

Yes. Only when the old, carnal nature is cut away can we become new creatures in Christ Jesus.

Therefore if any man be in Christ, he is a new creature: old things are passed away; behold, all things are become new. II Cor. 5:17.

For as many of you as have been baptized into Christ have put on Christ. Gal. 3:27.

735. WHAT IS THE NEW BIRTH?

The new birth (regeneration) is an entire change of the life and character of a believer. When a man is born again, the enmity against God is destroyed and the heart is filled with love for God. This love is exhibited by keeping God's commandments and by loving the people of God.

For this is the love of God, that we keep his commandments: and his commandments are not grievous. For whatsoever is born of God overcometh the world: and this is the victory that overcometh the world, even our faith. I John 5:3,4.

If a man say, I love God, and hateth his brother, he is a liar: for he that loveth not his brother whom he hath seen, how can he love God whom he hath not seen? I John 4:20.

We know that we have passed from death unto life, because we love the brethren ... I John 3:14a.

736. MUST EVERYONE BE BORN AGAIN?

Everyone should have two births—the natural and the spiritual. One is earthy and the other heavenly; one is of the body, the other is of the spirit. Without the first, we cannot see or enjoy this world. Without the second, we cannot see or enjoy the Kingdom of God.

Jesus answered and said unto him, Verily, verily, I say unto thee, Except a man be born again, he cannot see the Kingdom of God. Nicodemus saith unto him, How can a man be born when he is old? Can he enter the second time into his mother's womb, and be born? Jesus answered, Verily, verily, I say unto thee, Except a man be born of water and of the Spirit, he cannot enter into the kingdom of God. That which is born of the flesh is flesh, and that which is born of the Spirit is spirit. Marvel not that I said unto thee, Ye must be born again. John 3:3–7.

737.   WHO IS TO BE BAPTIZED?

Only those who believe and confess that Jesus is the Christ are to be baptized.

And as they went on their way, they came unto a certain water; and the eunuch said, See, here is water; what doth hinder me to be baptized? And Philip said, If thou believest with all thine heart, thou mayest. And he answered and said, I believe that Jesus Christ is the Son of God. Acts 8:36,37.

He saith unto them, But whom say ye that I am? And Simon Peter answered and said, Thou art the Christ, the Son of the living God. And Jesus answered and said unto him, Blessed art thou, Simon Bar-jona: for flesh and blood hath not revealed it unto thee, but my Father which is in heaven. Matt. 16:15–17.

738.   SHOULD CHILDREN BE BAPTIZED?

Children should be baptized only when they have had the Holy Spirit reveal Jesus, the Christ, to them and have been given full understanding of the significance of baptism.

He that believeth and is baptized shall be saved . . . Mark 16:16.

739.   WHAT IS THE SPIRITUAL STATE OF A CHILD?

Up to the age of accountability, a child is sanctified by a believing parent.

For the unbelieving husband is sanctified by the wife, and

*the unbelieving wife is sanctified by the husband: else were
your children unclean: but now they are holy. I Cor. 7:14.*

740.   HOW ARE WE TO BE BAPTIZED?

To receive the life and experience the Holy Spirit gives us in the
Sacrament of Baptism, we must follow the Bible pattern for baptism exactly as it is prescribed in the Scriptures.

1. *Repent* for our sins and the enmity that is in us against God.
2. *Believe* for an operation on our heart (circumcision) that will
   remove the old nature of sin.
3. *Be baptized* (completely immersed) into Jesus Christ so we
   may share His death, burial and resurrection.
4. Be baptized by a believer who has the authority to use the
   Name of the Lord Jesus Christ.

741.   WHO CAN ADMINISTER BAPTISM?

Administering baptism is the work of the minister who has had
the Holy Spirit reveal to him the identity of Jesus Christ and
who has the power and authority to use His name.

> *He (Jesus) saith unto them, But whom say ye that I am?
> And Simon Peter answered and said, Thou art the Christ,
> the Son of the living God. And Jesus answered and said
> unto him, Blessed art thou, Simon Bar-jona: for flesh and
> blood hath not revealed it unto thee, but my Father which
> is in heaven. And I say also unto thee, That thou art Peter,
> and upon this rock (revelation) I will build my church; and
> the gates of hell shall not prevail against it. And I will give
> unto thee the keys of the kingdom of heaven: and what-
> soever thou shalt bind on earth shall be bound in heaven:
> and whatsoever thou shalt loose on earth shall be loosed in
> heaven. Then charged he his disciples that they should tell
> no man that he was Jesus the Christ. Matt. 16:15–20.*

**742.   JESUS CHRIST INSTRUCTED HIS DISCIPLES TO BAP-
TIZE "IN THE NAME OF THE FATHER, AND OF THE
SON, AND OF THE HOLY GHOST". WHY DID THEY
BAPTIZE IN THE NAME OF JESUS CHRIST?**

The name of the Lord Jesus Christ is the name by which the
power of the Godhead is invoked.

For in Him the whole fulness of Deity (the Godhead), continues to dwell in bodily form—giving complete expression of the divine nature. And you are in Him, made full and have come to fullness of life—in Christ you too are filled with the Godhead: Father, Son and Holy Spirit, and reach full spiritual stature. And He is the head of all rule and authority—of every angelic principality and power. Col. 2:9,10. AMP.

743. WHY IS THERE SUCH CONTROVERSY ABOUT THE TITLES AND THE NAME OF THE GODHEAD TODAY?

This is a spiritual mystery that can only be solved with the aid of the Holy Spirit.

And to make all men see what is the fellowship of the mystery which from the beginning of the world hath been hid in God, who created all things by Jesus Christ: To the intent that now unto the principalities and powers in heavenly places might be known by the church the manifold wisdom of God, According to the eternal purpose which he purposed in Christ Jesus our Lord: Eph. 3:9–11.

But we speak the wisdom of God in a mystery, even the hidden wisdom, which God ordained before the world unto our glory: Which none of the princes of this world knew; for had they known it, they would not have crucified the Lord of Glory . . . But God hath revealed them unto us by his Spirit: for the Spirit searcheth all things, yea, the deep things of God. I Cor. 2:7,8,10.

744. WHAT IS THE NAME OF THE FATHER, SON, AND HOLY SPIRIT?

The disciples were commanded to go into all the world baptizing believers in the "name" of the Father and of the Son and of the Holy Spirit. The word is in the singular, the "name" not names. When the Holy Spirit revealed the identity of Jesus to the disciples they knew the final "name" of the one true God to be . . . The Lord Jesus Christ.

Therefore let all the house of Israel know assuredly, that God hath made that same Jesus, whom ye have crucified, both Lord and Christ. Acts 2:36.

And whatsoever ye do in word or deed, do all in the name of the Lord Jesus. Col. 3:17.

Then Peter said unto them, Repent, and be baptized every one of you in the name of Jesus Christ for the remission of sins, and ye shall receive the gift of the Holy Ghost. Acts 2:38.

745. WHAT IS THE DIFFERENCE BETWEEN THE BAPTISM OF JOHN THE BAPTIST AND THE BAPTISM OF JESUS CHRIST?

John the Baptist's baptism was a baptism of repentance and preparation for the Messiah. It was to show that those who had been baptized by him had repented of their sins and were looking forward to the Messiah. It was an outward act declaring their repentance. Christ's baptism, also a baptism of repentance, is an inward work for the circumcision of the heart and entrance into the Christ and the New Covenant.

And he (Paul) said unto them, Unto what then were ye baptized? And they said, Unto John's baptism. Then said Paul, John verily baptized with the baptism of repentance, saying unto the people, that they should believe on him which should come after him, that is, on Christ Jesus. Acts 19:3,4.

746. WHAT DID THE PEOPLE DO WHO RECEIVED JOHN'S BAPTISM?

When they heard of the baptism of Jesus Christ, they were baptized again in the name of the Lord Jesus.

When they heard this, they were baptized in the name of the Lord Jesus. Acts 19:5.

747. IS IT POSSIBLE TO BE BAPTIZED AND NOT RECEIVE A CIRCUMCISED HEART?

Yes! To receive a circumcised heart, the Holy Spirit must prepare the heart by giving us the desire and the faith to be born again. When baptism is not preceded by heart preparation, it is merely a rite and not an experience.

For unto us was the gospel preached, as well as unto them:

but the word preached did not profit them, not being mixed with faith in them that heard it. Heb. 4:2.

. . . For the letter killeth, but the Spirit giveth life. II Cor. 3:6.

748. WHAT SHOULD WE DO IF OUR BAPTISM HAS ONLY BEEN A RITE?

If our baptism has only been a rite, we should pray asking the Holy Spirit to prepare us for the promised experience. When we have the assurance that the heart has been fully prepared, we should be baptized.

For by one Spirit are we all baptized into one body, whether we be Jew or Gentile, whether we be bond or free; and have been all made to drink into one Spirit. I Cor. 12:13.

There is one body, and one Spirit, even as ye are called in one hope of your calling; One Lord, one faith, one baptism. Eph. 4:4,5.

STUDY QUESTIONS—Chapter 55

1. What is Water Baptism?
2. Why is baptism necessary?
3. What happens to original sin in baptism?
4. What happens to enmity when we are baptized?
5. What is circumcision of heart?
6. Why must the heart be circumcised?
7. What does circumcision of heart do for us?
8. In Biblical terms, where is the heart of man located?
9. Is the circumcision of heart an essential part of the new birth?
10. What is the new birth?
11. Does regeneration occur in baptism?
12. Why must we be born again?
13. Should children be baptized?
14. Why did the disciples (Apostles) baptize in the name of the Lord Jesus Christ?
15. What is the difference between the baptism of John the Baptist and the baptism of Jesus Christ?
16. How can we receive the experience of circumcision of heart when we are baptized?
17. What should we do if our baptism was only a rite?
18. Write John 3:5; Mark 16:16; Deut. 30:6; Heb. 8:10–13.

Chapter 56

THE SACRAMENT OF THE LORD'S SUPPER

749. WHAT IS THE LORD'S SUPPER?

The Lord's Supper is a sacrament instituted by Jesus Christ on the night before He died that confirms the covenant made with God through the blood of Christ. It is a fulfillment of the eternal covenant of the Passover Feast which God commanded the Israelites to observe. Through the blood of the lamb, the Israelites confirmed their covenant with God.

> *Purge out therefore the old leaven, that ye may be a new lump, as ye are unleavened. For even Christ our passover is sacrificed for us. I Cor. 5:7.*

> *... That the Lord Jesus the same night in which he was betrayed took bread: And when he had given thanks, he brake it, and said, Take, eat: this is my body, which is broken for you: this do in remembrance of me. After the same manner also he took the cup, when he had supped, saying, This cup is the new testament in my blood: this do ye, as oft as ye drink it, in remembrance of me. For as often as ye eat this bread, and drink this cup, ye do shew the Lord's death till he come. I Cor. 11:23–26.*

750. WHY WAS THE PASSOVER FEAST CELEBRATED?

The Passover Feast was celebrated by the Israelites commemorating their liberation from Egyptian slavery. The blood of a slain lamb was smeared on the doorposts of all their homes as protection from the divine judgment that was to pass through Egypt. God smote the first-born of the Egyptians as He struck the houses and cattle not protected by the blood of the lamb.

For I will pass through the land of Egypt this night, and will smite all the firstborn in the land of Egypt, both men and beasts; and against all the gods of Egypt I will execute judgment: I am the Lord. Exod. 12:12.

751. HOW IS THE LORD'S SUPPER A FULFILLMENT OF THE PASSOVER?

1. Christ became our Passover and was sacrificed for us. He took the place of the Paschal lamb—the lamb slain and eaten at the Passover.

   The next day John seeth Jesus coming unto him, and saith, Behold, the Lamb of God, which taketh away the sin of the world . . . And looking upon Jesus as he walked, he saith, Behold the Lamb of God! John 1:29,36.

2. When the Israelites ate the lamb, they received healing for their bodies. When we partake of the Lord's Supper, we receive healing for the body, soul and spirit.

   He brought them forth also with silver and gold: and there was not one feeble person among their tribes. Ps. 105:37.

   And I have led you forty years in the wilderness: your clothes are not waxen old upon you, and thy shoe is not waxen old upon thy foot. Deut. 29:5.

3. The Passover was a remembrance of the Israelites' exodus from the slavery of the Egyptians. The Lord's Supper is a remembrance of our own exodus from the slavery of sin.

   And Jesus said unto them, I am the bread of life: he that cometh to me shall never hunger; and he that believeth on me shall never thirst. John 6:35.

   The cup of blessing which we bless, is it not the communion of the blood of Christ? The bread which we break, is it not the communion of the body of Christ? For we being many are one bread, and one body: for we are all partakers of that one bread. I Cor. 10:16,17.

752. WHY DO WE CELEBRATE THE LORD'S SUPPER?

We celebrate the Lord's Supper for five reasons:

1. It was commanded by the Christ that we do so.

This do in remembrance of me. I Cor. 11:25.

And ye shall observe this thing for an ordinance to thee and to thy sons forever. Exod. 12:24.

2. To have in us the life of Christ, eternal life.

I am the living bread which came down from heaven: if any man eat of this bread, he shall live forever: and the bread that I will give is my flesh, which I will give for the life of the world . . . Then Jesus said unto them, Verily, verily, I say unto you, Except ye eat the flesh of the Son of man, and drink his blood, ye have no life in you. John 6:51,53.

3. To confirm the covenant made with God through the blood of Christ.

For this is my blood of the New Testament (covenant), which is shed for many for the remission of sins. Matt. 26:28.

4. To have health.

For he that eateth and drinketh unworthily, eateth and drinketh damnation to himself, not discerning the Lord's body. For this cause many are weak and sickly among you, and many sleep. I Cor. 11:29,30.

5. As a constant reminder of the great sacrifice Christ made for our redemption.

This do ye . . . in remembrance of me. I Cor. 11:25.

And it shall come to pass, when your children shall say unto you, What mean ye by this service? That ye shall say, It is the sacrifice of the Lord's passover. Exod. 12:26,27.

753. WHAT ARE THE VISIBLE EMBLEMS IN THE LORD'S SUPPER?

The visible emblems are the bread and the cup.

754. WHAT DO WE RECEIVE WHEN WE PARTAKE OF THE LORD'S SUPPER?

We receive the body and blood of Christ. It is His true presence that makes communion with Christ possible. This is the reason the Lord's Supper is called "Holy Communion".

The cup of blessing (of wine at the Lord's Supper) upon which we ask (God's) blessing, does it not mean (that in drinking it) we participate in and share a fellowship (a communion) in the blood of Christ, the Messiah? The bread which we break, does it not mean (that in eating it) we participate in and share a fellowship (a communion) in the body of Christ? For we (no matter how) numerous we are, are one body, because we all partake of the one Bread (the One Whom the communion bread represents). I Cor. 10:16,17 AMP.

755. **WHY DO WE BELIEVE IN THE REAL PRESENCE OF CHRIST IN THE LORD'S SUPPER?**

We believe in the real presence of Christ because:

A. Jesus said, "This IS my body and this IS my blood which was shed for you."

And he took bread, and gave thanks, and brake it, and gave unto them, saying, This is my body which is given for you: this do in remembrance of me. Luke 22:19.

B. The Bible clearly states that through the blood we have communion with Christ.

Likewise also the cup after supper, saying, This cup is the new testament in my blood, which is shed for you. Luke 22:20.

C. The Bible clearly states that unworthy communicants are guilty, not of the bread and the wine but of the body and blood of Christ.

Wherefore, whosoever shall eat this bread, and drink this cup of the Lord, unworthily, shall be guilty of the body and blood of the Lord. I Cor. 11:27.

D. No man has the right to change the meaning of a divine institution or covenant.

Brethren, I speak after the manner of men; Though it be but a man's covenant, yet if it be confirmed, no man disannulleth, or addeth thereto. Gal. 3:15.

756.   WHEN DO THE BREAD AND THE WINE (THE CUP) BE-COME THE BODY AND BLOOD OF JESUS CHRIST?

The moment we eat the bread and drink the wine, we partake of the real presence of Christ.

> *And after he had given thanks, he brake it, and said,* Take, eat: *this is my body, which is broken for you: this do in remembrance of me. After the same manner also he took the cup, when he had supped, saying, This cup is the new testament in my blood: this do ye, as oft as ye drink it, in remembrance of me. For as often as ye* eat *this bread and* drink *this cup ye do shew the Lord's death till he come. I Cor. 11:24–26.*

757.   WHAT SHOULD WE DO BEFORE WE PARTAKE OF THE LORD'S SUPPER?

The Scriptures tell us to examine ourselves carefully.

> *But let a man examine himself, and so let him eat of that bread, and drink of that cup. I Cor. 11:28.*

758.   WHAT DOES PAUL MEAN WHEN HE SAYS, "BUT LET A MAN EXAMINE HIMSELF"?

We are to be in complete communion with Christ when we partake of the Lord's Supper.

> *Wherefore whosoever shall eat this bread, and drink this cup of the Lord, unworthily, shall be guilty of the body and blood of the Lord. But let a man examine himself, and so let him eat of that bread, and drink of that cup. For he that eateth and drinketh unworthily, eateth and drinketh damnation to himself, not discerning the Lord's body. I Cor. 11:27–29.*

759.   HOW DO WE EXAMINE OURSELVES?

We examine ourselves by calling to mind the Ten Commandments of God and the laws of the Church, the particular duties of our calling and whether we have enmity against our brother. (See Foot Washing—Chapter 57.)

1. Ask the Holy Spirit to help us recall what sins we have committed and grant us repentance for them.

2. Confess our sins to God and ask for His forgiveness.

3. Make restitution wherever possible.

4. Be determined not to sin again.

760. WHAT WILL HAPPEN TO US IF WE EAT AND DRINK THE BODY AND BLOOD OF CHRIST UNWORTHILY?

We place ourselves in danger of sickness and death.

> *For he that eateth and drinketh unworthily, eateth and drinketh damnation (chastisement) to himself, not discerning the Lord's body. For this cause many are weak and sickly among you, and many sleep. I Cor. 11:29,30.*

761. WHAT BLESSINGS DO WE RECEIVE FROM THE LORD'S SUPPER?

When the members of the body of Christ come together repenting of sin and forgiving one another, the cleansing that is received strengthens and unites more firmly the entire body. Our sense of belonging to both God and each other is deepened as together we reaffirm our covenant. The Lord's Supper renews our fellowship with the Lord and His body, and our consecration to Him: and reminds us of the Lord's death, through which we are given eternal life.

> *Whoso eateth my flesh, and drinketh my blood, hath eternal life; and I will raise him up at the last day. John 6:54.*

> *For as often as ye eat this bread, and drink this cup, ye do shew the Lord's death till he come. I Cor. 11:26.*

> *But if we walk in the light as he is in the light, we have fellowship one with another, and the blood of Jesus Christ his Son cleanseth us from all sin. I John 1:7.*

762. WHY DOES CHRIST COMMAND US TO REMEMBER THE LORD'S SUPPER?

Jesus Christ said we should take the cup in remembrance of Him ... we remember the cup that He drank willingly for us, a cup He tried to avoid for He knew it held suffering and death. Nevertheless He drank that cup that He might redeem us from the power of the devil.

When we take the communion cup in our hand, the words of Jesus, "This do YE!" should move us to submit ourselves to the complete will of God accepting all things from His hand. Even if it be a cup of suffering, we willingly drink the cup. Submission to God's will enables us to share in a fellowship of Christ that gives us true communion.

Jesus said we should eat the bread, which is His body, in remembrance of Him. We remember that He gave His body willingly to cruel men who beat, bruised and mutilated it that we might have eternal life.

When we take the communion bread in our hand, the words of Jesus, "This do YE!" should move us to present our bodies to Him as a living sacrifice that His will might be accomplished in us.

> *. . . If any man will come after me, let him deny himself, and take up his cross, and follow me. Matt. 16:24.*

> *I beseech you therefore, brethren, by the mercies of God, that ye present your bodies a living sacrifice, holy, acceptable unto God, which is your reasonable service. Rom. 12:1.*

763. SHOULD CHILDREN PARTAKE OF THE LORD'S SUPPER?

Only after they have entered into covenant with Christ, are cleansed by His blood, and have been baptized into Christ for circumcision of heart, should children partake of the Lord's Supper. (See Chapter 60 on Dedication of Children.)

STUDY QUESTIONS—Chapter 56

1. What is the Lord's Supper?
2. How is the Lord's Supper related to the Passover Feast?
3. Why do we celebrate the Lord's Supper?
4. Why do we believe in the real presence of Christ in the Lord's Supper?
5. How do we examine ourselves?
6. What blessings do we receive from the Lord's Supper?
7. Write John 6:53; Matt. 26:28; I Cor. 11:27-29.

Chapter 57

THE SACRAMENT OF FOOT WASHING

764.   **WHAT IS FOOT WASHING?**

Foot Washing is a sacrament instituted by Jesus Christ to enable
man to fulfill the law of God ... "Thou shalt love thy neighbor
as thyself."

> *Thou shalt not avenge, nor bear any grudge against the
> children of thy people, but thou shalt love thy neighbour as
> thyself: I am the Lord. Lev. 19:18.*

> *Think not that I am come to destroy the law, or the proph-
> ets: I am not come to destroy, but to fulfil. For verily I say
> unto you, Till heaven and earth pass, one jot or one tittle
> shall in no wise pass from the law, till all be fulfilled.
> Matt. 5:17,18.*

> *Love worketh no ill to his neighbour: therefore love is the
> fulfilling of the law. Rom. 13:10.*

765.   **WHAT IS THE PURPOSE OF FOOT WASHING?**

Just as Baptism removes the enmity in us against God and enables us to love God, so foot washing removes the enmity in us
against our brother and enables us to love our brother as we love
ourselves.

> *Love worketh no ill to his neighbour: therefore love is the
> fulfilling of the law. Rom. 13:10.*

> *If I then, your Lord and teacher (Master), have washed
> your feet, you ought—it is your duty, you are under obliga-
> tion, you owe it—to wash one another's feet. For I have
> given you this as an example, so that you should do (in
> your turn) what I have done to you. John 13:14,15 Amp.*

766. **WHAT IS THE ENMITY THAT IS IN US AGAINST OUR BROTHER?**

We think too highly of ourselves; we long to rule over others; and we seek only after our own interests.

> ... Charity (love) ... vaunteth not itself, is not puffed up ... doth not behave itself unseemly, seeketh not her own ... I Cor. 13:4,5.

> For I say, through the grace given unto me, to every man that is among you, not to think of himself more highly than he ought to think; but to think soberly, according as God hath dealt to every man the measure of faith. Rom. 12:3.

767. **WHY DID JESUS WASH THE FEET OF THE DISCIPLES?**

He washed the feet of the disciples to show them that they were to become "servants" of the Lord by serving one another.

> And he sat down, and called the twelve, and saith unto them, If any man desire to be first, the same shall be last of all, and servant of all. Mark 9:35.

> ... but by love serve one another. For all the law is fulfilled in one word, even in this: Thou shalt love thy neighbor as thyself. Gal. 5:13,14.

> ... But whosoever will be great among you, let him be your minister; And whosoever will be chief among you, let him be your servant: Even as the Son of man came not to be ministered unto, but to minister, and to give his life a ransom for many. Matt. 20:26–28.

768. **DID THE DISCIPLES KNOW THEY WERE TO SERVE ONE ANOTHER?**

No. They had no thought or desire to serve anyone, and quarreled among themselves about who would be the greatest in God's Kingdom.

> And there was also a strife among them, which of them should be accounted the greatest. Luke 22:24.

> And he turned to the woman, and said unto Simon, Seest thou this woman? I entered into thine house, thou gavest

me no water for my feet: but she hath washed my feet with tears, and wiped them with the hairs of her head. Thou gavest me no kiss: but this woman since the time I came in hath not ceased to kiss my feet. My head with oil thou didst not anoint: but this woman hath anointed my feet with ointment. Luke 7:44–46.

Note: See Matt. 20:20–28.

769. WHY DID THE DISCIPLES NOT KNOW THEY WERE CALLED TO BE SERVANTS?

The Holy Spirit had not revealed this to them. We know nothing of spiritual matters until we receive a revelation from the Holy Spirit.

> *But as it is written, Eye hath not seen, nor ear heard, neither have entered into the heart of man, the things which God hath prepared for them that love him. But God hath revealed them unto us by his Spirit: for the Spirit searcheth all things, yea, the deep things of God. For what man knoweth the things of man, save the spirit of man which is in him? even so the things of God knoweth no man, but the Spirit of God. I Cor. 2:9–11.*

> *But the natural man receiveth not the things of the Spirit of God: for they are foolishness unto him: neither can he know them, because they are spiritually discerned. I Cor. 2:14.*

770. HOW DID JESUS TEACH THEM TO BE SERVANTS?

Jesus gave them an example to follow by washing their feet and becoming a servant to them.

> *He riseth from supper, and laid aside his garments; and took a towel, and girded himself. After that he poureth water into a bason, and began to wash the disciples' feet, and to wipe them with the towel wherewith he was girded. John 13:4,5.*

771. WHY DID JESUS DO THIS?

Jesus knew that if the disciples followed His example, the Holy Spirit would work a deep repentance in them and impart to them the gift of love for one another.

So after he had washed their feet, and had taken his garments, and was set down again, he said unto them, Know ye what I have done to you? Ye call me Master and Lord: and ye say well for so I am. If I then, your Lord and Master, have washed your feet; ye also ought to wash one another's feet. For I have given you an example, that ye should do as I have done to you ... A new commandment I give unto you, That ye love one another; as I have loved you, that ye also love one another. By this shall all men know that ye are my disciples, if ye have love one to another. John 13:12–15,34,35.

772.   WHY IS THE GIFT OF LOVE SO IMPORTANT?

1. The Gospel of the Kingdom cannot be preached effectively without the messenger possessing the gift of love.

Though I speak with the tongues of men and of angels, and have not charity (love), I am become-as sounding brass, or a tinkling cymbal. And though I have the gift of prophecy, and understand all mysteries, and all knowledge; and though I have all faith, so that I could remove mountains, and have not charity (love), I am nothing. I Cor. 13:1,2.

2. The Body of Christ is not able to function without the flow of love through each joint, nor can the members rightly esteem the value of every part.

That there should be no schism in the body; but that the members should have the same care one for another. I Cor. 12:25.

773.   HOW DO THE SCRIPTURES DESCRIBE THE SERVANTS OF CHRIST WHO POSSESS THE GIFT OF LOVE?

The Scriptures describe them as having "beautiful feet".

How then shall they call on him in whom they have not believed? and how shall they believe in him of whom they have not heard? and how shall they hear without a preacher? And how shall they preach, except they be sent? as it is written, How beautiful are the feet of them that preach the gospel of peace, and bring glad tidings of good things! Rom. 10:14–15.

774. WHOM DOES CHRIST SELECT TO PROCLAIM THE GOSPEL OF THE KINGDOM?

Christ selects believers who have beautiful feet to proclaim the Gospel of the Kingdom.

> *Behold upon the mountains the feet of him, that bringeth good tidings, that publisheth peace. O Judah, keep thy solemn feasts, perform thy vows . . . Nah. 1:15.*

> *As they ministered to the Lord, and fasted, the Holy Ghost said, Separate me Barnabas and Saul for the work whereunto I have called them. And when they had fasted and prayed, and laid their hands on them, they sent them away. Acts 13:2–3.*

> *. . . how can they preach except they be sent? as it is written, How beautiful are the feet of them that preach the gospel of peace, and bring glad tidings of good things! Rom. 10:15.*

775. IS THIS THE PURPOSE FOR WHICH CHRIST WASHED HIS DISCIPLES' FEET?

Yes. Christ washed the feet of His disciples to make their feet beautiful . . . to create a bond of unity among them that would make them a team, an army, to bring the Gospel to the world in word and example.

> *And your feet shod with the preparation of the gospel of peace; Eph. 6:15.*

> *Peter saith unto him, Thou shalt never wash my feet. Jesus answered him, If I wash thee not, thou hast no part with me. John 13:8.*

776. HOW DOES CHRIST SEE THE FEET OF HIS CHURCH BEFORE FOOTWASHING?

The feet of His body, the Church, are:

1. Defiled.

> *For all the law is fulfilled in one word, even in this; Thou shalt love thy neighbour as thyself. But if ye bite and devour one another, take heed that ye be not consumed one of another. Gal. 5:14,15.*

Note: See Num. 19 (waters of separation).

2. Broken, out of joint.

> *And cut through and make firm and plain and smooth, straight paths for your feet—(yes, make them) safe and upright and happy paths that go in the right direction—so that the lame and halting (limbs) may not be put out of joint, but rather may be cured. Heb. 12:13 (Amp.)*

> *From whom the whole body fitly joined together and compacted by that which every joint supplieth, according to the effectual working in the measure of every part, maketh increase of the body unto the edifying of itself in love. This I say therefore, and testify in the Lord, that ye henceforth walk not as other Gentiles walk, in the vanity of their minds, Having the understanding darkened, being alienated from the life of God through the ignorance that is in them, because of the blindness of their heart: Who being past feeling have given themselves over unto lasciviousness, to work all uncleanness with greediness. But ye have not so learned Christ; If so be that ye have heard him, and have been taught by him, as the truth is in Jesus. Eph. 4:16–21.*

777. DID THE WASHING OF THE DISCIPLES' FEET CHANGE THEM?

Yes. The disciples who quarreled among themselves for place and preferment, repented and received the gift of love. The multitudes marveled how they loved one another.

> *And the multitude of them that believed were of one heart and of one soul: neither said any of them that ought of the things which he possessed was his own; but they had all things common. And with great power gave the apostles witness of the resurrection of the Lord Jesus: and great grace was upon them all. Acts 4:32,33.*

778. HOW DO WE PREPARE OURSELVES FOR FOOTWASHING?

By repenting of our pride and enmity against our brother and by allowing the Spirit to give us understanding of the Word so that we have faith to receive the gift of love.

779. WHAT DOES THE SACRAMENT OF FOOT WASHING DO FOR US IN RELATIONSHIP TO OTHERS?

Through the Sacrament of Foot Washing:

1. The Holy Spirit reveals to us that we are servants of Christ and of one another.

2. The enmity against our brother is removed so that we can love one another.

3. Barriers are broken down and a bond of unity is produced among the members of the Body of Christ.

4. The alienated and wayward brother is restored back into the Body of Christ.

> *And make straight paths for your feet, lest that which is lame be turned out of the way; but let it rather be healed. Heb. 12:13.*

> *Brethren, if a man be overtaken in a fault, ye which are spiritual, restore such an one in the spirit of meekness; considering thyself, lest thou also be tempted. Gal. 6:1.*

> *. . . even as Christ also loved the church, and gave himself for it; That he might sanctify and cleanse it with the washing of water by the word, That he might present it to himself a glorious church, not having spot or wrinkle, or any such thing; but that it should be holy and without blemish. Eph. 5:25–26.*

780. WHAT DOES THE SACRAMENT OF FOOT WASHING DO FOR US AS INDIVIDUALS?

With every Sacrament of the church there is a spiritual experience for the believer. In the Sacrament of Foot Washing, the revelation that we are servants brings deep repentance and humility for the pride and selfishness that is in us. The gift of repentance in turn prepares our hearts to receive the gift of love from the Holy Spirit.

> *Let nothing be done through strife or vainglory; but in lowliness of mind let each esteem other better than themselves. Look not every man on his own things, but every man also on the things of others. Let this mind be in you, which was also in Christ Jesus: Who, being in the form of God, thought it not robbery to be equal with God: But*

made himself of no reputation and took upon him the form of a servant ... Phil. 2:3–7.

781. HOW OFTEN SHOULD FOOT WASHING BE OBSERVED?

Foot Washing should be observed whenever the members of the Local Church need cleansing from sin committed against the Body of Christ, the Church, or when the local oversight is directed to observe it. Sin committed against another member of the body manifests a need for love and repentance.

Foot Washing should precede the Lord's Supper when the communicants find that they are not worthy to partake of the body and blood of the Lord.

> *For whosoever exalteth himself shall be abased; and he that humbleth himself shall be exalted. Luke 14:11.*

> *Draw nigh to God, and he will draw nigh to you. Cleanse your hands, ye sinners; and purify your hearts, ye double minded. Be afflicted, and mourn, and weep: let your laughter be turned to mourning, and your joy to heaviness. Humble yourselves in the sight of the Lord, and he shall lift you up. James 4:8–10.*

> *But let a man examine himself . . . For he that eateth and drinketh unworthily, eateth and drinketh damnation to himself, not discerning the Lord's body. I Cor. 11:29.*

782. WHAT IS THE OLD TESTAMENT COUNTERPART OF THE NEW TESTAMENT FOOT WASHING?

The Hebrew priest was thoroughly cleansed before he could perform the duties of the priestly office. However, while performing his priestly duties, his hands and feet became defiled. To keep them clean, he washed them time and time again in the laver of water provided for this distinct purpose. This washing in the laver is the counterpart in the Old Testament for the Foot Washing sacrament in the New Testament.

> *And Aaron and his sons thou shalt bring unto the door of the tabernacle of the congregation, and shalt wash them with water. Exod. 29:4.*

> *And the Lord spake unto Moses, saying, Thou shalt also*

make a laver of brass, and his foot also of brass, to wash withal: and thou shalt put it between the tabernacle of the congregation and the altar, and thou shalt put water therein. For Aaron and his sons shall wash their hands and their feet thereat: When they go into the tabernacle of the congregation, they shall wash with water, that they die not; or when they come near to the altar to minister, to burn offering made by fire unto the Lord: So they shall wash their hands and their feet, that they die not: and it shall be a statute for ever to them, even to him and to his seed throughout their generation. Exod. 30:17–21.

783. WHAT HAPPENS TO US WHEN WE WASH ANOTHER'S FEET?

The Holy Spirit enables us to become true servants. We take the place of Christ and wash away the enmity that is in our brother.

That he might sanctify and cleanse it with the washing of water by the word, That he might present it to himself a glorious church, not having spot, or wrinkle, or any such thing; but that it should be holy and without blemish. For we are members of his body, of his flesh, and of his bones. Eph. 5:26,27,30.

784. WHAT HAPPENS TO US WHEN OUR FEET ARE WASHED?

We receive the one who washes our feet as we would Christ. This acknowledgement gives us an openness and closeness to the other members of the body and washes the enmity from us.

Verily, verily, I say unto you, He that receiveth whomsoever I send receiveth me; and he that receiveth me receiveth him that sent me. John 13:20.

Peter saith unto him, Thou shalt never wash my feet. Jesus answered him, If I wash thee not, thou hast no part with me. John 13:8.

To whom God would make known what is the riches of the glory of this mystery among the Gentiles; which is Christ in you, the hope of glory: Col. 1:27.

785.   WHAT IS THE PROCEDURE FOR FOOT WASHING?

The procedure used is the same as Jesus used.

> *He riseth from supper, and laid aside his garments; and took a towel, and girded himself. After that he poured water into a basin, and began to wash the disciples' feet, and to wipe them with the towel wherewith he was girded. John 13:4,5.*

The men and women are separated and each group conducts its own service. The men wash men's feet and the women wash women's feet.

> *Let all things be done decently and in order. I Cor. 14:40.*

786.   WHAT ARE THE BLESSINGS OF FOOT WASHING?

The blessings of Foot Washing are these:

1. It removes all that has defiled us in our daily walk as members of the Body of Christ.
2. It works a deep spiritual work in the heart.
3. It unites hearts in Christian fellowship and love.
4. It teaches humility and willingness to serve other followers of Christ.
5. It rebukes selfishness and the desire to rule others.
6. It makes us worthy communicants of the Lord's Supper.
7. It prepares our feet to take the Gospel of Peace to the world.

Note: Footwashing may be considered the continuing witness of the water just as Communion is the witness of the blood and the Holy Spirit is the witness of the Spirit on earth.

> *For there are three that bear record in heaven, the Father, the Word, and the Holy Ghost: and these three are one. And there are three that bear witness in earth, the Spirit, and the water, and the blood: and these three agree in one. I John 5:7,8.*

STUDY QUESTIONS—Chapter 57

1. Why is Foot Washing a Sacrament?
2. What is the purpose of Foot Washing?
3. What is the enmity that is in us against our brother?
4. Did the disciples know they were to serve one another?
5. Why is the gift of love so important?
6. What are "beautiful feet"?
7. How does footwashing prepare messengers of the Gospel?
8. What does the Sacrament of Foot Washing do for us individually, and in relationship to others?
9. How does Christ see the feet of His Body when Foot Washing is needed?
10. How do we prepare ourselves to receive a spiritual work through Foot Washing?

Chapter 58

THE SACRAMENT OF CONFIRMATION

787. WHAT IS CONFIRMATION?

Confirmation is a sacrament of the Church through which Christians are strengthened and established in the faith of Jesus Christ.

> And Judas and Silas, being prophets also themselves, exhorted the brethren with many words, and confirmed them. Acts 15:32.

> And when they had preached the gospel to that city, and had taught many, they returned again to Lystra, and to Iconium, and Antioch, confirming the souls of the disciples, and exhorting them to continue in the faith, and that we must through much tribulation enter into the kingdom of God. Acts 14:21,22.

> And he (Paul) went through Syria and Cilicia, confirming the churches. Acts 15:41.

788. WHY IS CONFIRMATION A SACRAMENT?

Confirmation is a sacrament because it was instituted by Christ, through his disciples, for the Church to observe to receive divine strength and establishment in the faith of Jesus Christ.

> As ye have therefore received Christ Jesus the Lord, so walk ye in him: Rooted and built up in him, and stablished in the faith, as ye have been taught, abounding therein with thanksgiving. Col. 2:6,7.

789. **WHY MUST WE BE STRENGTHENED AND ESTABLISHED?**

We must be strengthened so we can remain steadfast during times of testing. We must be established before we can begin to grow in the faith.

> *Wherefore I put thee in remembrance that thou stir up the gift of God, which is in thee by the putting on of my hands. For God hath not given us the spirit of fear: but of power, and of love, and of a sound mind. Be not thou therefore ashamed of the testimony of our Lord, nor of me his prisoner: but be thou partaker of the afflictions of the gospel according to the power of God. II Tim. 1:6–8.*

> *That we henceforth be no more children, tossed to and fro, and carried about with every wind of doctrine, by the sleight of men, and cunning craftiness, whereby they lie in wait to deceive; But speaking the truth in love, may grow up into him in all things, which is the head, even Christ. Eph. 4:14,15.*

790. **HOW IS THE SACRAMENT OF CONFIRMATION ADMINISTERED?**

The Sacrament of Confirmation is administered through the laying on of the hands of the presbytery (ministers).

> *Wherefore I put thee in remembrance that thou stir up the gift of God, which is in thee by the putting on of my hands. For God hath not given us the spirit of fear: but of power, and of love, and of a sound mind. Be not thou therefore ashamed of the testimony of our Lord, nor of me his prisoner: but be thou partaker of the afflictions of the gospel according to the power of God. II Tim. 1:6–8.*

791. **WHAT DO WE RECEIVE IN THE SACRAMENT OF CONFIRMATION?**

We receive the spirit of love, power and soundness of mind that firmly roots (establishes) us in the faith.

> *And he shall be like a tree planted by the rivers of water, that bringeth forth his fruit in his season; his leaf also shall not wither; and whatsoever he doeth shall prosper. Ps. 1:3.*

792.   WHO MAY BE CONFIRMED?

Believers may be confirmed after they have been taught the doctrines and sacraments of the church and have experienced them.

> *And Judas and Silas, being prophets also themselves,* exhorted the brethren with many words, *and confirmed them. Acts 15:32.*

793.   MUST CONFIRMANTS BE SPIRIT-FILLED?

Confirmation establishes and strengthens the Spirit (inner man) that is in man. You cannot confirm the work of the Holy Spirit if He is not there.

> *But if the Spirit of him that raised up Jesus from the dead dwell in you, he that raised up Christ from the dead shall also quicken your mortal bodies* by his spirit that dwelleth in you. *Rom. 8:11.*

794.   SHOULD CHILDREN BE CONFIRMED?

Yes. Children should be established in the faith after they have reached the age of accountability, have been instructed in the principles of the doctrines of Christ (catechism) and have been brought into the experience of each doctrine.

Note: Experience has taught us that when children reach the age of twelve, they are ready for catechism instruction. We call this "the age of accountability". The Lord Jesus was twelve years old when He was instructed in the law.

> *Now his parents went to Jerusalem every year at the feast of the passover. And when he (Jesus) was twelve years old, they went up to Jerusalem after the custom of the feast. Luke 2:41,42.*

795.   IS CONFIRMATION NECESSARY?

Yes. Without confirmation the Church of Jesus Christ is weak. If young Christians are not established firmly in the truth, they become discouraged and fall into confusion and bitterness when tribulation comes to them. The believer who has been confirmed will endure chastening and will become a mature son of God.

> *If ye endure chastening, God dealeth with you as with*

sons; for what son is he whom the father chasteneth not? Heb. 12:7.

They on the rock are they, which, when they hear, receive the word with joy; and these have no root, which for a while believe, and in time of temptation fall away. And that which fell among thorns are they, which, when they have heard, go forth, and are choked with cares and riches and pleasures of this life, and bring no fruit to perfection. Luke 8:13,14.

. . . that they might be called trees of righteousness, the planting of the Lord, that he might be glorified. Isa. 61:3b.

STUDY QUESTIONS—Chapter 58

1. What is confirmation?
2. Why is confirmation a sacrament?
3. Why do we need to be strengthened?
4. What do we receive in the sacrament of Confirmation?
5. Who may be confirmed?
6. When should children be confirmed?
7. Why is confirmation necessary?
8. Write II Tim. 1:7; Acts 15:32; Acts 14:21,22.

Chapter 59

THE SACRAMENT OF MATRIMONY

796. **WHAT IS MATRIMONY?**

Matrimony is a sacrament instituted by God through which a man and a woman enter into a lifetime agreement by vows (oaths) made to each other in the presence of God.

797. **WHAT KIND OF AGREEMENT IS MADE IN MATRIMONY?**

The husband and wife agree to become one flesh with each other exclusively that they might be joined together in a physical and spiritual union that can only be severed by death.

> *For this cause shall a man leave his father and mother, and ..hall be joined unto his wife, and they two shall be one flesh. This is a great mystery: but I speak concerning Christ and the church. Nevertheless let every one of you in particular so love his wife even as himself: and the wife see that she reverence her husband. Eph. 5:31–33.*

798. **WHY IS IT IMPORTANT THAT MATRIMONY SHOULD BE A SPIRITUAL UNION?**

Unless the husband and wife are joined in spirit, they miss the plan and purpose of God for matrimony . . . to make their love a reflection of the love of Christ for His bride, the Church.

> *So ought men to love their wives as their own bodies. He that loveth his wife loveth himself. For no man ever yet hated his own flesh; but nourisheth and cherisheth it, even as the Lord the church: For we are members of his body, of his flesh, and of his bones. Eph. 5:28–30.*

799.   HOW ARE HUSBAND AND WIFE MADE ONE IN SPIRIT?

The husband and wife are made one in spirit by God as they live in accordance to their vows. They become so dependent on one another that their thoughts, desires and faith blend so thoroughly that they become one in flesh, personality and spirit.

> *Wherefore they are no more twain, but one flesh. What therefore God hath joined together, let no man put asunder. Matt. 19:6.*

800.   WHAT DID CHRIST DO FOR MARRIAGE?

Christ restored marriage to the noble and holy institution it was meant to be, He restored marriage to the status of a sacrament and brought back the original teaching of God that one man was to be married to one woman until death. Christ also stressed the sublime purpose of marriage as being love between husband and wife and the procreation of children. He restored dignity to wives and mothers and clarified the teachings on divorce.

801.   WHAT TERMS DOES GOD SET DOWN FOR CHRISTIAN MATRIMONY?

The terms for Christian matrimony are:

1. There must be purity in body, soul and spirit.

> *Marriage is honourable in all, and the bed undefiled: but whoremongers and adulterers God will judge. Heb. 13:4.*

2. Christians are not permitted to marry unbelievers.

> *Be ye not unequally yoked together with unbelievers: for what fellowship hath righteousness with unrighteousness? and what communion hath light with darkness? and what concord hath Christ with Belial? or what part hath he that believeth with an infidel? II Cor. 6:14,15.*

3. Christians are not permitted to marry anyone who has been married unless the previous marriage has been dissolved by death.

> *For the woman which hath an husband is bound by the law to her husband so long as he liveth; but if the husband be dead, she is loosed from the law of her husband. So then if, while her husband liveth, she be married to another man, she shall be called an adulteress; but if her husband be*

dead, she is free from that law; so that she is no adulteress, though she be married to another man. Rom. 7:2,3.

4. Spiritual and emotional ties with the parents must be broken as husband and wife turn to each other and begin to establish their own family ties.

Therefore shall a man leave his father and mother, and shall cleave unto his wife: and they shall be one flesh. Gen. 2:24.

5. Husband and wife must recognize that in Christ both have equal standing. Neither is on a level above nor below the other.

The wife hath not power of her own body, but the husband: and likewise also the husband hath not power of his own body, but the wife. I Cor. 7:4.

Nevertheless, neither is the man without the woman; neither the woman without the man, in the Lord. For as the woman is of the man, even so is the man also by the woman; but all things of God. I Cor. 11:11,12.

There is neither Jew nor Greek, there is neither bond nor free, there is neither male nor female; for ye are all one in Christ Jesus. Gal. 3:28.

802.   WHAT IS REQUIRED OF A WIFE:

A wife is required:

1. To understand that Christian matrimony raises her to a position of equal dignity with her husband.

There is neither Jew nor Greek, there is neither bond nor free, there is neither male nor female; for ye are all one in Christ Jesus. Gal. 3:28.

2. To know that the command to submit to her husband's headship is addressed to her. She is told to do this willingly as an act of spiritual devotion to her husband.

Wives, submit yourselves unto your own husbands, as unto the Lord. Eph. 5:22.

3. To submit to her husband's headship so that God can place the responsibility for her spiritual welfare upon her husband.

For the husband is the head of the wife, even as Christ is the head of the church: and he is the savior of the body. Eph. 5:23.

4. To teach the children that the husband is the head of the home and she is to give him full support in his discipline and leadership of the family.

Children, obey your parents in the Lord: for this is right. Honour thy father and mother; (which is the first commandment with promise;) . . . And ye fathers, provoke not your children to wrath: but bring them up in the nurture and admonition of the Lord. Eph. 6:1,2,4.

5. To understand that she does not have exclusive rights over her own body that her husband is given certain rights. She must also know that she in turn has certain rights to her husband's body.

Let the husband render unto the wife due benevolence: and likewise also the wife unto the husband. The wife hath not power of her own body, but the husband: and likewise also the husband hath not power of his own body, but the wife. Defraud ye not one the other, except it be with consent for a time, that ye may give yourselves to fasting and prayer; and come together again, that Satan tempt you not for your incontinency. 1 Cor. 7:3–5.

6. To pray for and with her husband and children.

Finally, all (of you) should be of one and the same mind (united in spirit), sympathizing (with one another), loving (each the others) as brethren (of one household), compassionate and courteous—tender-hearted and humble-minded. Never return evil for evil or insult for insult—scolding, tongue-lashing, berating; but on the contrary blessing—praying for their welfare, happiness and protection, and truly pitying and loving them. For know that to this you have been called, that you may yourselves inherit a blessing (from God)—obtain a blessing as heirs, bringing welfare and happiness and protection. I Peter 3:8,9. AMP.

803. DOES GOD REQUIRE THE WIFE TO SUBMIT TO HER HUSBAND IN ALL THINGS?

A wife is required to submit to her husband in everything except sin. A wife is not asked to "obey" her husband but to willingly submit herself to him, not by force but as an act of spiritual devotion.

Note: Obedience is given to God, parents and superiors. Wives are not commanded by God to "obey". They are commanded to submit.

> *Wives, submit yourselves unto your own husbands, as unto the Lord. Eph. 5:22.*

804. WHY SHOULD THE WIFE SUBMIT HERSELF TO HER HUSBAND?

When the wife willingly submits herself to her husband, she is expressing love for him and for God.

> *Therefore as the church is subject unto Christ, so let the wives be to their own husbands in every thing. Eph. 5:24.*

805. WHAT IS THE WIFE'S POSITION IN THE HOME?

The wife's position in the home is that of an help-meet to her husband. Faith, spiritual insight and a sympathetic, loving nature were created within her that she might be his source of encouragement and strength in times of difficulty and distress.

> *Now the Lord God said, It is not good (sufficient, satisfactory) that the man should be alone; I will make him a helper meet (suitable, adapted, completing) for him. Gen. 2:18. AMP.*

806. WHAT IS REQUIRED OF A HUSBAND?

A husband is required:

1. To understand that Christian matrimony is based on the equal dignity of both marriage partners.

> *Submitting yourselves one to another in the fear of God. Eph. 5:21.*

2. To realize that he cannot command his wife to submit to him. The command to submit is not given to him to give to his wife but is a direct command from God to the wife.

> *Wives, submit yourselves unto your own husbands, as unto the Lord. Eph. 5:22.*

3. To regard his wife as his own flesh and bones and know that she is physically the weaker vessel. He must cherish her and be considerate of her so his prayers will be answered.

> *In the same way you married men should live considerately with (your wives), with an intelligent recognition (of the marriage relation), honoring the woman as (physically) the weaker, but (realizing that you) are joint heirs of the grace (God's unmerited favor) of life, in order that your prayers may not be hindered and cut off— Otherwise you cannot pray effectively. I Peter 3:7. AMP.*

4. To know that he is personally responsible before God for the welfare of his wife and children.

> *But if any provide not for his own, and specially for those of his own house, he hath denied the faith, and is worse than an infidel. I Tim. 5:8.*

5. To assume the leadership in the home in all things. This includes spiritual guidance.

> *One that ruleth well his own house, having his children in subjection with all gravity; I Tim. 3:4.*

6. To be qualified or disqualified for service in the Church by the way he governs his own house.

> *(For if a man know not how to rule his own house, how shall he take care of the church of God?) I Tim. 3:5.*

807. WHAT IS THE ROLE OF THE HUSBAND IN THE HOME?

The husband has the primary responsibility for the marriage and the family. He is the provider, protector, priest and father. His qualifications for leadership in the church are based on the skill he demonstrates in pastoring his family.

> *And did not he make one? Yet had he the residue of the spirit. And wherefore one? That he might seek a godly seed. Therefore take heed to your spirit, and let none deal treacherously against the wife of his youth. Mal. 2:15.*

> *But if any provide not for his own, and specially for those of his own house, he hath denied the faith, and is worse than an infidel. I Tim. 5:8.*

> *(For if a man know not how to rule his own house, how shall he take care of the church of God?) I Tim. 3:5.*

808. WHAT ARE THE RESPONSIBILITIES OF HUSBAND AND WIFE TOWARD THE CHILDREN?

The husband and wife are responsible for:

1. Setting a good example for a Christian marriage and home.
2. Teaching the children Christian truths.
3. Rooting out evil inclinations in their children. (See Chapter 33 on Iniquity.)
4. Fostering and encouraging prayer, modesty, self-respect, cleanliness, good companionship, good reading, self-denial and self-control.
5. Making the children responsible for certain household chores.
6. Teaching the children love for God, Church and country.
7. Teaching the children discipline . . . to obey their parents and all in authority over them.
8. To teach and foster love within the home.

809. WHY DID GOD INSTITUTE CHRISTIAN MATRIMONY?

God instituted Christian matrimony that:

1. Husband and wife can express the divinely given instincts of love. Man inherently must love someone beyond himself and give himself to that person.

   Husbands, love your wives, even as Christ also loved the church, and gave himself for it; Eph. 5:25.

2. Husband and wife might complete one another.

   And the Lord God said, It is not good that the man should be alone; I will make him an help meet for him. Gen. 2:18.

3. Husband and wife might share in God's creative work through the procreation of children.

   And God blessed them, and God said unto them, Be fruitful, and multiply, and replenish the earth, and subdue it: Gen. 1:28.

4. The marriage partners might fully develop and perfect Christian traits in each other by learning to adjust and overcome the character defects and weaknesses in their lives.

   Therefore as the church is subject unto Christ, so let the wives be to their own husbands in every thing. Husbands, love your wives, even as Christ also loved the church, and gave himself for it; That he might sanctify and cleanse it with the washing of water by the word, That he might present it to himself a glorious church, not having spot, or wrinkle, or any such thing; but that it should be holy and without blemish. Eph. 5:24–27.

810. WHAT PREPARATIONS SHOULD PRECEDE MATRIMONY?

Because matrimony is a sacrament, it must be entered into prayerfully, soberly and with purity of body, mind and spirit. It should be preceded by proper betrothal or engagement.

BIBLE NARRATIVES: The institution of marriage. Gen. 2:18–24; The angel calls Mary, who was engaged to Joseph, Joseph's wife, and called Joseph Mary's husband. Matt. 1:19,20,24; Eliezer prayed for a wife for Isaac. Gen. 24:12.

811. DOES GOD EVER GIVE PERMISSION TO DISSOLVE A MARRIAGE?

Yes. God gives permission to dissolve a marriage when one of the marriage partners is guilty of fornication. Jesus said that this sin would warrant the complete annulment of the marriage covenant.

Whosoever shall put away his wife, except it be for fornication, and shall marry another, committeth adultery: Matt. 19:9.

812. WHAT DOES THE WORD "FORNICATION" MEAN?

The word "fornication" is a translation of the Greek word "porneia" which means adultery, homosexuality, incest."—(Analytical Greek Lexicon.)

For this ye know and understand: That no fornicator . . . hath inheritance in the kingdom of Christ and of God. Eph. 5:5.

813. CAN A MARRIAGE BE DISSOLVED FOR ANY OTHER REASON?

No. According to Christ only one offense ("porneia") warrants divorce.

814.   WHAT IS DIVORCE?

Divorce is a decree of the government which declares the marriage bond broken.

815.   IS IT WRONG TO SEEK A DIVORCE?

No. If a marriage partner is guilty of fornication ("porneia") and refuses to repent, the innocent party may seek a divorce.

> *But I say unto you, That whosoever shall put away his wife, saving for the cause of fornication, causeth her to commit adultery . . . Matt. 5:32.*

816.   UNDER THE OLD COVENANT, WHAT WAS THE PENALTY FOR PORNEIA?

In the Old Testament God commanded those committing "porneia" to be put to death by stoning.

> *And the man that committeth adultery with another man's wife, even he that committeth adultery with his neighbour's wife, the adulterer and the adulteress shall surely be put to death. Lev. 20:10.*

817.   UNDER THE NEW COVENANT, WHAT IS TO BE DONE WHEN A MARRIAGE PARTNER IS INVOLVED IN PORNEIA?

Christian marriage is a type of Christ and His Church. Members of the Body of Christ are not "cut off" when they forsake Him for another but are brought to repentance and restored whenever possible. However, if they persist in sin and refuse to repent, the day will come when the Lord will no longer strive with them and they will be "cut off" from the Church, His Body, with no hope of being restored. So it is with the marriage partner who commits "porneia". Every means must be used to bring repentance and restoration.

> *He, that being often reproved hardeneth his neck, shall suddenly be destroyed, and that without remedy. Prov. 29:1.*

> *When Jesus had lifted up himself, and saw none but the woman, (taken in adultery), he said unto her, Woman, where are those thine accusers? hath no man condemned*

thee? She said, No man, Lord. And Jesus said unto her, Neither do I condemn thee: go, and sin no more. John 8:10,11.

Brethren, if a man be overtaken in a fault, ye which are spiritual, restore such an one in the spirit of meekness; considering thyself, lest thou be tempted. Gal. 6:1.

Then came Peter to him, and said, Lord, how oft shall my brother sin against me, and I forgive him? till seven times? Jesus saith unto him, I say not unto thee, Until seven times: but, Until seventy times seven. Matt. 18:21,22.

818. IF WE ARE THE INJURED PARTY, HOW CAN WE HELP TO RESTORE THE MARRIAGE?

There are several steps we can take to help restore the marriage. Among them are:

1. Learning that when someone misuses or wrongs us, we cannot retaliate.

   Ye have heard that it hath been said, An eye for an eye, and a tooth for a tooth: But I say unto you, That ye resist not evil: but whosoever shall smite thee on thy right cheek, turn to him the other also. Matt. 5:38,39.

2. Forgive.

   And when ye stand praying, forgive . . . Mark 11:25.

3. We continue to walk in the ways of the Lord and refuse to heed the counsel of those who advise us that divorce is the answer and will solve all our problems.

   Trust in the Lord with all thine heart; and lean not unto thine own understanding. In all thy ways acknowledge him, and he shall direct thy paths. Prov. 3:5,6.

4. We commit our ways to the Lord and put our trust in Him.

   Thou wilt keep him in perfect peace, whose mind is stayed on thee: because he trusteth in thee. Isa. 26:3.

5. We must examine ourselves and confess our sins to God asking Him to forgive us and reveal to us where we have failed in the marriage. We reach a state where we feel completely helpless and hopeless and realize there is nothing more we can do.

We then become totally dependent upon God and resign ourselves completely to His will.

And having in a readiness to revenge all disobedience, when your obedience is fulfilled. II Cor. 10:6.

And shall not God avenge his own elect, which cry day and night unto him, though he bear long with them? I tell you that he will avenge them speedily . . . Luke 18:7,8.

819. CAN THERE BE TRUE RESTORATION?

Yes. True repentance opens the way for God to reunite the marriage partners and bring true restoration. Grace is imparted to both parties to forgive and forget and to heal the stinging wounds.

The Spirit of the Lord is upon me, because he hath anointed me . . . to heal the broken-hearted . . . Luke 4:18.

But he giveth more grace. Wherefore he saith, God resisteth the proud, but giveth grace unto the humble. Humble yourselves in the sight of the Lord, and he shall lift you up. James 4:6,10.

820. WHAT CAN BE DONE WHEN RESTORATION IS IMPOSSIBLE?

In a Christian marriage, the pastor of the Church should be consulted. He will advise the injured party how to pray and "war in the Spirit." He will seek to restore the one who has fallen into sin. If the sinning partner secures a divorce and refuses all attempts of restoration, the Church Council will be called to determine the innocence of the injured party and whether the marriage is beyond restoration.

And if he shall neglect to hear them, tell it unto the church: but if he neglect to hear the church, let him be unto thee as an heathen man and a publican. Matt. 18:17.

Dare any of you, having a matter against another, go to law before the unjust, and not before the saints? Do ye not know that the saints shall judge the world? And if the world shall be judged by you, are ye unworthy to judge the smallest matters? Know ye not that we shall judge angels? how much more things that pertain to this life? I Cor. 6:1-3.

821. IS REMARRIAGE EVER PERMITTED?

Remarriage is permitted if the pastor and the Church Council judge the marriage of a member of the Local Church beyond any possible restoration, know all the facts concerning the adulterous affair and can find the injured party innocent. After a reasonable period of time has elapsed during which the injured person has received healing and peace, the Church Council may grant permission to remarry in the Lord.

> *. . . Whosoever shall put away his wife, except it be for fornication and shall marry another, committeth adultery: and whoso marrieth her which is put away doth commit adultery. His disciples say unto him, If the case of the man be so with his wife, it is not good to marry. But he said unto them, All men cannot receive this saying, save they to whom it is given. Matt. 19:9–11.*

822. IS A BELIEVER ALLOWED TO SEPARATE FROM OR DIVORCE AN UNBELIEVER?

No. The Bible does not allow separation or divorce for this reason but tells us that the faith of the believer will sanctify the unbelieving mate.

> *And the woman which hath an husband that believeth not, and if he be pleased to dwell with her let her not leave him. For the unbelieving husband is sanctified by the wife, and the unbelieving wife is sanctified by the husband: else were your children unclean; but now are they holy.*
> *I Cor. 7:13,14.*

> *Likewise, ye wives, be in subjection to your own husbands; that, if any obey not the word, they also may without the word be won by the conversation of the wives; while they behold your chaste conversation coupled with fear.*
> *I Peter 3:1,2.*

823. HOW IS THE UNBELIEVING MATE SANCTIFIED BY THE BELIEVER?

The unbeliever shares the blessings God bestows upon the believer as long as he or she remains under the same roof.

BIBLE NARRATIVES: Joseph's blessings upon Potiphar's house, Gen. 39:2–5; . . . "that the Lord blessed the Egyptian's house for Joseph's sake." Gen. 39:5b. Jacob's blessing upon Laban's household. Gen. 30:27. . . . "for I have learned by experience that the Lord hath blessed me for thy sake." Gen. 30:27.

824.   WHAT IF THE UNBELIEVER LEAVES?

If the unbeliever leaves the place of blessing, the believer is not to live under condemnation but is to be assured that the unbeliever will no longer experience the blessings of God. Often, the withdrawing of the blessings of God will cause the unbeliever to return and be converted.

> But if the unbelieving depart, let him depart. A brother or a sister is not under bondage in such cases: but God hath called us to peace. For what knowest thou, O wife, whether thou shalt save thy husband? or how knowest thou, O man, whether thou shalt save thy wife? I Cor. 7:15,16.

825.   IF THE UNBELIEVER DOES NOT RETURN, MAY THE BELIEVER REMARRY?

No. The Scriptures teach that they should remain unmarried or be reunited with their mate.

> And unto the married I command, yet not I, but the Lord, Let not the wife depart from her husband: But and if she depart, let her remain unmarried, or be reconciled to her husband: and let not the husband put away his wife. I Cor. 7:10,11.

826.   WHAT IS THE STATE OF A DIVORCED PERSON WHO BECOMES A BELIEVER?

According to the Scriptures, a person who is divorced before he is saved is instructed to remain as he is when the Lord saves him.

> Every one should remain after God calls him in the station or condition of life in which the summons found him. I Cor. 7:20. AMP.

> . . . And Jesus said, I do not condemn you either. Go on your way, and from now on sin no more. John 8:11. AMP.

> . . . for I have learned, in whatsoever state I am, therewith to be content. Phil. 4:11.

827. IS SUCH A PERSON ENTITLED TO HOLD A POSITION IN THE CHURCH?

The person who has been divorced is restricted from holding the office of bishop, elder and deacon, if he remarries. The leaders must be an example to the members of the church. Anyone in the place of leadership must be free from any criticism that could bring reproach to the Church of Jesus Christ.

> *Now a bishop (superintendent, overseer) must give no grounds for accusation but must be above reproach, the husband of one wife, circumspect and temperate and self-controlled; (he must be) sensible and well behaved and dignified and lead an orderly (disciplined) life; (he must be) hospitable—showing love for and being a friend to the believers, especially strangers or foreigners—(and) be a capable and qualified teacher ... Let deacons be the husbands of but one wife, and let them manage (their) children and their own households well; I Tim. 3:2,12. AMP.*

STUDY QUESTIONS—Chapter 59

1. What is matrimony?
2. What agreement is made in matrimony?
3. What is the purpose of God for matrimony?
4. How are husband and wife made one in Spirit?
5. What terms does God set down for Christian matrimony?
6. What is required of a wife?
7. What is required of a husband?
8. What are the responsibilities of husband and wife toward the children?
9. Why did God institute Christian matrimony?
10. What preparations should precede matrimony?
11. Does God ever give permission to dissolve a marriage?
12. What does the word "fornication" mean?
13. Under the Old Covenant, what was the penalty for porneia?
14. Under the New Covenant, what is to be done when a marriage partner is involved in porneia?
15. Is a believer allowed to separate from or divorce his partner because he is an unbeliever?
16. What if the unbeliever leaves?
17. If the unbeliever does not return, may the believer remarry?
18. Write: Eph. 5:28,29,31; II Cor. 6:14,15; Eph. 5:22–24.

Chapter 60

THE SACRAMENT OF
THE DEDICATION OF CHILDREN

828. WHAT IS THE DEDICATION OF CHILDREN?

The Dedication of Children is a sacrament in which the parents give their child to God for the purpose of having the Lord direct the spiritual growth and development of the child.

> *Suffer little children, and forbid them not, to come unto me; for of such is the kingdom of heaven. Matt. 19:14.*

> *And he took them up in his arms, put his hands upon them, and blessed them. Mark 10:16.*

829. WHAT AGREEMENT IS MADE IN THIS SACRAMENT?

The parents acknowledge that the child belongs to them and to the Lord and agree to raise the child that he might be of service to God. God accepts the child dedicated to Him and promises to bless him with peace, guidance and knowledge.

> *All thy children shall be taught of the Lord; and great shall be the peace of thy children. Isa. 54:13.*

830. WHAT DOES THE SACRAMENT DO FOR THE CHILD?

The child that is dedicated to God is sanctified (set apart) for a special place of blessing and care. The steps of the child are ordered of the Lord and even when the path seems to lead to tragedy, victory and fulfillment are the end results.

> *Take heed that ye despise not one of these little ones; for I say unto you, That in heaven their angels do always behold the face of my Father which is in heaven. Matt. 18:10.*

BIBLE NARRATIVES: The story of Joseph, Gen. 37:39–47; The story of Samson, Judges 13,14.

831. WHAT DOES THE SACRAMENT DO FOR THE PARENTS?

The parents are given peace and confidence knowing that the child they have presented to God will be under His constant care and guidance.

> . . . *for I know whom I have believed, and am persuaded that he is able to keep that which I have committed unto him against that day. II Tim. 1:12b.*

832. WHAT PREPARATION SHOULD BE MADE BEFORE ENTERING INTO THIS SACRAMENT?

A time of prayer and meditation should precede the formal dedication of a child to God asking the Holy Spirit to enable the parents to relinquish their hold on the child and to submit their wills to God so that wisdom can be imparted to them for the rearing of the child.

> *O my Lord . . . teach us what we shall do unto the child you have given us to rear for thee. Judges 13:8 RSV.*

> *Except the Lord build the house, they labour in vain that build it; except the Lord keep the city, the watchman waketh in vain. It is vain for you to rise up early, to sit up late, to eat the bread of sorrows: for so he giveth his beloved sleep. Lo, children are an heritage of the Lord: and the fruit of the womb is his reward. As arrows are in the hand of a mighty man; so are children of the youth. Happy is the man that hath his quiver full of them: they shall not be ashamed, but they shall speak with the enemies in the gate. Ps. 127.*

833. WHAT IS THE PARENTS' RESPONSIBILITY?

Parents are responsible to God to train the child to obey the commandments of the Lord and to serve Him. By word and example they are to lead the child to experience every doctrine and sacrament of the church of Jesus Christ.

> *Train up a child in the way he should go: and when he is old, he will not depart from it. Prov. 22:6.*

834. DOES THE PARENTS' RESONSIBILITY FOR THE CHILD EVER END?

No. Parents are never relieved of the responsibility of praying for and admonishing their child in proper living. The parent who does not raise his voice when he sees an adult child in sin is held accountable to God.

> In that day I will perform against Eli all things which I have spoken concerning his house: when I begin, I will also make an end. For I have told him that I will judge his house for ever for the iniquity which he knoweth; because his sons made themselves vile, and he restrained them not. And therefore I have sworn unto the house of Eli, that the iniquity of Eli's house shall not be purged with sacrifice nor offering for ever. I Sam. 3:12–14.

835. WHAT IS THE AGE OF ACCOUNTABILITY?

A child becomes responsible for his own salvation at approximately twelve years of age. Until this time the child is under the protection of the covenant his parents made with God. At twelve years of age, he should be enrolled in catechism class to study and experience the doctrines and sacraments of the Church and to dedicate his life anew for the service of God and His Kingdom.

> And when he (Jesus) was twelve years old, they went up to Jerusalem after the custom of the feast. Luke 2:42.

836. WHAT HAPPENS TO A CHILD IF HE DIES BEFORE HE IS OLD ENOUGH TO REPENT AND BE BAPTIZED?

A dedicated child is under the protection of the covenant his parents made with God and is made holy by their faith. If he dies before he is old enough to repent and be baptized, he is guaranteed entrance into the Kingdom of God.

> For the unbelieving husband is set apart, separated, withdrawn from heathen contamination and affiliated with the Christian people, by union with his consecrated, set-apart wife; and the unbelieving wife is set apart and separated through union with her consecrated husband. Otherwise, your children would be unclean, unblessed heathen, out-

side the Christian covenant. But as it is, they are prepared for God, pure and clean. I Cor. 7:14 AMP.

837.   IN WHAT STATE IS THE CHILD OF UNBELIEVING PARENTS?

The child of unbelieving parents is considered unclean, unblessed heathen, outside the Christian covenant and subject to the wrath of God.

> *Otherwise your children would be unclean, unblessed, heathen, outside the Christian covenant, but as it is they are prepared for God, pure and clean. I Cor. 7:14. AMP.*

BIBLE NARRATIVES: The children of Achan were destroyed with their father and mother because of Achan's sin, Josh. 7:1-26; The children of the wicked were destroyed at the time of the flood, Gen. 7:17; The children of the wicked were destroyed at the destruction of Sodom and Gomorrah, Gen. 19:24.

838.   WHAT DOES THE BIBLE TEACH ABOUT DISCIPLINING CHILDREN?

There can be no love without discipline and the Bible commands parents to discipline their children in love.

> *For whom the Lord loveth he chasteneth, and scourgeth every son whom he receiveth. Heb. 12:6.*

> *He that spareth his rod hateth his son: but he that loveth him chasteneth him betimes. Prov. 13:24.*

839.   WHY IS DISCIPLINE NECESSARY?

In the fifth commandment, God requires us to honor our parents and we are taught to do this by discipline. Children that are taught discipline in their early years learn to honor all those in authority over them. This valuable training lasts a lifetime and affects all areas of life . . . social as well as spiritual.

> Train *up a child in the way he should go: and when he is old, he* will not depart *from it. Prov. 22:6.*

> *Correct thy son, and he shall give thee rest; yea, he shall give delight unto thy soul. Prov. 29:17.*

Note: Prov. 22:6 says *train* up a child. Training demands discipline and perseverance.

840. WHAT METHOD OF DISCIPLINE DOES THE BIBLE RECOMMEND?

The Bible recommends children be spanked by their parents when they need it.

> *The rod and reproof give wisdom; but a child left to himself bringeth his mother to shame. Prov. 29:15.*

> *Foolishness is bound in the heart of a child; but the rod of correction shall drive it far from him. Prov. 22:15.*

> *Chasten thy son while there is hope, and let not thy soul spare for his crying. Prov. 19:18.*

Note: "Spanking"—to strike the buttocks as with an open hand, or *rod* (a straight or slender stick, as one cut fresh from a tree). Webster.

841. HOW SHOULD A SPANKING BE ADMINISTERED?

A spanking should be administered in love and only when the parent is in complete control of himself. Correction should never be done in anger for anger in the parent stirs up anger in the child thwarting the whole purpose for correction. Violence or physical abuse should never be used nor should correction be administered for the purpose of breaking the will of the child, but rather for the purpose of directing the will and bringing it into proper subjection. It is well to pray with a child before correcting him. Frequent, mild but firm admonition is all part of good child-training and coupled with prayer is the best training he can have.

> *Fathers, provoke not your children to anger, lest they be discouraged. Col. 3:21.*

> *And, ye fathers, provoke not your children to wrath: but bring them up in the nurture and admonition of the Lord. Eph. 6:4.*

> *Even a child is known by his doings, whether his work be pure, and whether it be right. Prov. 20:11.*

842. WHAT SHOULD BE THE ATTITUDE OF CHILDREN TO-WARD THOSE IN AUTHORITY OVER THEM?

Children should be taught to respect, honor and obey those in authority over them. This includes God, government officials, teachers, employers, ministers, and the elderly.

> *Let every soul be subject unto the higher powers. For there is no power but of God: the powers that be are ordained of God. Whosoever therefore resisteth the power, resisteth the ordinance of God: and they that resist shall receive to themselves damnation. Rom. 13:1,2.*

843. WHAT IS THE PARENTS' ROLE IN SECURING THE PROMISES OF THIS SACRAMENT?

The parents are responsible for:

1. Training their children by word and example in holy living.
2. Proper discipline.
3. Teaching them to respect God, His Word, His ministers and His people.

Note: Children learn to respect God, His Word, His ministers and His people by the example their parents place before them. Criticism of God and His ministers before children destroys faith and confidence that can seldom be renewed.

> *... The fathers have eaten sour grapes, and the children's teeth are set on edge. Ezek. 18:2.*

4. Prayer that never ceases.
5. Admonishing their children to follow God.

STUDY QUESTIONS—Chapter 60

1. What is the Dedication of Children?
2. What agreement is made by the parents?
3. What benefits does the child receive from this sacrament?
4. What do the parents receive?
5. What is the age of accountability?
6. In what state is a child of unbelieving parents?
7. Why is it necessary to discipline children?
8. What method of discipline does the Bible recommend?
9. How should discipline be administered?

Chapter 61

THE SACRAMENT OF ANOINTING WITH OIL

844. **WHAT IS THE SACRAMENT OF ANOINTING WITH OIL?**

It is a sacrament for the healing of the body, soul or spirit.

> *Is there any sick among you? Let him call for the elders of the church: and let them pray over him, anointing him with oil in the name of the Lord. And the prayer of faith shall save the sick, and the Lord shall raise him up; and if he have committed sins, they shall be forgiven him. James 5:14,15.*

845. **WHAT VISIBLE SIGN IS USED IN THE SACRAMENT?**

Olive oil that has been consecrated by the prayers of the presbytery is used in this sacrament.

BIBLE NARRATIVE: Holy anointing oil was compounded with perfumes for special times of consecration and sanctifying vessels in the temple. Exod. 30:22–25.

846. **WHY IS OIL USED IN THE SACRAMENT?**

A. Oil symbolizes the presence of the Holy Spirit.

> *Thou hast loved righteousness and hated iniquity; therefore God, even thy God, hath anointed thee with the oil of gladness above thy fellows. Heb. 1:9.*

B. It is the symbol of the sacrament that secures the promised blessings of God.

> *. . . See, that thou make all things according to the pattern shewed to thee in the mount. Heb. 8:5.*

847. HOW IS OIL USED IN THE SACRAMENT?

The consecrated oil is smeared, rubbed or poured on the sick individual for healing and deliverance in the Name of the Lord.

> ... and let them pray over him, anointing him with oil in the name of the Lord. James 5:14.

848. WHO CAN ADMINISTER THE SACRAMENT?

The anointing of oil is administered by the elders of the Church.

> Is there any sick among you? Let him call for the elders of the church; and let them pray over him, anointing him with oil in the name of the Lord. James 5:14.

849. WHY IS THIS SACRAMENT ADMINISTERED?

This sacrament is administered for healing and deliverance of the sick and oppressed. Many are weak and sickly because of sins committed against Christ or His body, the Church.

> Wherefore whosoever shall eat this bread, and drink this cup, of the Lord, unworthily, shall be guilty of the body and blood of the Lord. But let a man examine himself, and so let him eat of that bread, and drink of that cup. For he that eateth and drinketh unworthily, eateth and drinketh damnation to himself, not discerning the Lord's body. For this cause many are weak and sickly among you, and many sleep. I Cor. 11:27–30.

> For to be carnally minded is death ... Because the carnal mind is enmity against God: for it is not subject to the law of God, neither indeed can be. Rom. 8:6,7.

850. WHAT SINS ARE COMMITTED AGAINST CHRIST OR HIS BODY, THE CHURCH?

Sins against Christ or His body, the Church, include:

1. Becoming offended when we are chastened by the Lord.

> And blessed is he, whosoever shall not be offended in me. Luke 7:23.

2. Taking offense at a thoughtless word or act of another believer and harboring resentment or bitterness toward another believer.

Great peace have they which love thy law: and nothing shall offend them. Ps. 119:165.

3. Having an unforgiving spirit.

But if ye do not forgive, neither will your Father which is in heaven forgive your trespasses. Mark 11:26.

4. Having a disobedient spirit that will not obey the commandments of God.

And having a readiness to revenge all disobedience, when your obedience is fulfilled. II Cor. 10:6.

5. Robbing God of tithes and offerings.

Will a man rob God? Yet ye have robbed me. But ye say, Wherein have we robbed thee? In tithes and offerings. Mal. 3:8.

6. Hiding or condoning sin.

He that covereth his sins shall not prosper: but whoso confesseth and forsaketh them shall have mercy. Prov. 28:13.

7: Gossiping.

If any man among you seem to be religious, and bridleth not his tongue, but deceiveth his own heart, this man's religion is vain. James 1:26.

8. Partaking of the Lord's Supper unworthily.

Wherefore whosoever shall eat this bread, and drink this cup of the Lord, unworthily, shall be guilty of the body and blood of the Lord. But let a man examine himself, and so let him eat of that bread, and drink of that cup. For he that eateth and drinketh unworthily, eateth and drinketh damnation to himself, not discerning the Lord's body. For this cause many are weak and sickly among you, and many sleep. I Cor. 11:27–30.

851. HOW IS HEALING RECEIVED WHEN WE HAVE SINNED AGAINST CHRIST OR HIS CHURCH?

We call for the elders of the Church, confessing our sins to them and asking God for forgiveness through prayer.

Confess your faults one to another, and pray for one another that ye may be healed . . . James 5:16.

852. WHAT DO THE ELDERS DO?

The elders hear the confession of sins and pray to the Lord on behalf of the afflicted believer to remit his sins. Then they anoint the sick person with oil in the Name of the Lord and pray the prayer of faith.

> *Is any one among you sick? He should call in the church elders—the spiritual guides. And they should pray over him, anointing him with oil in the Lord's name. And the prayer (that is) of faith will save him that is sick, and the Lord will restore him; and if he has committed sins, he will be forgiven. James 5:14,15, AMP.*

853. WHAT DOES THE LORD DO?

According to the Scriptures, the Lord forgives the confessed sins of the believer, restores him to right standing in the Body of Christ, and sometimes restores him to physical health.

> *And the prayer (that is) of faith will save him that is sick, and the Lord will restore him; and if he has committed sins, he will be forgiven. James 5:15 AMP.*

854. ISN'T THE BELIEVER ALWAYS RESTORED TO PHYSICAL HEALTH?

No. Many times healing will follow the administering of the sacrament. However, this sacrament is primarily for the healing and saving of the soul from death. (See Healed by His Stripes—Chapter 35.)

> *My brethren, if any one among you strays from the Truth and falls into error, and another (person) brings him back (to God), Let the (latter) one be sure that whoever turns a sinner from his evil course will save (that one's) soul from death and will cover a multitude of sins (that is, procure the pardon of the many sins committed by the convert). James 5:19,20. AMP.*

855. WHEN SHOULD THE ELDERS BE CALLED?

The elders should be called in all cases of serious illness. The family or doctors cannot always judge whether the sickness is of spiritual or of an organic origin.

> *And Asa in the thirty and ninth year of his reign was diseased in his feet, until his disease was exceeding great: yet in his disease he sought not to the Lord, but to the physicians. And Asa slept with his fathers, and died in the one and fortieth year of his reign. II Chron. 16:12,13.*

856. IS THERE ANY OCCASION WHEN LAYMEN ARE PERMITTED TO ANOINT WITH OIL?

Yes. Laymen are permitted to anoint the sick for physical healing. However, only the elders can administer the Sacrament of Anointing for spiritual healing and restoration.

> *And they cast out many devils, and anointed with oil many that were sick, and healed them. Mark 6:13.*

> *And these signs shall follow them that believe; In my name shall they cast out devils; they shall speak with new tongues; They shall take up serpents; and if they drink any deadly thing it shall not hurt them; they shall lay hands on the sick, and they shall recover. Mark 16:17,18.*

STUDY QUESTIONS—Chapter 61

1. What is the sacrament of Anointing with Oil?
2. Why is oil used in this sacrament?
3. How is oil used in the sacrament?
4. Who can administer this sacrament?
5. Why is this sacrament administered?
6. What sins are committed against the body of Christ?
7. How do we receive healing when we have sinned against the church?
8. What do the elders do when called by the sick?
9. What does the Lord do when we are anointed with oil by the elders?
10. Why should the elders be called?

INDEX

This index is set up to serve also as a glossary of important definitions used throughout this book. The first number given under each entry locates the question and answer which defines the entry. Other references to the same entry are indicated in chronological order by question number.

CATECHISM TEACHINGS ON TAPE

In Detroit, the students of *Understanding God* receive a special aid in understanding their lessons. They participate in weekly lectures given by Patricia Beall Gruits. These lectures supplement the lesson and help the students immensely.

Because of a great demand, these lectures have been transcribed on sixty and ninety minute cassette tapes and are available to you. There is a taped lecture to accompany each of the sixty-one chapters of this book.

Through these tapes, you and your Bible study group can enjoy hearing Mrs. Gruits teach catechism to you in your homes and churches.

There are sixteen tapes, which contain approximately eighteen hours of instruction. They come beautifully packaged in a portfolio which can be easily transported. They make a lovely gift and can be purchased from Rhema International for $85.00 for the full set of sixteen tapes, including the carrying case. These tapes are now being translated into other languages and will soon be available in Spanish, Italian, German, French, Japanese, Yugoslavian, Polish and Russian.

HOW TO TEACH CATECHISM SEMINARS

For those of you who are interested in the teaching methods employed in instructing catechism, there are regular Rhema Seminars on *How to Teach Catechism*. These seminars take place in various parts of the country at different times of the year. Check with Rhema International to see when one will be in your area.

If you are a minister or Christian educator and want to see the spiritual gifts more operative in your church, this seminar may suggest ways to put that plan into motion. Among the many subjects covered are:

How to Bring People into Spiritual Experiences
The Foundation Stones of the Bible
The Gifts and Callings of the Holy Spirit
Spiritual Ministries
Prayer and Fasting
Worship and Praise
Teaching with Rhema Tapes
The Power of Confirmation . . . and many more.

If you are interested in either the Catechism tapes or the Rhema Seminars fill out and mail the coupon below today.

. . . .

RHEMA INTERNATIONAL HEADQUARTERS
Bethesda Missionary Temple
P.O. Box 4832
Detroit, Michigan 48234

[ ] Please send me _____ sets of the 16-tape series, *Catechism On Tape*, at $85 each. I enclose _____.

[ ] Please send information on the next *How to Teach Catechism* seminar in my area.

Name _____
Address _____

City _____ State _____ Zip _____

. . . .